An Empirical Study of the Fair and Equitable Treatment Standard Clause

How Tribunals Have Examined Its Relationship with the Minimum Standard

Patrick Dumberry

Wolters Kluwer

Published by:
Kluwer Law International B.V.
PO Box 316
2400 AH Alphen aan den Rijn
The Netherlands
E-mail: lrs-sales@wolterskluwer.com
Website: www.wolterskluwer.com/en/solutions/kluwerlawinternational

Sold and distributed by:
Wolters Kluwer Legal & Regulatory U.S.
920 Links Avenue
Landisville, PA 17538
United States of America
E-mail: customer.service@wolterskluwer.com

ISBN 978-94-035-2508-2

e-Book: ISBN 978-94-035-2518-1
web-PDF: ISBN 978-94-035-2528-0

Table of Contents

List of Abbreviations

AJIL	American Journal of International Law
American Rev. Int'l Arb.	American Review of International Arbitration
Am Univ Int L Rev	American University International Law Review
Arb. Int.	Arbitration International
ASDI	Annuaire Suisse de droit international
ASEAN	Association of Southeast Asian Nations
ASIL Proc.	American Society of International Law Proceedings
B.C. Int'l & Comp. L. Rev.	Boston College International and Comparative Law Review
BITs	Bilateral Investment Treaties
British IICL	British Institute of International and Comparative Law
British YIL	British Yearbook of International Law
CAFTA-DR	Central America-Dominican Republic Free Trade Agreement
Canadian YIL	Canadian Yearbook of International Law
CETA	Comprehensive Economic and Trade Agreement
Chicago JIL	Chicago Journal of International Law
COMESA	Common Market for Eastern and Southern Africa
CPTPP	Comprehensive and Progressive Agreement for Trans-Pacific Partnership
CUSMA	Canada-United States-Mexico Agreement
ECT	Energy Charter Treaty
EU	European Union
FET	Fair and Equitable Treatment
FPS	Full Protection and Security
FTA	Free Trade Agreement
FTC	Free Trade Commission

FTC Note	Free Trade Commission Notes of Interpretation of 31 July 2001
GA Res.	General Assembly of the United Nations
Howard LJ	Howard Law Journal
ICJ	International Court of Justice
ICJ Rep.	International Court of Justice Reports of Judgments, Advisory Opinions and Orders
ICJ Statute	Statute of the International Court of Justice
ICLQ	International and Comparative Law Quarterly
ICSID	International Centre for Settlement of Investment Disputes
ICSID Rev.	ICSID Review – Foreign Investment Law Journal
ILA	International Law Association
ILC	International Law Commission
ILM	International Legal Materials
IMS	International Minimum Standard
Indian JIL	Indian Journal of International Law
J. E. Asia & Int'l L.	Journal of East Asia and International Law
J. Int. Arb.	Journal of International Arbitration
J. Int. Disp. Settl.	Journal of International Dispute Settlement
J.Int'l Econ. L.	Journal of International Economic Law
J. World Invest.	Journal of World Investment
J. World Invest. & Trade	Journal of World Investment & Trade
J. World Trade	Journal of World Trade
J.P.L.	Journal of Public Law
L. & Bus. Rev. Am.	Law and Business Review of the Americas
LNTS	League of Nations Treaty Series
LPICT	Law and Practice of International Courts and Tribunals
MAI	Multilateral Agreement on Investment
Max Planck Yrbk. UNL	Max Planck Yearbook of United Nations Law
McGill LJ	McGill Law Journal
MFN	Most-Favoured-Nation
Mich. L. Rev.	Michigan Law Review
MST	Minimum Standard of Treatment
NAFTA	North American Free Trade Agreement
Northwestern J. Int'l L.	Northwestern Journal of International Law
OECD	Organisation for Economic Co-operation and Development
PACER Plus	Pacific Agreement on Closer Economic Relations Plus
RBDI	Revue belge de droit international

Rec des cours	Collected Courses of the Hague Academy of International Law
Rev Intern Dr Econ	Revue Internationale De Droit Économique
Rev. arb.	Revue De L'arbitrage
Suffolk Transnat'l L. Rev.	Suffolk Transnational Law Review
TDM	Transnational Dispute Management
TTIP	Transatlantic Trade and Investment Partnership
U. Pa. J. Int'l L.	University of Pennsylvania Journal of International Law
UN	United Nations
UNCTAD	United Nations Conference on Trade and Development
UNRIAA	United Nations Reports of International Arbitral Awards
UNTS	United Nations Treaty Series
US	United States
USTS	United States Treaty Series
VCLT	Vienna Convention on the Law of Treaties
World Arb. & Med. Rev.	World of Arbitration and Mediation Review
Yb Int'l Invest. L. & Pol.	Yearbook on International Investment of Law and Policy

Acknowledgements

On 7 November 2023, I gave a presentation in Paris before the Member States of the Organisation for Economic Co-operation and Development (OECD), and other States invited to the event (99 countries in total). The event was part of the OECD Track 2 programme ('Future of Investment Treaties'). In this context, I conducted a comprehensive empirical research project examining how investment tribunals have assessed the status, scope and content of 'Fair and Equitable Treatment' (FET) clauses and matters of liability and compensation. I examined all publicly available awards rendered by arbitral tribunals in the last 25 years dealing with FET clauses. I have found 279 relevant awards. My findings are published in this book.

I am indebted to several bright and talented students from the University of Ottawa who have assisted me over the past year with research and editing. Their assistance was invaluable to the completion of this book. I want to sincerely thank: Khairul Islam (PhD student), Ramy Daniel Sarouf (LLM student) and Eloïse Alarie Beiger. All of them have done an amazing job. I would furthermore like to thank all the people at Kluwer (and especially Eleanor Taylor) for their patience and support during the process of creating this book.

Finally, I would like to dedicate this study to my mother and my two beautiful and intelligent children, Ophelie and Florent. Special thanks to Fatima for her love and support throughout this journey.

Patrick Dumberry
Montréal, Québec, Canada
March 2024

General Introduction

I THE SCOPE OF THIS BOOK

In recent years, a number of books,[1] including one by the present author,[2] and numerous articles have been published on the 'Fair and Equitable Treatment' (FET) standard. The standard is found in an overwhelming majority of Bilateral investment treaties (BITs) and has become, in the last decades, one of the most controversial provisions examined by arbitral tribunals. According to a 2023 Organisation for Economic Co-operation and Development (OECD) paper, examining 2,670 treaties concluded by 99 jurisdictions, the FET clause is found in 95% of them.[3] This figure confirms a study I conducted some 10 years ago.[4] The aim of this publication is not to offer a comprehensive analysis of the scope and content of the FET standard. The goal is more modest. The book intends to empirically examine two questions. First, I will

1. I. Tudor, *The Fair and Equitable Treatment Standard in International Foreign Investment Law* (Oxford UP 2008); G. Cavazos Villanueva, *The Fair and Equitable Treatment Standard: The Mexican Experience* (VDM Verlag 2008); R. Kläger, *Fair and Equitable Treatment in International Investment Law* (Cambridge UP 2011); A. Diehl, *The Core Standard of International Investment Protection: Fair and Equitable Treatment* (Wolters Kluwer 2012); M. Paparinskis, *The International Minimum Standard and Fair and Equitable Treatment* (Oxford UP 2013); T. Weiler, *The Interpretation of International Investment Law: Equality, Discrimination and Minimum Standards of Treatment in Historical Context* (Martinus Nijhoff 2013); A. Schernbeck, *Der Fair and Equitable Treatment Standard in internationalen Investitionsschutzabkommen* (Nomos 2013); F. Maria Palombino, *Fair and Equitable Treatment and the Fabric of General Principles* (TMC Asser 2018); R. Islam, *The Fair and Equitable Treatment (FET) Standard in International Investment Arbitration: Developing Countries in Context* (Springer 2018).
2. P. Dumberry, *The Fair and Equitable Treatment Standard: A Guide to NAFTA Case Law on Article 1105* (Wolters Kluwer 2013).
3. OECD, *'Fair' And 'Equitable' Treatment Provisions in Investment Treaties; A Large-Sample Survey of Treaty Provisions* (2023) 4.
4. P. Dumberry, *Has the Fair and Equitable Treatment Standard Become a Rule of Customary international Law?* 8(1) J. Int. Disp. Settl. 155-178 (2016) DOI: 10.1093/jnlids/idw002, examining 1,964 BITs that were available on the UNCTAD website at the time (February 2014) and finding that only 50 of them did not include an FET clause (and 25 others only referred to the FET in their preamble). Thus, less than 5% of the BITs examined do not include any formal and binding FET obligation for the host State of investments.

analyse how investment tribunals have assessed FET clauses in the last 25 years regarding the complex question of the relationship between that standard and the Minimum Standard of Treatment (MST) under custom. For instance, are tribunals interpreting FET clauses as offering the same level of protection as the one existing under customary international law? Do they instead believe that it offers investors a level of protection that is different, i.e., 'autonomous' from the MST under custom? Second, I will assess whether the answer given by tribunals to this first question has had any impact on how they have examined the content of the standard and how they have addressed matters of liability and compensation.

The idea for this book has its origin in a presentation I gave in Paris in 2023 before the Member States of the OECD, and other States invited to the event (99 countries in total). The event was part of the OECD Track 2 programme ('Future of Investment Treaties').[5] My presentation examined how tribunals have assessed FET clauses and their relationship with the MST and whether their analysis has had any impact on how they have addressed matters of liability and compensation. In the context of this comprehensive empirical research project, I have examined all publicly available awards/decisions dealing with FET clauses rendered by arbitral tribunals in the last 25 years. I have found 279 relevant awards. A summary of my findings has been published on the OECD website.[6] My findings are found in Part II of this book. As further explained below, while the vast majority of investment treaties include an FET clause, a considerable degree of variation in the actual content of the clause remains. I have examined awards separately for each of the following three types of FET clauses:

- Clauses containing an unqualified formulation of the FET obligation, i.e., a stand-alone obligation to provide FET without any reference to international law or any other standards.
- Clauses containing an explicit reference to the standard existing under 'international law'. In this category, there are two distinct types of clauses, those providing for treatment 'in accordance with international law' and others indicating that the treatment should be 'no less than that required under international law'.
- Clauses where the FET obligation is expressly linked to the MST under custom.

Previous studies have shown that these different formulations of FET clauses significantly impact how tribunals interpret the scope and content of the obligation.[7] United Nations Conference on Trade and Development (UNCTAD) published an important report in 2012 indicating that the drafting variations in FET clauses have had an impact on how tribunals have assessed matters of liability.[8] UNCTAD noted a

5. *See*, https://www.oecd.org/daf/inv/investment-policy/investment-treaties.htm.
6. See, P. Dumberry, 'The Cost of Inaction: Arbitral Practice in Respect of Earlier Generation FET Clauses and Current Approaches to FET Clauses', 7 November 2023, at: https://www.oecd.org/investment/investment-policy/Expert-contribution-Prof-Dumberry-on-FET.pdf.
7. OECD, *Fair and Equitable Treatment Standard in International Investment Law* (2004), No. 2004/3, Working Papers on International Investment Law, 40.
8. UNCTAD, *Fair and Equitable Treatment*, Series on Issues in International Investment Agreements II (2012) 8: '[The] identification of the correct source of the FET standard – whether it is grounded

significant statistical difference between the lower success rates (22%) of FET claims filed under the North American Free Trade Agreement (NAFTA) (where the FET clause is linked to the MST) compared to the much higher one (62%) under FET clauses found in other BITs.[9] The goal of my research project was to assess whether the picture described by UNCTAD (assessing only 88 awards) is still accurate 10 years later. To the best of my knowledge, this is the first comprehensive survey of case law on the FET since the 2012 UNCTAD Report. My analysis of 279 relevant awards confirms some of the patterns identified in the Report. It also identifies new trends.

On the one hand, my analysis of 174 awards examining stand-alone FET clauses shows that less than 25% of these awards actually addressed the question of the status of the clause and its relationship with the MST. Yet, the vast majority of awards where tribunals took a position on the issue concluded that the clause should be interpreted to have an 'autonomous' character (80% of awards). Very few awards interpreted a stand-alone FET clause as an implicit reference to the MST under custom. The success rate of FET claims is higher for tribunals that have expressly stated that a stand-alone FET clause has an 'autonomous' character compared to those which did not take a position on this question (2\3 versus 50%). These findings suggest that when a tribunal discusses the question of the status of the FET clause and takes a position on the matter, it is more likely that it will conclude that a breach has been committed. On the contrary, if a tribunal does not take a position on this question, it is less likely to find a breach. In any event, the overall success rate of 50% for all awards examining stand-alone FET clauses is much higher compared to the way tribunals have assessed other types of FET clauses.

Thus, in 42 awards where tribunals have examined FET clauses expressly linked to the MST in NAFTA, CAFTA, and other BITs, they have consistently followed the contracting parties' intention and applied a strict standard. I have found no award interpreting this type of clause as a stand-alone 'autonomous' FET clause. Interpreting the clause in accordance with the MST led tribunals to define the content of the FET standard narrowly. For instance, the vast majority have not considered investors' legitimate expectations to be a stand-alone element, but rather as a factor to be taken into account when assessing other elements contained in the standard. They have also systematically required a high threshold of severity to find a breach. As a result of this narrow interpretation, NAFTA tribunals concluded that the host State violated the FET clause in a limited number of cases. The success rate of NAFTA claims is thus significantly lower (25%) when compared to awards interpreting other types of FET clauses. These findings therefore confirm UNCTAD's analysis published 10 years ago.

On the other hand, my survey also shows other patterns which, to the best of my knowledge, had not been empirically identified before. These developments concern FET clauses which refer to 'international law' (63 awards). How a tribunal analyses the

in customary international law or is a self-standing obligation – can have important consequences in terms of the standard's content and, more precisely, of the types of State measures that can be challenged as well as the required threshold for finding a violation, that is, the required degree of seriousness of the breach.'

9. These BITs contain stand-alone FET clauses without any reference to the MST or provisions referring to 'international law'.

status of such an FET clause and the question of its relationship with the MST has a direct impact on the interpretation (broad or narrow) it gives to the standard's content and to matters of liability and compensation. The pattern is very clear if one examines the two different types of clauses referring to 'international law' separately.

First, let's examine FET clauses where the treatment must be 'in accordance with international law'. The vast majority of awards where tribunals have taken a position on the status of this type of clause have concluded that this is *not* a reference to the MST under custom. They have considered that under this clause the FET standard offers better protection than under the MST. In practice, they interpreted the clause in very much the same way as other tribunals have regarding stand-alone FET clauses having an autonomous character. These broad interpretations led the majority of tribunals (two-thirds of awards) to find a breach of FET and to award compensation.

Second, let's look at FET clauses where the treatment must be 'no less' than that required by international law. Tribunals assessing this type of clause have been evenly divided on the interpretation to be given to this provision and its relationship to the MST. Yet, there is a clear link between the approach adopted by a tribunal on this question and how it assesses matters of liability and compensation. Tribunals which have considered 'no less' clauses as offering better protection than under the MST have given broad interpretations which led *all of them* to conclude that a breach had been committed. On the contrary, tribunals which have interpreted 'no less' clauses as meaning that the level of treatment is the same as the one existing under MST, have adopted narrower approaches which led the vast majority of them to not find a breach.

The findings in this book are important given that new trends are emerging regarding how States are drafting FET clauses in their new investment treaties. States are increasingly adopting investment treaties that contain FET clauses which are explicitly linked to the MST. The 2023 OECD Report indicates that about half of all treaties concluded in the past decade which include an FET clause have adopted this approach.[10] Many recent treaties also contain FET clauses with a closed list of specific elements of the FET obligation (e.g., the CETA between the European Union (EU) and Canada). The OECD Report also noted that no new treaty signed in the last five years contains a 'stand-alone' FET clause.[11] Notwithstanding these new developments, these types of provisions remain the most frequently used FET clause in all investment treaties that are in force. Stand-alone FET clauses are found in almost 80% of treaties concluded between 1959 and 2023.[12]

States are also increasingly expressing their willingness to adopt new FET clauses (or to modify existing ones) to protect their needs and interests better. In fact, the goal of the OECD 'Track 2' program is for States to have a 'discussion to consider whether it would be better if specific substantive provisions of older treaties were more similar to those now almost universally used in newer treaties'.[13] The OECD has, so far,

10. OECD, *supra* n. 3, 16.
11. *Ibid.*, 15.
12. *Ibid.*
13. *See*, https://www.oecd.org/investment/investment-policy/investment-treaties.htm.

examined expropriation and MFN clauses.[14] One of the clauses currently studied in the context of this program is the FET clause.

In the current context where States are increasingly willing to make substantive changes to FET clauses in their treaties, it is, in my view, essential for all stakeholders to have a clear global picture. Apart from the 2012 UNCTAD Report, this book is the first to provide solid empirical evidence of some of the possible pitfalls which are associated with the inclusion of a stand-alone FET clause in a treaty. It is also the first study to explain that only a minority of tribunals examining FET clauses linked to 'international law' concluded that it should be considered a reference to the MST under custom. The majority of tribunals examining these clauses have, in fact, viewed them in very much the same way as stand-alone FET clauses. This book also shows that there are undeniable potential benefits for States in adopting detailed FET clauses linked to the MST in their treaties.

II THE STRUCTURE OF THIS BOOK

Part I examines the interaction between the MST and the FET standard. It analyses the fascinating story of how the concept of the MST emerged in the early twentieth century, its subsequent decline from the 1960s until the 1990s and its surprising recent 'resurrection' in the year 2000. This evolution has had a direct impact on the emergence and subsequent development of the FET standard. Thus, why have States started referring to the FET standard instead of the MST in their investment treaties? In answering this question, I will address the controversial question of whether the FET is an autonomous standard of protection to be accorded to foreign investors, or is a mere reference to the MST under customary international law.

Part II examines how tribunals have concretely interpreted FET clauses and their interaction with the MST. Furthermore, it assesses if their reasoning has had any impact on the interpretation they gave to the content of the standard and regarding matters of liability and compensation.

After having examined the theoretical aspects of the relationship between FET clauses and the MST (in Part I) and concretely assessed how tribunals have dealt with the issue (in Part II), I will finally address, in Part III, the soundness of the arguments put forward by the supporters of the 'convergence' theory. According to the tribunals which have endorsed this theory, the level of protection offered to foreign investors under the MST has rapidly evolved in recent years. As a result, the level of protection under custom is now said to be the same as that existing under BITs containing a stand-alone FET clause. Accordingly, all FET clauses, whatever their differences in language, would now provide investors with the *same* standard of treatment. My

14. *See*, OECD, *The Interaction Between Most-Favoured-Nation Clauses and Dispute Settlement Arrangements in Investment Treaties*, OECD Secretariat background note, 30 Nov. 2022 meeting: https://www.oecd.org/daf/inv/investment-policy/most-favoured-nation-clauses-dispute-settlement-investment-treaties.pdf; *The Notion of 'Indirect Expropriation' in Investment Treaties Concluded by 88 Jurisdictions: A Large Sample Survey of Treaty Provisions*, OECD Secretariat background note, October 2021 meeting: https://www.oecd.org/investment/investment-policy/oecd-future-investment-treaties-indirect-expropriation-meeting-background.pdf.

empirical analysis of awards in Part II shows that this is *not at all* how tribunals have concretely analysed FET clauses. In fact, the way they have generally assessed the content of the standard of protection (broad or narrow) and matters of liability very much depends on the type of FET clause they were applying. I will explain the reasons why the 'convergence' theory should be rejected.

Finally, Part IV provides a summary of my findings.

PART I 'The Interaction Between the FET and the MST'

Introduction

The first Part of this book examines the question of the interaction between the Minimum Standard of Treatment (MST) and the Fair and Equitable Treatment (FET) standard.

Chapter I examines the emergence of the MST in the early twentieth century as a basic threshold of protection meant to be imposed on all States and accorded to all *foreign* investors, notwithstanding the level of treatment already offered by States to their own nationals. In the 1920s and 1930s, international jurisprudence slowly developed the concept, and by the end of World War II, it was well-established as a rule of custom. In the 1960s and 1970s, Newly Independent States began to challenge the existence of any such MST. While the standard ultimately survived these events, the opposition by many States had another more subtle consequence: both developing and developed States now perceived the MST as ineffective in providing basic legal protection to foreign investors doing business abroad. It is in this historical context that both developed and developing States began frenetically signing bilateral treaties for the promotion and protection of foreign investments (BITs) that provided clearer rules on investment protection.

Chapter II examines the emergence of the FET standard in investment treaties and its interaction with the MST. One of the most controversial questions discussed in scholarship is why States began using the FET expression in their BITs instead of the well-established customary rule of the MST. According to one view, Western States incorporated the concept of FET into their BITs to simply reflect the MST that existed under international law. In other words, the FET was simply used as a convenient, neutral and acceptable reference to the MST. In my view, a more convincing approach explains that Western States began to use the expression *because* of the ambiguities surrounding the concept of the MST and the fact that it had been heavily contested by many States in the past. The drafting language used by States in their BITs supports this approach insofar as the vast majority of them contain stand-alone (or autonomous) references to the FET standard without mention of international law or the MST. According to a recent Organisation for Economic Co-operation and Development (OECD) paper, these clauses represent almost 80% of FET provisions in treaties concluded between 1959 and 2023.[1] In my view, the FET standard should *generally* be considered an *independent* treaty standard with an autonomous meaning from the MST. Yet, there are some *particular situations* where this is not the case: when a treaty *explicitly* links the FET to the standard existing under 'international law' or the MST (one example is North American Free Trade Agreement (NAFTA) Article 1105).[2]

In any event, by the end of the 1990s, the MST, as a source of investment protection for foreign investors, was in sharp decline. Chapter III examines the phenomenon of the 'return' of the MST to centre stage. Its return was the consequence of many tribunals (notably in the context of NAFTA) beginning to interpret FET clauses in the early 2000s and concluding that they provided investors with *more extensive* rights than under the MST. States reacted strongly to these controversial awards. For instance, the NAFTA Parties issued a binding Note of Interpretation explaining that they had always intended for the FET standard to be interpreted strictly as a reference to the MST. The NAFTA Parties, as well as a number of other States, also began to refer explicitly to the MST in FET clauses contained in their investment treaties. Their clear aim was to limit the scope of investors' rights under these clauses. The novel FET clause contained in the European Union (EU)-Canada *Comprehensive Economic and Trade Agreement* (CETA), which includes a detailed list of the elements considered to be in breach of the standard, is clearly the most explicit attempt by States to achieve that goal.

I THE EMERGENCE OF THE MST AS A RULE OF CUSTOMARY INTERNATIONAL LAW

The first section defines the concept of MST and examines its customary status (section 1.1). The following sections examine its historical foundation (section 1.2) and the subsequent challenges to its customary status that was led by developing States in the 1960s and 1970s (section 1.3), which resulted in the new phenomenon of 'treatification' in the 1990s (section 1.4).

1.1 The Concept of the MST and Its Customary Status

Despite some disagreement between States on the existence of the MST in the last few decades (a point that will be examined further below), the concept is now predominantly recognised as a rule of customary international law. Many States have explicitly recognised the customary status of the MST in their pleadings in investment arbitration proceedings.[3] The customary nature of the MST has also been recognised by several

1. OECD, *'Fair' and 'Equitable' Treatment Provisions in Investment Treaties; A Large-Sample Survey of Treaty Provisions* (2023).
2. For an analysis of this provision, *see*: P. Dumberry, *The Fair and Equitable Treatment Standard: A Guide to NAFTA Case Law on Article 1105* (Wolters Kluwer 2013).
3. *See*, for instance, the following non-exhaustive list of cases: *Azurix Corp v. Argentina*, ICSID Case No. ARB/01/12, Award, 14 Jul. 2006, paras 332-333; *Bayindir Insaat Turizm Ticaret ve Sanayi A Şv.*

NAFTA awards.[4] It has also been endorsed by the three NAFTA Parties in their respective pleadings[5] as well as in the Free Trade Commission's (FTC's) 2001 Note of Interpretation.[6] Numerous other awards (outside NAFTA) have also explicitly (or implicitly) acknowledged the customary nature of the MST.[7] The majority of writers

---

Pakistan, ICSID Case No. ARB/03/29, Award, 27 Aug. 2009, paras 164, 173; *Bureau Veritas, Inspection, Valuation, Assessment and Control, BIVAC BV v. Paraguay*, ICSID Case No. ARB/07/9, Further Decision on Objections to Jurisdiction, 9 Oct. 2012, paras 105, 152-153; *Biwater Gauff (Tanzania Ltd) v. Tanzania*, ICSID Case No. ARB/05/22, Award and Concurring and Dissenting Opinion, 24 Jul. 2008, para. 587; *Chevron Corporation and Texaco Petroleum Corporation v. Ecuador*, UNCITRAL, Partial Award on Merits, 30 Mar. 2010, para. 227; *CMS Gas Transmission Company v. Argentina*, ICSID Case No. ARB/01/8, Award, 25 Apr. 2005, paras 270-271, 282; *Compañía de Aguas del Aconquija SA and Vivendi Universal SA v. Argentina*, ICSID Case No. ARB/97/3, Award, 20 Aug. 2007, paras 5.2.2, 6.6.2; *Continental Casualty Company v. Argentina*, ICSID Case No. ARB/03/9, Award, 5 Sep. 2008, paras 56, 248, 253; *Duke Energy Electroquil Partners and Electroquil SA v. Ecuador*, ICSID Case No. ARB/04/19, Award, 18 Aug. 2008, para. 331; *EDF International SA et al v. Argentina*, ICSID Case No. ARB/03/23, Final Award, 11 Jun. 2012, para. 343; *Electrabel SA v. Hungary*, ICSID Case No. ARB/07/19, Decision on Jurisdiction, Applicable Law and Liability, 30 Nov. 2012, para. 7.157; *El Paso Energy International Company v. Argentina*, ICSID Case No. ARB/03/15, Award, 31 Oct. 2011, para. 329; *Enron Corporation and Ponderosa Assets, LP v. Argentina*, ICSID Case No. ARB/01/3, Award, 22 May 2007, para. 253; *Kardassopoulos v. Georgia and joined case*, ICSID Case Nos ARB/05/18 and ARB/07/15, Award, 3 Mar. 2010, paras 409, 417; *LG&E Energy Corp., LG&E Capital Corp. and LG&E International Inc. v. Argentina*, ICSID Case No. ARB/02/1, Decision on Liability, 3 Oct. 2006, para. 113; *MCI Power Group LC and New Turbine Inc v. Ecuador*, ICSID Case No. ARB/03/6, Award, 31 Jul. 2007, para. 250; *Metalpar S.A. and Buen Aire S.A. v. Argentina*, ICSID Case No. ARB/03/5, Award on the Merits, 6 Jun. 2008, para. 117; *National Grid PLC v. Argentina*, UNCITRAL, Award, 3 Nov. 2008, para. 161; *Railroad Development Corporation (RDC) v. Guatemala*, ICSID case No. ARB/07/23, Award, 29 Jun. 2012, paras 159, 207-211 (referring also to the same position adopted by El Salvador and Honduras); *Rumeli Telekom AS and Telsim Mobil Telekomikasyon Hizmetleri AS v. Kazakhstan*, ICSID Case No. ARB/05/16, Award, 29 Jul. 2008, para. 611; *Saluka Investments BV v. Czech Republic*, UNCITRAL, Partial Award, 17 Mar. 2006, para. 289; *SAUR International SA v. Argentina*, ICSID Case No. ARB/04/4, Decision on Jurisdiction and Liability, 6 Jun. 2012, para. 472; *Sempra Energy International v. Argentina*, ICSID Case No. ARB/02/16, Award, 28 Sep. 2007, paras 292, 294; *Suez, Sociedad General de Aguas de Barcelona S.A., and Vivendi Universal S.A. v. Argentina*, ICSID No. ARB/03/19, Decision on Liability, 30 Jul. 2010, para. 183; *Ulysseas, Inc v. Ecuador*, UNCITRAL, Final Award, 12 Jun. 2012, paras 206-207; *Unglaube and Unglaube v. Costa Rica*, ICSID Case Nos ARB/08/1 and ARB/09/20, Award, 16 May 2012, para. 242.

4. *Mondev International Ltd. v. United States*, ICSID Case No. ARB/AF/99/2, Award, 2 Oct. 2012, para. 121; *Waste Management, Inc. v. Mexico ('Number 2')*, ICSID Case No. ARB/AF/00/3, Award, 30 Apr. 2004, para. 91; *Glamis Gold Ltd v. United States*, UNCITRAL, Award, 8 Jun. 2009, para. 627; *Apotex Holdings Inc & Apotex Inc. v. United States*, ICSID Case No. ARB/AF/12/1, Award, 25 Aug. 2014, paras 2.64, 9.15, 9.16, 9.25, 9.27; *ADF Group Inc. v. United States*, ICSID Case No. ARB/AF/00/1, Award, 6 Jan. 2003, para. 179; *Cargill, Inc. v. Mexico*, ICSID Case No. ARB/AF/05/02, Award, 18 Sep. 2009, para. 278; *Merrill & Ring Forestry L.P. v. Canada*, UNCITRAL, Award, 31 Mar. 2010, para. 190; *Eli Lilly and Company v. Canada*, UNCITRAL, Case No. UNCT/14/2, Final Award, 16 Mar. 2017, para. 223; *William Ralph Clayton, William Richard Clayton, Douglas Clayton, Daniel Clayton and Bilcon of Delaware, Inc v. Canada*, UNCITRAL PCA Case No. 2009-04, Award on Jurisdiction and Liability, 17 Mar. 2015, para. 436; *Windstream Energy LLC v. Canada*, UNCITRAL, Award, 27 Sep. 2016, para. 350.
5. *See*, for instance, *ADF, supra* n. 4, para. 112 (referring to the position of the US); *Glamis, supra* n. 4, para. 543 (referring to the position of the US); *Apotex, supra* n. 4, para. 2.64; *Mondev, supra* n. 4, para. 111.
6. FTC, 'Note of Interpretation of Certain Chapter 11 Provisions', 31 Jul. 2001.
7. *See*, for instance: *Impregilo S.p.A. v. Argentina*, ICSID Case No. ARB/07/17, Award, 21 Jun. 2001, para. 285; *Bayindir, supra* n. 3, para. 164; *Biwater, supra* n. 3, para. 592; *CMS, supra* n. 3, paras 270-271, 282, 284 (referring to an 'international law minimum standard'); *Compañía de Aguas,*

have also recognised that the MST is a rule of customary international law;[8] only a few have rejected such a claim.[9]

supra n. 3, paras 5.2.2, 6.6.2, 7.4.5, 7.4.6, 7.4.7; *EDF, supra* n. 3, paras 343, 999; *El Paso Energy, supra* n. 3, paras 329, 335-336; *Enron, supra* n. 3, paras 253, 258, *see also,* Decision on the Application for Annulment of the Argentine Republic, Annulment Committee, paras 302, 304; *Lauder v. Czech Republic,* UNCITRAL, Final Award, 3 Sep. 2001, para. 292; *Lemire v. Ukraine,* ICSID No. ARB/06/18, Decision on Jurisdiction and Liability, 21 Jan. 2010, paras 250-254, *see also,* Award, 28 Mar. 2011, para. 139; *National Grid, supra* n. 3, paras 167, 169, 170; *Occidental Exploration and Production Co v. Ecuador,* LCIA Case No. UN3467, Award, 1 Jul. 2004, paras 188-192; *Railroad Development, supra* n. 3, para. 218; *Rumeli, supra* n. 3, para. 611; *Saluka, supra* n. 3, paras 289, 291-295; *SAUR, supra* n. 3, para. 491; *Sempra, supra* n. 3, para. 302; *Siemens AG v. Argentina,* ICSID No. ARB/02/8, Award, 17 Jan. 2007, paras 289, 291, 293; *Suez, supra* n. 3, para. 184; *Total SA v. Argentina,* ICSID Case No. ARB/04/1, Decision on Liability, 27 Dec. 2010, para. 125; *Ulysseas, supra* n. 3, paras 206-207, 245; *Spence International Investments, LLC, Berkowitz, et al v. Costa Rica,* ICSID Case No. Unct/13/2, Interim Award, 30 May 2017, para. 282; *Rusoro Mining Ltd. v. Venezuela,* ICSID Case No. ARB/AF/12/5, Award, 22 Aug. 2016, paras 513, 520; *Murphy Exploration & Production Company International v. Ecuador,* PCA Case No. 2012-16, Partial Final Award, 6 May 2016, paras 206-208; *Crystallex International Corporation v. Venezuela,* ICSID Case No. ARB/AF/11/2, Award, 4 Apr. 2016, para. 530; *Quiborax S.A., Non Metallic Minerals S.A. and Allan Fosk Kaplún v. Bolivia,* ICSID Case No. ARB/06/2, Award, 16 Sep. 2015, paras 290-291; *ECE Projektmanagement v. The Czech Republic,* UNCITRAL, PCA Case No. 2010-5, Award, 19 Sep. 2013, para. 4.760; *Mr. Franck Charles Arif v. Moldova,* ICSID Case No. ARB/11/23, Award, 8 Apr. 2013, para. 529; *Deutsche Bank AG v. Sri Lanka,* ICSID Case No. ARB/09/2, Award, 31 Oct. 2012, para. 419; *Continental Casualty, supra* n. 3, para. 254; *Oko Pankki Oyj, VTB Bank Deutschland AG and Sampo Bank Plc v. Estonia,* ICSID Case No. ARB/04/6, Award, 19 Nov. 2007, para. 216; *Abengoa, S.A. y COFIDES, S.A. v. Mexico,* ICSID Case No. ARB/AF/09/2, Award, 18 Apr. 2013, paras 642-643; *TECO Guatemala Holdings, LLC v. Guatemala,* ICSID Case No. ARB/10/23, Award, 19 Dec. 2013, para. 455; *Binder v. Czech Republic,* UNCITRAL, Final Award, 15 Jul. 2001, para. 484; *Electrabel, supra* n. 3, paras 7.158-7.159; *OAO Tatneft v. Ukraine,* PCA UNCITRAL, Award on the Merits, 29 Jul. 2014, para. 392;*Teinver S.A., Transportes de Cercanías S.A. and Autobuses Urbanos del Sur S.A. v. Argentina,* ICSID Case No. ARB/09/01, Award, 21 Jul. 2017, para. 666; *Addiko Bank AG v. Montenegro,* ICSID Case No. ARB/17/35, Award, 24 Nov. 2021, paras 543-544; *Spoldzielnia Pracy Muszynianka v. Slovak Republic,* UNCITRAL, PCA Case No. 2017-08, 7 Oct. 2020, para. 459; *Veolia Propreté v. Arab Republic of Egypt,* ICSID Case No. ARB/12/15, Award, 25 May 2018, para. 162; *Abed El Jaouni and Imperial Holding SAL v. Lebanon,* ICSID Case No. ARB/15/3, Decision on Jurisdiction and Liability, 25 Jun. 2018, and Award, 14 Jan. 2021, para. 509; *SunReserve Luxco Holdings S.à.r.l. (Luxembourg) et al. v. Italy,* SCC Case No. 2016/32, Final Award, 25 Mar. 2020, paras 672-673; *Silver Ridge Power BV v. Italian Republic,* ICSID Case No. ARB /15/37, Award, 26 Feb. 2021, para. 401; *Belenergia S.A. v. Italy,* ICSID Case No. ARB/15/40, Award, 6 Aug. 2019, para. 568; *LSG Building Solutions GmbH and others v. Romania,* ICSID Case No. ARB/18/19, Decision on Jurisdiction, Liability and Principles of Reparation, 11 Jul. 2022, para. 1019; *Valores Mundiales, S.L. and Consorcio Andino S.L. v. Venezuela,* ICSID Case No. ARB/13/11, Award, 25 Jul. 2017, para. 530; *Koch Minerals Sarl and Koch Nitrogen International Sarl v. Venezuela,* ICSID Case No. ARB/11/19, Award, 30 Oct. 2017, para. 8.42; *Flughafen Zürich A.G. and Gestión e Ingenería IDC S.A. v. Venezuela,* ICSID Case No. ARB/10/19, Award, 12 Nov. 2014, para. 573; *Iberdrola Energia, S.A. v. Guatemala,* ICSID Case No. ARB/09/5, August 2012, para. 427; *The Lopez-Goyne Family Trust and Others v. Nicaragua,* ICSID, Case No. ARB/17/44, Award, 1 Mar. 2023, para. 428; *Adel A Hamadi Al Tamimi v. Oman,* ICSID Case No. ARB/11/33, Award, 27 Oct. 2015, paras 382, 384, 386; *OI European Group B.V. v. Venezuela,* ICSID Case No. ARB/11/25, Award, 10 Mar. 2015, para. 484; *Windstream, supra* n. 4, para. 350.

8. J.C. Thomas, *Fair and Equitable Treatment under NAFTA's Investment Chapter; Remarks'* 96 ASIL Proc. 14 (2002); R. Dolzer & M. Stevens, *Bilateral Investment Treaties* (Martinus Nijhoff 1995) 58; Sir R. Jenning & Sir A. Watts, *Oppenheim's International Law* (9th ed., vol. I, Part 1, Longman 1996) 931; L. Reed, J. Paulsson & N. Blackaby, *A Guide to ICSID Arbitration* (Kluwer Law 2004) 48; I. Tudor, *The Fair and Equitable Treatment Standard in International Foreign Investment Law* (Oxford UP 2008) 61-62, 67; A. Newcombe & L. Paradell, *Law and Practice of Investment Treaties:*

What is more controversial is determining the actual *content* of the standard. The MST is an *umbrella concept* that incorporates different elements. As pointed out by Roth in 1949, 'the international standard is nothing else but a set of rules, correlated to each other and deriving from one particular norm of general international law, namely that the treatment of an alien is regulated by the laws of nations'.[10] Similarly, according to Newcombe and Paradell, the MST 'consists of a series of interconnecting and overlapping elements or standards that apply to both the treatment of foreigners and their property'.[11] A number of NAFTA tribunals have also endorsed the description of the MST as an umbrella concept.[12]

A number of writers have emphasised that the concept of the MST is vague and lacks precise content.[13] For instance, in a 2012 report, the United Nations Conference

Standards of Treatment (Kluwer 2009) 234; A. Diehl, *The Core Standard of International Investment Protection: Fair and Equitable Treatment* (Wolters Kluwer 2012) 145; G. Cavazos Villanueva, *The Fair and Equitable Treatment Standard: The Mexican Experience* (VDM Verlag 2008) 63-64; D. Carreau, *Investissements*, in: *Répertoire de droit international* (Dalloz 1998) para. 135; H. Dickerson, *Minimum Standards*, 9 Max Planck Encyclopedia of Public International Law, para. 1 (2013); M. Klein Bronfman, *Fair and Equitable Treatment: An Evolving Standard*, 10 Max Planck Yrbk. UNL 624 (2006) DOI: 10.1163/138946306783559986; J.C. Thomas, *Reflections on Article 1105 of NAFTA: History, State Practice and the Influence of Commentators*, 17(1) ICSID Rev. 29ff. (2002) DOI: 10.1093/icsidreview/17.1.21; J. Roman Picherack, *The Expanding Scope of the Fair and Equitable Treatment Standard: Have Recent Tribunals Gone Too Far?*. 9(4) J. World Invest. & Trade 265 (2008) DOI: 10.1163/221190008x00061; G. Mayeda, *Playing Fair: The Meaning of Fair and Equitable Treatment in Bilateral Investment Treaties*, 41(2) J. World Trade 273-291, 280 (2007) DOI: 10.54648/trad2007011; M. Audit & M. Forteau, *Investment Arbitration Without BIT: Toward a Foreign Investment Customary Based Arbitration?*, 29 J. Int. Arb. 640 (2012) DOI: 10.54648/joia2012036; M. Paparinskis, *The International Minimum Standard and Fair and Equitable Treatment* (Oxford UP 2013) 16, 163; T. Gazzini, *The Role of Customary International Law in the Field of Foreign Investment*, 8 J. World Invest. & Trade 699 (2007) DOI: 10.1163/221190007x00143; T. Kill, *Don't Cross the Streams: Past and Present Overstatement of Customary International Law in Connection with Conventional Fair and Equitable Treatment Obligations*, 106 Mich. L. Rev 853, 856 (2008); J.-P. Laviec, *Protection et promotion des investissements, étude de droit international économique* (PUF 1985) 86-88; M.A. Orellana, *International Law on Investment: The Minimum Standard of Treatment (MST)*, 3 TDM 1-2 (2004); J.W. Salacuse, *The Law of Investment Treaties* (Oxford UP 2010) 311; J.P. Trachtman, *The Obsolescence of Customary International Law*, SSRN 87-88 (2014).

9. M.C. Porterfield, *An International Common Law of Investor Rights?*, 27 U. Pa. J. Int'l Econ. L. 81-82, 98, 103, 113 (2006); M. Sornarajah, *The International Law on Foreign Investment* (2nd ed., Cambridge UP 2004) 64, 92-93 (but *see also* at 328-329); S. Schwebel, *The United States 2004 Model Bilateral Investment Treaty: An Exercise in the Regressive Development of International Law*, in: *Global Reflections on International Law, Commerce and Dispute Resolution, Liber Amicorum in honour of Robert Briner* (ICC Pub. 2005) 647.
10. H. Roth, *The Minimum Standard of International Law Applied to Aliens* (A.W. Sijthoff 1949) 127.
11. Newcombe & Paradell, *supra* n. 8, 236.
12. *See*, for instance: *Glamis, supra* n. 4, para. 618; *Cargill, supra* n. 4, para. 268; *Mobil Investments Canada Inc. & Murphy Oil Corporation v. Canada*, ICSID Case No. ARB/AF/07/4, Decision on Liability and on Principles of Quantum, 22 May 2012, para. 135.
13. M. Sornarajah, *The Fair and Equitable Standard of Treatment: Whose Fairness? Whose Equity?*, in: Federico Ortino et al. (eds) *Investment Treaty Law: Current Issues II* (BIICL 2007) 172; Sornarajah, *supra* n. 9, 328; Porterfield, *supra* n. 9, 80; Gazzini, *supra* n. 8, 699; J. d'Aspremont, *International Customary Investment Law: Story of a Paradox*, in: T. Gazzini & E. de Brabandere (eds), *International Investment Law: The Sources of Rights and Obligations* (Martinus Nijhoff 2012) 33; R. Islam, *The Fair and Equitable Treatment (FET) Standard in International Investment Arbitration: Developing Countries in Context* (Springer 2018) 58.

on Trade and Development (UNCTAD) stated that the minimum standard is 'highly indeterminate, lacks a clearly defined content and requires interpretation'.[14] The report suggested that '[t]he MST is a concept that does not offer ready-made solutions for deciding modern investment disputes; at best, it gives a rough idea of a high threshold that the challenged governmental conduct has to meet for a breach to be established'.[15] As a result, it has been argued that the MST lacks the necessary *normative requirement*, as identified by the International Court of Justice (ICJ) in the *North Sea Continental Shelf* case,[16] in order to be considered a rule of custom.[17]

An OECD report stated that 'case law points to a number of areas across which the notion of an international minimum standard applies' including 'the administration of justice in cases involving foreign nationals, usually linked to the notion of denial of justice', 'the treatment of aliens under detention', full protection and security, and finally, the 'general right of expulsion by the host State' which 'should be the least injurious to the person affected'.[18] The 2012 UNCTAD report came to the same conclusion as that of the OECD.[19] Other writers have defined the content of the minimum standard more broadly.[20] The present author has concluded elsewhere that the MST encompasses (at the very least) an obligation for host States to prevent the denial of justice in the administration of justice, to provide due process, to prevent arbitrary conduct and to provide investors with 'full protection and security'.[21] One of the most controversial questions in the field of investor-State arbitration is whether the FET standard is one of the elements *encompassed* within the larger umbrella concept of the MST or whether it is an autonomous standard. This question is examined below.

---

14. UNCTAD, *Fair and Equitable Treatment*, UNCTAD Series on Issues in International Investment Agreements II (2012) 28, *see also* 44.
15. *Ibid.*, 46-47.
16. *North Sea Continental Shelf Cases (Federal Republic of Germany v. Denmark / Federal Republic of Germany v. Netherlands)*, 1969 ICJ Rep. 42, para. 72, indicating that a provision must be of a 'fundamentally norm-creating character such as could be regarded as forming the basis of a general rule of law'.
17. d'Aspremont, *supra* n. 13, 33-34, *see also* at 10-12, 23-24.
18. OECD, *International Investment Law: A Changing Landscape: A Companion Volume to International Investment Perspectives* (2005) 82. This definition is endorsed by Tudor, *supra* n. 8, 62.
19. UNCTAD, *supra* n. 14, 44, referring also to: OECD, *Fair and Equitable Treatment Standard in International Investment Law* (2004) (Working Papers on International Investment Law No. 2004/3). A similar approach is adopted by Sornarajah, *supra* n. 13, 172; Sornarajah, *supra* n. 9, 329.
20. Based on the list mentioned by the tribunal in *Waste Management, supra* n. 4, para. 98, Newcombe & Paradell, *supra* n. 8, 238, indicate that a 'number of specific elements of the minimum standard of treatment where state responsibility may arise for mistreatment of foreign investors and investment, including, but not exhaustively: denial of justice, lack of due process, lack of due diligence, and instances of arbitrariness and discrimination'. Paparinskis, *supra* n. 8, 182, 239, 246-247, 256, argues that denial of justice, arbitrariness and non-discrimination are elements of the MST.
21. Dumberry, *supra* n. 2, 25-28.

1.2 The Historical Foundation of the MST

The historical aspects surrounding the emergence of the MST have already been the subject of substantial scholarship.[22] Moreover, a number of articles[23] and books[24] published in the last 20 years have also made a significant contribution to the understanding of the concept.

The origin of the MST is grounded in the international law doctrine of State responsibility for injuries to aliens.[25] It is rooted in a due diligence obligation for States to respect the rights of foreigners within their country. Before the twentieth century, there was a prevailing view that individuals conducting business in another State should be subject to the law of that State.[26] This point of view stemmed from the fact that many States, especially in Latin America, strongly opposed other solutions. Several States adopted this position to counter so-called gunboat diplomacy and other types of interferences by Western States in their internal affairs that were often made under the pretext of protecting the interests of their nationals abroad.[27] It is in this context that many States rejected the idea of the existence of any obligation under international law to accord a 'minimum' level of protection to foreigners.[28]

Despite this opposition, an MST gradually emerged in the early twentieth century,[29] which at the time, focused almost exclusively on the non-discriminatory aspects of the treatment and on preventing denial of justice.[30] The development of this standard of treatment stemmed from capital-exporting States' concern that many host States of investments lacked the most basic measures of protection for aliens and their property.[31] They argued that all governments were bound under international law to

22. *See*, for instance, E. Borchard, *The 'Minimum Standard' of the Treatment of Aliens*, 33 ASIL Proc. 55 (1939) DOI: 10.1017/s0272503700041215; E. Borchard, *The Diplomatic Protection of Citizen Abroad* (Bank Law Publishing Co. 1915); E. Borchard, *The 'Minimum Standard' of the Treatment of Aliens*, 38 Mich. L. Rev. 445 (1940) DOI: 10.2307/1282834; E. Root, *The Basis of Protection to Citizens Residing Abroad*, 4 AJIL 521 (1919) DOI: 10.2307/2186238; C. Eagleton, *The Responsibility of States in International Law* (New York U. Press 1928) 103; Roth, *supra* n. 10.
23. *See, inter alia*: Orellana, *supra* n. 8; T. Weiler, *An Historical Analysis of the Function of the Minimum Standard of Treatment in International Investment Law*, in: T. Weiler & F. Baetens (eds), *New Directions in International Economic Law: In Memoriam Thomas Wälde* (Martinus Nijhoff, 2011); A. Falsafi, *The International Minimum Standard of Treatment of Foreign Investors' Property: A Contingent Standard*, 30 Suffolk Transnat'l L. Rev. 317 (2006-2007); H. Haeri, *A Tale of Two Standards: 'Fair and Equitable Treatment' and the Minimum Standard in International Law*, 27 Arb. Int. 31-32 (2011) DOI: 10.1093/arbitration/27.1.27.
24. Paparinskis, *supra* n. 8, 39-83; T. Weiler, *The Interpretation of International Investment Law: Equality, Discrimination and Minimum Standards of Treatment in Historical Context* (Martinus Nijhoff 2013).
25. Dickerson, *supra* n. 8, para. 2.
26. Tudor, *supra* n. 8, 60. This period is examined in detail in: Weiler, *supra* n. 23, 337ff.
27. Weiler, *supra* n. 23, 345, providing several examples of such interventions and referring to 'no fewer than one hundred instances of "protection by force" between 1813 and 1927 by the United States alone, including two dozen in the 20th century'.
28. S. Schill, *The Multilateralization of International Investment Law* (Cambridge UP 2009) 26-27.
29. Paparinskis, *supra* n. 8, 64.
30. Weiler, *supra* n. 23, 351.
31. Orellana, *supra* n. 8, 1.

treat foreigners with at least a minimum standard of protection[32] because the existing standard in many countries was considered too low.[33] The reasons for establishing such a standard were explained by the United States (US) Secretary of State, Mr Elihu Root, in an article published in 1910[34] and they were reiterated some 90 years later by the NAFTA *S.D. Myers* Tribunal explaining that the 'minimum standard' is a 'floor below which treatment of foreign investors must not fall'.[35] The *Glamis* Tribunal subsequently explained that the standard is 'meant to serve as a floor, an absolute bottom, below which conduct is not accepted by the international community', adding that the standard 'cannot vary between nations as thus the protection afforded would have no minimum'.[36]

International jurisprudence slowly developed the concept of a minimum standard of protection.[37] While a number of cases have had a significant impact on the emergence of this standard,[38] the best known is certainly the *Neer* case in 1926. This case was decided by the US-Mexico Claims Commission, which was established in the 1920s to adjudicate claims arising out of widespread unrest in Mexico.[39] The Commission held that the 'propriety of governmental acts should be put to the test of international standards' and that 'the treatment of an alien, in order to constitute an international delinquency, should amounts to an outrage, to bad faith, to wilful neglect of duty, or to an insufficiency of governmental action so far short of international standards that every reasonable and impartial man would readily recognize its insufficiency'.[40]

As noted by one writer, 'the Commission attempted to define the international standard by means of analogy, deriving criteria of procedural outrage from the better-established rules of denial of justice and then applying these more generally'.[41] Although the *Neer* case did not expressly use the expression MST, it has had

32. C. Schreuer & R. Dolzer, *Principles of International Investment Law* (Oxford UP 2008) 12-13.
33. Salacuse, *supra* n. 8, 47; Thomas, *supra* n. 8, 26.
34. Root, *supra* n. 22, 521: 'Each country is bound to give to the nationals of another country in its territory the benefit of the same laws, the same administration, the same protection, and the same redress for injury which it gives to its own citizens, and neither more nor less: *provided the protection which the country gives to its own citizens conforms to the established standard of civilization*. There is, however a standard of justice very simple, very fundamental, and of such general acceptance by all civilized countries as to form a part of the international law of the world. The … system of law and administration shall conform to this general standard. If any country's system of law and administration does not conform to that standard, although the people of the country may be content to live under it, no other country can be compelled to accept it as furnishing a satisfactory measure of treatment of its citizens,' emphasis added. On this question, *see* Paparinskis, *supra* n. 8, 39-46.
35. *S.D. Myers Inc. v. Canada*, UNCITRAL, First Partial Award, 13 Nov. 2000, para. 259.
36. *Glamis*, *supra* n. 4, para. 615.
37. M. Kinnear, A. Biorklund & J.F.G. Hannaford, *Investment Disputes under NAFTA: An Annotated Guide to NAFTA Chapter 11* (Kluwer Law 2006), section on Art. 1105, at 11-12; Orellana, *supra* n. 8, 2.
38. *See, inter alia*: *Roberts v. Mexico*, Award, 2 Nov. 1926, 4 UNRIAA 77; *Chevreau v. United Kingdom*, Award, 9 Jun. 1931, 2 UNRIAA 1113; *George W. Hopkins v. Mexico*, Award, 31 Mar. 1926, 4 UNRIAA 41, 50.
39. *USA (LF Neer) v. Mexico*, Award, 15 Oct. 1926, 4 UNRIAA 60.
40. *Ibid.*, 61-62.
41. Paparinskis, *supra* n. 8, 64.

considerable influence on the emergence of the concept.[42] This conclusion has since then been contested by a number of tribunals.[43] Several writers have argued that little weight should be accorded to a three-page award that only makes a general statement and is not substantiated by State practice.[44] In *Windstream,* the Tribunal stated:

> the Tribunal notes that Neer is also an award (or more accurately, a decision of an international claims commission), not direct evidence of State practice, and that the Neer tribunal itself did not have any direct evidence relating to State practice before it. The Tribunal is therefore unable to determine the content of the customary international law minimum standard of treatment by revisiting the evidence before the Neer tribunal. Nor did the Neer decision deal with the treatment of foreign investors, and consequently the factual circumstances of the case are in any event not directly relevant here.[45]

In the *Railroad Development Corporation* case, the Tribunal also stated that the Commission 'did not formulate the minimum standard of treatment after an analysis of

42. Roth, *supra* n. 10, 95. The case is discussed in detail in: Thomas, *supra* n. 8, 29ff.; Paparinskis, *supra* n. 8, 48-54.
43. *See, Mondev, supra* n. 4, para. 115: 'The Tribunal would observe, however, that the *Neer* case, and other similar cases which were cited, concerned not the treatment of foreign investment as such but the physical security of the alien. Moreover the specific issue in *Neer* was that of Mexico's responsibility for failure to carry out an effective police investigation into the killing of a United States citizen by a number of armed men who were not even alleged to be acting under the control or at the instigation of Mexico. In general, the State is not responsible for the acts of private parties, and only in special circumstances will it become internationally responsible for a failure in the conduct of the subsequent investigation. Thus there is insufficient cause for assuming that provisions of bilateral investment treaties, and of NAFTA, while incorporating the *Neer* principle in respect of the duty of protection against acts of private parties affecting the physical security of aliens present on the territory of the State, are confined to the *Neer* standard of outrageous treatment where the issue is the treatment of foreign investment by the State itself.' Another example is *Merrill & Ring, supra* n. 4, para. 197, noting that the *Neer* and other cases were 'dealing with situations concerning due process of law, denial of justice and physical mistreatment, and only marginally with matters relating to business, trade or investments' (*see also*, para. 204: 'No general rule of customary international law can thus be found which applies the *Neer* standard, beyond the strict confines of personal safety, denial of justice and due process'). *See also, Elliott Associates L.P. v. Republic of Korea*, PCA Case No. 2018-51, Award, 20 Jun. 2023, 576: 'The Tribunal notes that judicial and arbitral pronouncements such as those in Neer must be considered with due care. First, in contrast with Neer, which arose out of an alleged "failure to apprehend or punish," the present case deals with the protection of foreign investment. Accordingly, leaving aside the question whether the standard articulated in Neer has evolved in the almost one hundred years that have elapsed since it was adopted (an issue that the Tribunal need not address, in view of its findings below), the Tribunal notes that the Treaty envisages and indeed specifically confirms that the MST standard applies not only in circumstances such as those in Neer, but also to treatment of foreign investment, and requires "fair and equitable treatment" of covered investments.'
44. S.M. Schwebel, *Is Neer far from Fair and Equitable?*, 27(4) Arb. Int. 555-561 (2011) DOI: 10.1093/arbitration/27.4.555; J. Paulsson, *Neer-lv Misled?*, Miami Law Research Paper 247 (*see also*: J. Paulsson & G. Petrochilos, *Neer-ly Misled?*, 22(2) ICSID Rev. 242-257(2007) DOI: 10.1093/icsidreview/22.2.242). *See also*: Newcombe & Paradell, *supra* n. 8, 237; Tudor, *supra* n. 8, 64; R. Kläger, *Fair and Equitable Treatment in International Investment Law* (Cambridge UP 2011) 53.
45. *Windstream, supra* n. 4, para. 352.

State practice' and further noted that it was 'ironic that the decision considered reflecting the expression of the minimum standard of treatment in customary international law is based on the opinions of commentators and, on its own admission, went further than their views without an analysis of State practice followed because of a sense of obligation'.[46] Interestingly, the *RDC* Tribunal criticised the *Neer* award precisely on that point by making this rather ironic statement: 'by the strict standards of proof of customary international law applied in Glamis Gold, Neer would fail to prove its famous statement (...) to be an expression of customary international law'.[47] The same can arguably be said about the *RDC* award. As noted by Alschner, 'the tribunal chose to substitute the findings by a different tribunal under a different treaty for its own analysis' of State practice and *opinio juris*.[48] He further noted that this is, in fact, what CAFTA Article 10.5 and its Annex 'had urged the tribunal *not* to do'.[49] In any event, other writers have rightly highlighted the fact that the case does not involve any issue related to the protection of investments per se,[50] therefore arguing that the award would only be relevant for 'cases of failure to arrest and punish private actors of crimes against aliens'.[51]

It suffices to conclude (in the context of the present book)[52] that the *Neer* case offers little value when determining the *actual* content of the MST in contemporary international investment law due to the fact that the standard has evolved substantially since the 1920s. This position has been adopted by several tribunals[53] as well as by many scholars.[54] Other tribunals[55] have come to the same conclusion regarding the *Roberts* case, which was decided by the US-Mexico General Claims Commission in 1926 and involved a US citizen who had been imprisoned in Mexico in what he held to be

46. *Railroad, supra* n. 3, para. 216.
47. *Ibid.*
48. W. Alschner, *Investment Arbitration and State-Driven Reform* (Oxford UP 2022). *See also*, M. Porterfield, 'A Distinction Without a Difference? The Interpretation of Fair and Equitable Treatment Under Customary International Law by Investment Tribunals,' Investment Treaty News (22 Mar. 2013), indicating that the tribunal 'accepted, without any evidence of state practice or opinio juris, the pronouncements of previous tribunals as definitive evidence of the standard under CIL'.
49. Alschner, *supra* n. 48, emphasis in the original.
50. R. Jennings, *General Course on Principles of International Law*, 121 Rec. des cours (1967-II) 487; Laviec, *supra* n. 8, 88.
51. Paulsson, *supra* n. 44, 247. *See also*: Schwebel, *supra* n. 44.
52. *See*, analysis in Dumberry, *supra* n. 2, 16-19.
53. *ADF, supra* n. 4, para. 181; *Mondev, supra* n. 4, paras 116, 117; *Loewen Group, Inc. and Raymond L. Loewen v. United States*, ICSID Case No. ARB/AF/98/3, Award on Merits, 26 Jun. 2003, para. 132; *Philip Morris Brands Sàrl, Philip Morris Products S.A. and Abal Hermanos S.A. v. Uruguay*, ICSID Case No. ARB/10/7, Award, 8 Jul. 2016, para. 319; *Crystallex, supra* n. 7, para. 534; *Gold Reserve Inc. v. Venezuela*, ICSID Case No. ARB/AF/09/1, Award, 22 Sep. 2014, para. 567; *Windstream, supra* n. 4, para. 352; *Bilcon, supra* n. 4, paras 434-435; *Mesa Power Group, LLC v. Canada*, UNCITRAL PCA Case No. 2012-17, Award, 24 Mar. 2016, paras 496-501.
54. Newcombe & Paradell, *supra* n. 8, 237; Tudor, *supra* n. 8, 64; Kläger, *supra* n. 44, 53; Paulsson, *supra* n. 44, 257. For Paparinskis, *supra* n. 8, 216, the *Neer* case 'operates as the default rule', to be 'replaced by more specific and detailed rules on the Issue when they exist or are developed'.
55. *Rusoro, supra* n. 7, paras 517-519; *OI European, supra* n. 7, para. 489.

inhumane conditions.[56] The Commission defined the minimum treatment as that required 'in accordance with ordinary standards of civilization'.[57]

The question of whether or not any customary rule in the field of investment arbitration had firmly crystallised after the Second World War has solicited plenty of controversy.[58] However, it is safe to say that the MST was an established rule of custom at the time.[59] One writer has, however, recently argued that in the period before the Second World War, the MST which emerged was originally based on the concept of 'general principles recognized by civilized nations' (which are found in the *domestic laws* of States), and was therefore *not* based on customary international law.[60]

The next section will examine a number of dramatic developments that occurred in the decades following the Second World War.

1.3 The Challenge to Existing Customary Rules, Including the MST, Led by Newly Independent States in the 1960s and 1970s

In the 1960s and 1970s, a group of States revived opposition to the existence of any custom rules in the field of investment law. This era was fundamentally marked by the arrival on the international scene of a growing number of 'Newly Independent States' who were emerging from colonialism in both Asia and Africa. These new States openly contested the *legitimacy* of existing customary international law.[61] They demanded a revision of the 'outdated' rules that did not take into account the fundamental changes that had occurred in the international community since the end of the colonisation

56. *Roberts*, *supra* n. 38, 296.
57. *Ibid.*: 'Facts with respect to equality of treatment of aliens and nationals may be important in determining the merits of a complaint of mistreatment of an alien. But such equality is not the ultimate test of the propriety of the acts of authorities in the light of international law. That test is, broadly speaking, whether aliens are treated in accordance with ordinary standards of civilization. We do not hesitate to say that the treatment of Roberts was such as to warrant an indemnity on the ground of cruel and inhumane imprisonment.' According to *Lemire*, *supra* n. 7, para. 249: 'Roberts is understood to stand for the propositions that a certain treatment may give rise to international responsibility notwithstanding that it affects citizens and aliens alike, and that administrative and legislative actions may amount to a violation of the customary minimum treatment even if the State did not act in bad faith or with willful neglect of duty.'
58. P. Juillard, *L'évolution des sources du droit des investissements*, 250 Rec. des Cours 76 (1994).
59. This is indeed the position taken by these writers in the 1950s: R.R. Wilson, *The International Law Standard in Treaties of the United States* (Harvard UP 1953) 103-104; G. Schwarzenberger, *International Law* (3rd ed., vol. 1, Stevens & Sons 1957) 206-207. *See also*: Paparinskis, *supra* n. 8, 64-67, 83ff.
60. A.C. Blandford, *The History of Fair and Equitable Treatment Before the Second World War*, 32(2) ICSID Rev. 294ff. (2017), referring, *inter alia*, to the famous 1910 speech by former US Secretary of State Elihu Root and to the early work of Borchard. On the *Neer* case, he noted that: 'Today, the Neer standard is often cited as a classic formulation of the minimum standard under customary international law. However, the Neer Commission did not purport to articulate customary international law. It derived the standard from the general principles of justice and equity.'
61. A.T. Guzman, *Why LDCs Sign Treaties That Hurt Them: Explaining the Popularity of Bilateral Investment Treaties*, 38(4) Va.J.Int'l L. 64 (1998); Juillard, *supra* n. 58, 76.

period.[62] According to Abi-Saab, these States '[did] not easily forget that the same body of international law that they [were] now asked to abide by, sanctioned their previous subjugation and exploitation and stood as a bar to their emancipation'.[63]

Specifically, these States rejected the obligation of providing any minimum standard of protection to foreign investors under customary international law.[64] They insisted that 'States were bound to accord the foreign investor only national treatment, only what their domestic law provided.'[65] They also contested the existence of any international law norms requiring compensation for expropriated foreign properties and supported a less stringent compensation requirement than the Hull formula.[66] At the time, the developing States took the debate to the United Nations General Assembly where they represented the majority of States.[67] They used their status within the international body to advance their interests by way of resolutions and declarations,[68] which included Resolution 3171 adopted in 1973[69] and the 1974 *Charter of Economic Rights and Duties of States*.[70]

What has been the impact of this contestation on custom? One thing is clear: considering the opposition between developed and developing States, the *Charter of Economic Rights and Duties of States* could hardly be considered a reflection of existing international law at the time.[71] Another question raised is whether or not the effect of the attack by new States had been to *destroy* the few rules of custom that existed after the Second World War. A number of writers believe that this was the case.[72] Without specifically taking a position on the impact that the contestation may have had on

62. G. Abi-Saab, *The Newly Independent States and the Rules of International Law: An Outline*, 8 Howard LJ 118 (1962).
63. *Ibid.*, 100. *See also*: S.N. Guha-Roy, *Is the Law of Responsibility of States for Injuries to Aliens A Part of Universal International Law?*, 55 AJIL 866 (1961) DOI: 10.2307/2196271.
64. Sornarajah, *supra* n. 9, 140ff.; OECD, *supra* n. 19, 982. *See*, for instance: *Report of the Fourth Session of the Asian African Legal Consultative Committee*, 2 ILC YB 78, 82-84 (1961).
65. Schwebel, *supra* n. 9, 3.
66. Guzman, *supra* n. 61, 647; UNCTAD, *Bilateral Investment Treaties 1995-2006: Trends in Investment Rulemaking* (2007) 48.
67. Juillard, *supra* n. 58, 84ff.
68. M. Byers, *Custom, Power and the Power of Rules: International Relations and Customary International Law* (Cambridge UP 1999) 41.
69. UN GA Res 3171, 1974 GAOR, 28th Session Supp. 30, 52, U.N. Doc. A/9030 in (1974) 13 ILM 238.
70. UN GA Res 3281, 1974 U.N. GAOR, 29th Session Supp. 31, 50-55, U.N. Doc. A/9631 in (1975) 14 ILM 251.
71. S.M. Schwebel, *Investor-State Disputes and the Development of International Law: The Influence of Bilateral Investment Treaties on Customary International Law*, 98 ASIL Proceedings 28 (2004) DOI: 10.1017/s0272503700060699; Schwebel, *supra* n. 9, 1; C. Brower & J. Tepe, *Charter of Economic Rights and Duties of States-A Reflection or Rejection of International Law?*, 9 Int'l Law 295 (1975); D. Carreau & P. Juillard, *Droit international économique* (LGDJ 1998) 464; Salacuse, *supra* n. 8, 75.
72. Carreau & Juillard, *Ibid.*, 464-465; Sornarajah, *supra* n. 9, 19-20, 89-93, 213; A. Akinsanya, *International Protection of Direct Foreign Investments in the Third World*, 36 ICLQ 58 (1987) DOI: 10.1093/iclqaj/36.1.58; A. Al Faruque, *Creating Customary International Law Through Bilateral Investment Treaties: A Critical Appraisal*, 44 Indian JIL 312-313 (2004); d'Aspremont, *supra* n. 13, 14.

custom, the ICJ in the famous *Barcelona Traction* case of 1970 simply noted that *no rule* of customary international law existed in the field of international investment law:

> Considering the important developments of the last half-century, the growth of foreign investments and the expansion of international activities of corporations, in particular of holding companies, which are often multinational, and considering the way in which the economic interests of states have proliferated, it may at first sight appear surprising that the evolution of the law has not gone further and that no generally accepted rules in the matter have crystallized on the international plane.[73]

The more established position, as mentioned above, is that some customary rules *already existed* at the time when developing States started opposing them. Thus, while contested by many States, it remains that the MST had long been established as a basic rule of custom.[74] In the 1990 *ELSI* case, the ICJ indeed referred explicitly to the existence of a 'minimum international standard'.[75] In fact, while it seems that the MST survived the assault by developing States, it did not do so without some casualties. Thus, as noted by one writer, the strong contestation of a large segment of States has 'served to undermine the solidity of the traditional international legal framework for foreign investment'.[76] Thus, while developed States held the view that customary rules existed, they also acknowledged that their effectiveness was limited as a result of the vehement opposition of a large number of States.[77] In fact, both developed and developing States perceived these rules as ineffective in providing basic legal protection to foreign investors.[78] As discussed further below, it is in this historical context that in the 1990s States began signing numerous BITs that provided clearer rules on investment protection.

73. *Barcelona Traction, Light and Power Co., Ltd. (Belgium v. Spain)*, 1970 ICJ Rep. 3, paras 46-47.
74. *See*, P. Dumberry, *The Formation and Identification of Rules of Customary International Law in International Investment Law* (Cambridge UP 2016), 96; Paparinskis, *supra* n. 8, 83ff.; J.E. Alvarez, *Bit on Custom*, 42 NYU J. Int'l L. & Pol. 39 (2009-2010); J.E. Alvarez, *The Public International Law Regime Governing International Investment*, 344 Rec. des cours 292 (2009) DOI: 10.1163/9789004249936. But *see*, Schwebel, *supra* n. 9, 4 for whom 'There was, and is, no agreement within the international community on the content of "the customary international law minimum standard of treatment of aliens", or even on whether such a minimum standard existed or exists.'
75. *Sicula S.p.A. ELSI (US v. Italy)*, Judgment, 1989 ICJ Rep. 115, para. 111 ('The primary standard laid down by Article V is "the full protection and security required by international law", in short the "protection and security" must conform to the minimum international standard').
76. Salacuse, *supra* n. 8, 45-46, 75; Al Faruque, *supra* n. 72, 294-295.
77. The Member States of the OECD certainly believed at the time that these customary rules existed. Thus, the OECD, *Draft Convention on the Protection of Foreign Property*, 7 ILM 117 (1967), Art. 1 cmt., explicitly used the expression 'minimum standard which forms part of customary international law'. It should be noted that the OECD used a different expression ('general principles of international law') in its 1984 study: OECD Committee on International Investment and Multinational Enterprise, *Inter-Governmental Agreements Relating to Investment in Developing Countries*, Doc. No. 84/14, 27 May 1984, at 12, para. 36. On this question, *see*, OECD, *supra* n. 19, 97.
78. d'Aspremont, *supra* n. 13, 16; Salacuse, *supra* n. 8, 76. *See also*: J.W. Salacuse, *The Three Laws of International Investment National, Contractual, and International Frameworks for Foreign Capital* (Oxford UP 2013) 329-330.

1.4 The New Phenomenon of 'Treatification' in the 1990s

This new phenomenon of numerous States starting to sign BITs in the early 1990s has been referred to as 'treatification'. This was a period marked by globalisation whereby private foreign investments were (almost) universally deemed by States as essential tools for their economic development.[79] At the time, a newly found consensus emerged regarding the necessity to offer better legal protections to foreign investments in order to accelerate such development. Yet, there was still great uncertainty surrounding the types of legal protections that existed for foreign investors under custom. Not surprisingly, efforts by the OECD to negotiate a comprehensive Multilateral Agreement on Investment (MAI) in 1995 were unsuccessful.[80] As explained by two scholars, it is due to the fact that 'customary law was deemed to be too amorphous and not be able to provide sufficient guidance and protection' to foreign investors that the capital-exporting and the developing States started frenetically concluding ad hoc BITs.[81] The same conclusion is reached by many writers,[82] including Kläger:

> Many states felt that an international minimum standard – whatever concrete contours it had – existed, but also that it had been challenged every now and again. Due to the failure to establish a multilateral framework for foreign investments, states pursued the reaffirmation and clarification of the legal status of foreign investments through the conclusion of bilateral treaties. In this way, states tried to overcome the uncertainty pertaining to the customary law in this field and to establish a firmer set of rules that applied at least *inter partes*.[83]

According to Schreuer and Dolzer, as a result of the new climate of international economic relations in the 1990s, 'the fight of previous decades against customary rules protecting foreign investment had abruptly become anachronistic and obsolete'.[84] Consequently, by the 1990s, 'the tide had turned' and developing States were no longer opposed to the application of a minimum standard of protection under custom. Instead,

79. Thus, the 1992 *World Bank Guidelines* on the Treatment of Foreign Direct Investment explained in its preamble that it 'recognizes' that 'a greater flow of foreign direct investment brings substantial benefits to bear on the world economy and on the economies of developing countries in particular'.
80. For a draft text, *see Multilateral Agreement on Investment*, Draft Consolidated Text, DAFFE/MAI 987/REV1, 22 Apr. 1998.
81. R. Dolzer & A. von Walter, *Fair and Equitable Treatment: Lines of Jurisprudence on Customary Law*, in: F. Ortino (ed.), *Investment Treaty Law, Current Issues II* (2007) 99.
82. Orellana, *supra* n. 8, 3; Laviec, *supra* n. 8, 87-88; Campbell McLachlan, *Investment Treaties and General International Law*, 57 ICLQ 365 (2008) DOI: 10.1017/s0020589308000225; J.W. Salacuse, *BIT by BIT: The Growth of Bilateral Investment Treaties and Their Impact on Foreign Investment in Developing Countries*, 24 Int'l L. 659 (1990); B. Kishoiyan, *The Utility of Bilateral Investment Treaties in the Formulation of Customary International Law*, 14(2) Northwestern J. Int'l L. 332, 372 (1993); Al Faruque, *supra* n. 72, 293; d'Aspremont, *supra* n. 13, 16-18.
83. Kläger, *supra* n. 44, 263-4. *See also*: J.W. Salacuse, *Towards a Global Treaty on Foreign Investment: The Search for a Grand Bargain*, in: N. Horn & S. Kröll (eds), *Arbitrating Foreign Investment Disputes: Procedural and Substantive Legal Aspects* (2004) 58; Salacuse, *supra* n. 8, 77; C. McLachlan, L. Shore & M. Weiniger, *International Investment Arbitration: Substantive Principles* (Oxford UP 2007) 17.
84. Schreuer & Dolzer, *supra* n. 32, 16.

they granted 'more protection to foreign investment than traditional customary law did, now on the basis of treaties negotiated to attract additional foreign investment'.[85]

It is now estimated that 3,265 international investment agreements (IIAs) provide investors with investment protection,[86] including 2,830 BITs.[87] As a result of these developments, the number of arbitration cases between investors and States is booming. The most recent UNCTAD Report mentions a total of 1,257 known cases.[88]

The next chapter examines how this new phenomenon of 'treatification' was marked by the emergence of the FET standard and the decline of the MST as a source of investment protection for foreign investors.

II THE EMERGENCE OF THE FET STANDARD IN INVESTMENT TREATIES AND ITS INTERACTION WITH THE MST

I will first examine the early appearance of the FET standard in multilateral instruments after the Second World War and the fact that it is now contained in the overwhelming majority of BITs (section 2.1). The following sections examine the question of the interaction between the FET standard and the MST. The central question analysed is why States started referring to the FET standard instead of the MST in their investment treaties? (section 2.2). I will then address the implications of the answer to this question. I will argue that FET should be considered a standard independent of the MST (except in some specific situations) (section 2.3).

2.1 Early Appearance of the Standard in Multilateral Instruments and Current Overwhelming Presence in BITs

The history of the emergence of the FET clause has previously been examined in detail by several authors.[89] For the purposes of this book, it suffices to simply highlight some of the most salient features of these important historical developments.

The first reference to 'equitable treatment' can be found in Article 23(e) of the League of Nations Covenant, which commits its Member States 'to secure and maintain

85. *Ibid. See also*: Schwebel, *supra* n. 44, 28.
86. UNCTAD, 'Trends in the Investment Treaty Regime and a Reform Toolbox for The Energy Transition' (2023) IIA Issues Note.
87. *Ibid.*
88. *Ibid.*
89. *See, inter alia*: S. Vasciannie, *The Fair and Equitable Treatment Standard in International Investment Law and Practice*, 70 British YIL 99 (1999) DOI: 10.1093/bybil/70.1.99; Thomas, *supra* n. 8; Kinnear et al., *supra* n. 37, 23; UNCTAD, *Fair and Equitable Treatment*, Series on Issues in International Investment Agreements (1999); UNCTAD, *supra* n. 14, 5ff.; Haeri, *supra* n. 23, 83ff.; Blandford, *supra* n. 60, 287-303. *See also*, more recently M. Pinchis-Paulsen, *The Life and Death (and Re-Birth) of 'Fair and' 'Equitable Treatment:' A Historical Examination of Twentieth Century International Trade and Investment Law Treaty-Making and Political Decision-Making* (Ph.D. Thesis, University of London, King's College, 2017); Islam, *supra* n. 13, 31ff.; Kill, *supra* n. 8, 869.

... equitable treatment for the commerce of all Members of the League'.[90] The 1948 *Havana Charter for an International Trade Organization* is generally considered the first legal instrument making reference to the FET standard.[91] The Havana Charter never came into force. At the same time, the Organization of American States adopted the *Economic Agreement of Bogotá* in 1948, which mentioned in Article 22 that 'foreign capital shall receive equitable treatment'.[92] The document was, however, never ratified.[93] Ten years later in 1959, a group of European businesspersons and lawyers under the leadership of Mr Hermann Abs and Lord Shawcross drafted the Abs-Shawcross *Draft Convention on Investments Abroad*. The document specifically offered protection in terms of 'fair and equitable treatment' to foreigner's property.[94] The clause offered wide protection and covered 'the most constant protection and security' and forbade discrimination against a foreigner's property.

In 1967, the OECD developed a convention to protect private property: the *Draft Convention on the Protection of Foreign Property* (hereinafter 'Draft Convention').[95] It provides that 'each party shall at all times ensure FET to the property of the nationals of the other parties'.[96] One of the reasons why the Draft Convention included such a reference to FET may be because several OECD members had, at the time, already started to adopt the FET clause in their respective BITs (a point discussed below).[97] Although the Draft Convention was never opened for signature, its importance should not be underestimated since it 'represented the collective view and dominant trend of OECD countries on investment issues'.[98] The Draft Convention also provided OECD Member States with guidelines that were subsequently used by them as a model to

90. *See*, analysis of Kill, *supra* n. 8, 869ff. A detailed account of this provision can be found in: M. Pinchis, *The Ancestry of 'Equitable Treatment' in Trade: Lessons from the League of Nations During the Inter-War Period*, 15 J. World Invest. & Trade, 13-72 (2014) DOI: 10.1163/2212900 0-01502002.
91. Havana Charter for an International Trade Organization, 24 Mar. 1948, Art. II(2), in: U.N. Conference on Trade & Employment, Final Act and Related Documents 8-9, U.N. Doc. E/Conf. 2/78, U.N. Sales No. 1948.II.D.4 (1948). Although the Havana Charter focused on trade issues, it also contained provisions related to investments including a reference that a future organisation would be authorised to 'make recommendations for and promote bilateral or multilateral agreements on measure designed ... to assure just and equitable treatment for the enterprise ...'. *See*: Thomas, *supra* n. 8, 40ff.; Kill, *supra* n. 8, 871-873. Several other initiatives are discussed in: Weiler, *supra* n. 22, 358ff.
92. Organization of American States, Economic Agreement of Bogotá, Art. 22, May 1948, L. Treaty Ser. No. 25, OAS Doc. No. OEA/Ser.A/4 (SEPF). The full provision reads as follows: 'foreign capital shall receive equitable treatment. The States therefore agree not to take unjustified, unreasonable or discriminatory measures that would impair the legally acquired rights or interests of nationals of other countries in the enterprises, capital, skills, arts or technology they have supplied'.
93. Kill, *supra* n. 8, 873.
94. Article 1. Hermann Abs & Hartley Shawcross, *The Proposed Convention to Protect Private Foreign Investment: A Round Table – Comment on the Draft Convention by Its Authors*, 9 JPL 115-132 (1960).
95. OECD, *supra* n. 77.
96. Article 1(a).
97. K.J. Vandevelde, *Bilateral Investment Treaties: History, Policy and Interpretation* (Oxford UP 2010) 199.
98. OECD, *supra* n. 77, 2ff.

draft their own BITs.[99] In fact, it has been observed that the many textual similarities between the different treaty models used by developed OECD Member States as a basis for treaty negotiation with developing countries have led to greater uniformity in the BIT language.[100] Thus, the origin of the FET clause that is now commonly found in modern BITs can (at least in part) be traced to this 1967 OECD Draft Convention.[101]

On the bilateral front, the first group of BITs that mentioned the FET were those concluded by European States (including Germany and Switzerland) in the early 1960s.[102] By the 1970s, FET was specifically mentioned in most BITs between capital-exporting and capital-importing countries.[103] According to some estimates, the standard was mentioned in over 300 BITs between the 1960s and 1990s.[104]

From the 1990s onwards, States have included the FET standard in an overwhelming majority of BITs.[105] A detailed analysis conducted in the early 1990s of 335 BITs shows that only 28 BITs did not include a reference to FET.[106] This is confirmed by Tudor's book published in 2008 examining 365 BITs with only 19 of them not containing a reference to FET.[107] The present author has examined elsewhere all 1,964 BITs that were available on the UNCTAD website[108] at the time (February 2014) and found that only 50 of them did not include an FET clause at all, while 25 others only referred to the FET in their preambles.[109] Thus, less than 5% of the BITs examined did not include any formal and binding FET obligation for the host State of investments. These figures were recently confirmed in a 2023 paper by the OECD: 'Among the 2,670 sample treaties concluded by the 99 jurisdictions that are invited to participate in OECD-hosted work on the *Future of Investment Treaties*, almost 95% contain such references.'[110] Yet, it should be added that even when a BIT does *not* contain an FET clause, an investor may invoke a broadly worded most favoured nation (MFN) clause contained in that treaty to rely on provisions found in *another* treaty entered into by the host State that provides for 'better' treatment (i.e., the presence of an FET clause rather than no such protection at all).[111]

---

99. *Ibid.*; Tudor, *supra* n. 8, 19; Bronfman, *supra* n. 8, 161; Islam, *supra* n. 13, 37ff.
100. K.J. Vandevelde, *The Political Economy of a Bilateral Investment Treaty*, 92 AJIL, 621, 628 (1988) DOI: 10.2307/2998126; Vasciannie, *supra* n. 89, 113.
101. Vasciannie, *supra* n. 89, 113.
102. Vandevelde, *supra* n. 97, 196.
103. UNCTAD, *supra* n. 14, 8-9; OECD, *supra* n. 19, 78.
104. M. Khalil, *Treatment of Foreign Investment in BITs*, 8 ICSID Rev. 355 (1992) DOI: 10.1093/icsidreview/7.2.339.
105. Tudor, *supra* n. 8, 23.
106. Khalil, *supra* n. 104, 351-355.
107. Tudor, *supra* n. 8, 23.
108. *See*, http://investmentpolicyhub.unctad.org/IIA. I examined BITs available in English, French, Spanish, etc., but not those in Arabic or Russian.
109. P. Dumberry, *Has the Fair and Equitable Treatment Standard Become a Rule of Customary International Law?*, 8(1) J. Int. Disp. Settl. 155-178 (2016) DOI: 10.1093/jnlids/idw002.
110. OECD, *supra* n. 1, 4.
111. This is the conclusion reached so far by investment tribunals which have accepted the importation of FET protection through broad MFN clauses (one exception is: *İçkale İnşaat Limited Şirketi v. Turkmenistan*, ICSID Case No. ARB/10/24, Award, 8 Mar. 2016, paras 326ff.). *See*, analysis: P. Dumberry, *The Importation of the Fair and Equitable Treatment Standard Through MFN Clauses: An Empirical Study of BITs*, 17 ICSID Rev. 229-259 (2016), examining all publicly available BITs with no FET clause and concluding that all of them (except for two)

While the vast majority of BITs include an FET clause, there nevertheless remains a considerable degree of variation in the actual content of the clause. These variations can be summarised as follows:[112]

- Reference to the FET solely in a treaty preamble without imposing any binding obligations on the host State.
- Autonomous and unqualified reference to the FET.
- Reference to the FET in combination with other standards of protection (such as national treatment and the most-favoured-nations clause).
- Reference to the FET with an additional specification that this treatment prohibits arbitrary and discretionary measures.
- Reference to the FET combined with a reference to international law.
- Reference to the FET combined with a reference to customary international law.

To this list can now be added another rather novel type of clause which first appeared in the CETA: a closed list enumerating the different elements which are considered to be in breach of the treatment. This type of clause is further examined below (section 3.4).

As further discussed below, the most significant distinction is between three types of clauses. On the one hand, many treaties contain 'stand-alone' clauses containing an 'unqualified' reference to the obligation to accord an FET. On the other hand, BITs often contain clauses referring to an FET obligation linked to 'international law'. Importantly, there are an increasing number of treaties that contain FET clauses specifically referring to the MST, including notably the NAFTA and the Central America-Dominican Republic Free Trade Agreement (CAFTA-DR) (a point discussed further below).[113] How tribunals have addressed these different types of clauses is examined in Part II of this book.

---

contain MFN clauses that are broad enough to allow for the importation of FET clauses from other treaties. The author has also examined a related different question: P. Dumberry, *Shopping for a Better Deal: The Use of MFN Clauses to Get 'Better' Fair and Equitable Treatment Protection*, Arb. Int. 1-16 (2016) DOI: 10.1093/arbint/aiw036; P. Dumberry, *The Importation of 'Better' Fair and Equitable Treatment Standard Protection Through MFN Clauses: An analysis of NAFTA Article 1103*, TDM (2016).

112. The present typology is based on the work of Tudor, *supra* n. 8, 22ff.; Kläger, *supra* n. 44, 9ff.; Diehl, *supra* n. 8, 129ff. UNCTAD, *supra* n. 14, xiii, identifies four different approaches: '(a) Unqualified obligation to accord fair and equitable treatment; (b) FET obligation linked to international law; (c) FET obligation linked to the minimum standard of treatment of aliens under customary international law; (d) FET obligation with additional substantive content such as denial of justice.'

113. One rare older example of such a clause is found in the Protocol to the BIT between the Netherlands and Venezuela, which was signed on the same day as the BIT, and providing at Art. 3(1): 'The Contracting Parties agree that the treatment of investments shall be considered to be fair and equitable as mentioned in Article 3, paragraph 1, if it conforms to the treatment accorded to investments of their own nationals, or to investments of nationals of any third State, whichever is more favorable to the national concerned, as well as to the *minimum standard for the treatment of foreign nationals under international law*' (emphasis added). The provision is examined in: *ConocoPhillips Petrozuata B.V. et al. v. Venezuela*, ICSID Case No. ARB/07/30, Decision on Jurisdiction and Merits, 3 Sep. 2013, paras 291ff. The Tribunal

The next section will examine the controversial question as to why States started referring to the FET standard instead of the MST in their investment treaties.

2.2 Why Did States Start Referring to the FET Standard Instead of the MST in Their Investment Treaties?

As noted by the *Cairn* Tribunal, 'the history of how the FET standard has been included in investment treaties suggests that the FET standard was inspired by the MST'.[114] One of the most controversial questions discussed in scholarship is why States first began including the term FET in their BITs throughout the 1960s and 1970s and why they have continued to do so (almost) uniformly thereafter in the 1990s.[115]

According to one view, Western States incorporated the concept of FET in their BITs to simply reflect the MST that existed under international law.[116] This approach has been endorsed by a number of writers.[117] These writers typically refer to the 1967 OECD Draft Convention[118] as representative of the position of developed States at the time on matters of protection of foreign investments.[119] This is because the OECD's Commentary to the 1967 Draft Convention indicated that the concept of FET flowed

---

referred to the 'Explanatory Statement for the Dutch Treaty presented to the Congress of the Republic of Venezuela,' dated 19 Nov. 1991, indicating that this 'minimum required by International Law for the treatment of foreign nationals' is 'by definition, a pre-existing obligation of the Parties, independently of the Agreement' and therefore a reference to the MST under custom. It also noted that it 'specifies' the expression FET 'and thus limits the discretion of eventual arbitrators when examining the behaviour of any of the Parties'. The same type of clause was also examined in: *OI European*, *supra* n. 7, para. 477. The case is further examined in Part II.

114. *Cairn Energy PLC and Cairn UK Holdings Limited (CUHL) v. India*, PCA Case No. 2016-07, Award, 21 Dec. 2020, para. 1704.
115. *See*, discussion in Dumberry, *supra* n. 2, 31-35.
116. *See*, analysis in Newcombe & Paradell, *supra* n. 8, 268; Thomas, *supra* n. 8, 44, 47; Carreau & Juillard, *supra* n. 71, 454.
117. *See*, for instance: Picherack, *supra* n. 8, 264 ('When the language of fair and equitable treatment first began to emerge in draft multilateral instruments and investment agreements in the 1950s and 1960s, it was likely then intended to serve as a reference to the minimum standard of treatment existing in international law. ... The desire to set down a fair and equitable treatment provision in the text of multilateral instruments and investment agreements could be seen as an attempt at the time to solidify the minimum international standard in the face of the Calvo doctrine and many developing countries' assertions which denied the existence of a minimum standard of treatment in customary international law separate from a national treatment standard'); Paparinskis, *supra* n. 8, 160-163 ('If one takes together the pre- and post-Second World War materials pre-dating investment arbitrations, it seems permissible to conclude that the ordinary meaning of fair and equitable treatment was a reference to customary minimum standard, in particular regarding administration of justice'); S. Montt, *State Liability in Investment Treaty Arbitration* (Hart Publ. 2009) 69 ('If the historical background is to be taken seriously, then the FET standard, when first used, could not have meant anything higher than IMS. At a time when the opposing North-South legal camps were, respectively, IMS and national treatment, the FET standard could not have referred to either an autonomous standard or to a higher standard than those minima'); Blandford, *supra* n. 60, 302 ('at the time when the United States introduced FET provisions to post-war treaty negotiations, "just and equitable treatment" was already a term of art for what we now call the minimum standard').
118. OECD, *supra* n. 77.
119. Vasciannie, *supra* n. 89, 112-113; UNCTAD, *supra* n. 14, 8; OECD, *supra* n. 19, 4.

from the 'well established general principle of international law that a State is bound to respect and protect the property of nationals of other States'.[120] The Drafting Committee also added that the phrase FET refers to 'the standard set by international law for the treatment due by each State with regard to the property of foreign nationals' and that 'the standard required conforms in effect to the minimum standard which forms part of customary international law'.[121] The same position was also taken by OECD Member States in 1984.[122] This position is also confirmed by the practice of some Western States.[123] This narrative has, however, been subject to dissent by many scholars.[124] While it is possible that the OECD commentary reflected how their Member States (all developed States) *themselves* viewed customary international law at the time, it was certainly not representative of what developing States believed were their legal obligations in the 1960s.[125]

As explained by two scholars, the use of a 'different and more politically neutral term [FET] might be explained by the historical political sensitivities regarding the minimum standard of treatment', which was 'historically viewed with suspicion because of the legacy of gun-boat diplomacy and imperialism'.[126] For these writers, the concept of the FET 'may simply have been viewed as a convenient, neutral and acceptable reference' to the MST.[127]

This is also the position endorsed by Judge Nikken in his separate opinion in the *Suez v. Argentina* case.[128] The majority of the Tribunal noted that the FET clause in the France-Argentina BIT refers to 'the principles of international law', not to the MST, and then made this comment:

> The formulation 'minimum standard under customary international law' or simply 'minimum international standard' is *so well known and so well established* in international law that one can assume that if France and Argentina had intended to limit the content of fair and equitable treatment to the minimum international

120. OECD, *supra* n. 77, 119.
121. *Ibid.*
122. Thomas, *supra* n. 8, 48 referring to: OECD Committee, *supra* n. 77, 12, para. 36 ('according to all Member countries which have commented on this point, fair and equitable treatment introduced a substantive legal standard referring to general principles of international law even if this is not explicitly stated').
123. *See*, examples examined by Newcombe & Paradell, *supra* n. 8, 268 (referring to US, UK, Swiss and Canadian treaty practice); Thomas, *supra* n. 8, 48-51; Paparinskis, *supra* n. 8, 162 ('pleadings in the ICJ (...) show that such States as Belgium, Spain, the UK, and the US used the language of fair and equitable treatment to refer to the customary of law administration of justice'). On Swiss practice, *see*: Statement of the Swiss Department of External Affairs (Mémoire, JAAC 1979, fasc. 43/IV, No. 113), in: L. Caflisch, *La pratique suisse en matière de droit international public*, 36 ASDI 178 (1980) ('On se réfère ainsi au principe classique du droit des gens selon lequel les États doivent mettre les étrangers se trouvant sur leur territoire et leurs biens au bénéfice du "standard minimum" international, c'est-à-dire leur accorder un minimum de droits personnels, procéduraux et économiques').
124. Kill, *supra* n. 8, 876-877; Bronfman, *supra* n. 8, 615.
125. Kill, *supra* n. 8, 879.
126. Newcombe & Paradell, *supra* n. 8, 263-264.
127. *Ibid.*, 263-264. *See also*, Montt, *supra* n. 117, 69-70.
128. *Suez, supra* n. 3, Judge Nikken's separate opinion.

> standard they would have used that formulation specifically. In fact, they did not.[129]

Judge Nikken rejected this argument about the MST being 'so well-known and so well established in international law' for the following reasons:

> Therefore, it is not so easy to say that the concept of international minimum standard was a *well-established* concept. It certainly was for the capital-exporting countries, but not for the rest of the world (...). However, although from the late twentieth century the debate on this concept could be considered overcome, the historical burden of its phrasing has not vanished. Clauses on the treatment of foreign investment referring to the 'international minimum standard' could hardly be agreed upon, as some of the Parties to those treaties were not willing to accept it *expressis verbi*. 'International minimum standard' was a 'forbidden phrase' in a treaty for the very many countries that had rejected that standard, because it was associated with unjust international relations, as has been recognized by scholars who have addressed the issue. The explanation suggested by the NAFTA Free Trade Commission interpretation, which reveals the intention of the NAFTA Parties to consider fair and equitable treatment and international minimum standard as identical, was that a formula had to be found for saying the same thing but with different words, neutral words, which were not historically demonized. The phrase 'fair and equitable treatment' is a neutral expression in relation to which there was no controversy and it had been used in another context in the Havana Charter signed in 1948 and in the Economic Agreement of Bogota, also signed in 1948.[130]

He believed that the terms 'principles of international law' found in the BIT was 'a clear reference to the minimum standard, the only standard on Treatment of aliens in general international law at the time when the treaty was concluded'.[131]

A more convincing approach has been adopted by other writers who suggest that the growing use of the term FET by Western States in their BITs was intended to counter the assertion made by developing States about the inexistence of any MST under international law.[132] Thus, Western States started including references to the FET standard *because* of the ambiguities surrounding the concept of the MST.[133] In the words of the *PSEG v. Turkey* Tribunal, the FET standard 'has acquired prominence in investment arbitration as a consequence of the fact that other standards traditionally provided by international law might not in the circumstances of each case be entirely appropriate'.[134] They started using this term as a result of the challenge mounted by developing States against the MST.

Weiler provides a detailed account explaining that the US started using the expression FET after the War in its investment treaty negotiation because it had already been used in its commercial and reciprocal trade treaties and it was a familiar

129. *Ibid.*, para. 184, emphasis added.
130. *Ibid.*, Judge Nikken's separate opinion, paras 14-15.
131. *Ibid.*, para. 8.
132. *See*, Thomas, *supra* n. 8, 48. *Contra*: Paparinskis, *supra* n. 8, 163.
133. Weiler, *supra* n. 24, 199, 211-212, 216, 227, 239-240; Vasciannie, *supra* n. 89, 157-158.
134. *PSEG Global, Inc and Konya Ilgin Electrik Uretim ve Ticaret Limited Sirketi v. Turkey*, ICSID Case No. ARB/02/5, Award, 19 Jan. 2007, para. 238.

diplomatic term of art.[135] Recent research has indeed shown that the term 'just and equitable treatment' was used by the US in diplomatic correspondence with other States in the 1930s regarding protection of its nationals abroad.[136] Having examined these commercial treaties in some detail, he concludes that their common thread had been the 'objective of promoting equality of access and non-discrimination for Americans in the decision-making of foreign States and State enterprises'.[137] For him, 'it should be unsurprising, therefore, that the FET clause was pressed into service when officials were casting about for treaty terms that could be used to broaden and deepen access and protection for U.S. investors abroad'.[138] There was also another reason for using the expression:

> Given how the global political atmosphere of the 1950s and 1960s was not conducive to safeguarding private foreign investment, U.S. Department of State officials did not hesitate in offering the more ambiguous FET language in their model treaties, rather than resigning themselves to a perpetual debate over the scope and meaning of the [MST].[139]

The term 'equitable' was indeed attractive to US treaty drafters after the Second World War because it [was] capable of bearing multiple meanings'[140] and could 'mean different things to different people'.[141] Thus, while it could be construed as a manifestation of the principle of sovereign equality of States for some, others could rely on it to further legal protection to foreign investors.[142] Yet, as explained by Weiler, in the context of BIT negotiation Western States 'shared the same agenda: use all available legal means to boost the standard of treatment owed to foreign investors'.[143] For him, 'it should also appear beyond doubt that they were not confusing the FET standard with the [MST] in their own minds, although they were undoubtedly hopeful that their official from less developed countries might not be savvy to these interpretative slights of hand'.[144] For the Western States, 'it was essential to identify treaty terms capable of acceptance by potential treaty partners whilst nonetheless ginning up the discretion of future arbitrators to apply more stringent norms of establishment and protection'.[145] In other words, US negotiators embraced the FET standard in the 1960s because the MST 'controversy had otherwise poisoned the well for treaty drafters'.[146] The point is well-explained by Vandevelde:

135. Weiler, *supra* n. 24, 191, 194. *See also*, M. Pinchis-Paulsen, 'The Forgotten Purpose of "Fair and Equitable Treatment" Clauses in Post-War United States' Commercial Treaties,' 29 Sep. 2014. Available at SSRN: https://ssrn.com/abstract=2502803.
136. Blandford, *supra* n. 60, 300ff.
137. Weiler, *supra* n. 24, 195.
138. *Ibid.*, 199.
139. *Ibid.*
140. *Ibid.*, 205.
141. *Ibid.*, 199.
142. *Ibid.*
143. *Ibid.*, 211.
144. *Ibid.*, 211-212.
145. *Ibid.*, 211.
146. *Ibid.*, 215.

> Full protection and security had been identified as an element of customary international law since the inter-war FCNs, though it was then called 'most constant protection and security'. During the 1950s, with the concept of an international minimum standard under attack, the United States moved away from references to customary law in its FCNs and sought to establish new standards of a requirement of fair and equitable treatment and a prohibition on arbitrary and discriminatory treatment to complement the most constant protection and security standard.[147]

The actual drafting language used by States in their BITs supports this approach. As pointed out by two authors, 'if the parties to a treaty want to refer to customary international law, one would assume that they will refer to it as such rather than using a different expression'.[148] For the vast majority of BITs that contain an FET clause that does *not* make any reference to international law, the standard should *not* be considered an implicit reference to the MST.[149] As pointed out by two writers, '[a]s a matter of textual interpretation, it seems implausible that a treaty would refer to a well-known concept like the "minimum standard of treatment in customary international law" by using the expression "fair and equitable treatment"'.[150] This is especially the case considering the (above-mentioned) contentious debates between developed and developing States as to the very existence of an MST.[151]

2.3 FET Should Be Considered a Treaty Standard Independent from the MST, Except in Specific Situations

In my view, the historical analysis examined in the previous section shows that the FET standard should *generally* be considered an *independent* treaty standard having an autonomous meaning from the MST. This is the position adopted by the majority of writers.[152] It should be noted, however, that several scholars have rejected this

147. K. Vandevelde, *United States International Investment Agreements* (Kluwer 2002) 263.
148. Schreuer & Dolzer, *supra* n. 32, 124. *See also*: Bronfman, *supra* n. 8, 621; Laviec, *supra* n. 8, 94; Salacuse, *supra* n. 8, 226; Vasciannie, *supra* n. 89, 105; UNCTAD, *supra* n. 14, 13.
149. UNCTAD, *supra* n. 14, 13.
150. Schreuer & Dolzer, *supra* n. 32, 124. *See also*: Bronfman, *supra* n. 8, 621; Laviec, *supra* n. 8, 94; Salacuse, *supra* n. 8, 226; Vasciannie, *supra* n. 89, 105; UNCTAD, *supra* n. 14, 13. This position is adopted in: *Suez, supra* n. 3, para. 184, but rejected in the Separate opinion of Nikken, paras 10ff.
151. Diehl, *supra* n. 8, 151; Vasciannie, *supra* n. 89, 131; UNCTAD, *supra* n. 14, 13; Salacuse, *supra* n. 8, 226-227.
152. F.A. Mann, *British Treaties for the Promotion and Protection of Investments*, 52 British YIL 241, 244 (1981) DOI: 10.1093/bybil/52.1.241('The terms "fair and equitable treatment" envisage conduct which goes far beyond the minimum standard and afford protection to a greater extent and according to a much more objective standard than any previously employed form of words. A tribunal would not be concerned with a minimum, maximum or average standard. It will have to decide whether in all the circumstances the conduct in issue is fair and equitable or unfair and inequitable. No standard defined by other words is likely to be material. The terms are to be understood and applied independently and autonomously'); Newcombe & Paradell, *supra* n. 8, 263; Dolzer & Stevens, *supra* n. 8, 60; Vasciannie, *supra* n. 89, 144 ('These considerations point ultimately towards the conclusion that the two standards in question are not identical: both standards may overlap significantly with respect to issues such as arbitrary treatment, discrimination and unreasonableness, but the presence of a provision assuring fair

interpretation.[153] Interpreting FET as an independent treaty standard is certainly the better approach when the clause is unqualified and contains no reference whatsoever to international law.[154]

Yet, as logical and sound as it may be, this interpretation is *not* convincing *in certain particular cases* where a treaty *explicitly* links the FET to the standard existing under 'international law'. In Part II, I will show that tribunals have, however, adopted different interpretations on that issue. In the present author's view, any possible ambiguities should disappear when there is clear and undeniable evidence that the intention of the State parties was, in fact, that the FET standard be considered a reference to the MST under custom.[155] This is clearly the case under NAFTA Article 1105.[156]

Under Article 1105, the FET standard must be considered *one of the elements* included in the umbrella concept of the MST. In fact, this is evident because the provision requires NAFTA Parties to provide foreign investors treatment in accordance with 'international law', *including* FET. NAFTA tribunals have endorsed this approach.[157] Moreover, as further discussed below, the NAFTA parties have expressly

---

and equitable treatment in an investment instrument does not automatically incorporate the international minimum standard for foreign investors'); P. Muchlinski, *Multinational Enterprises and the Law* (2nd ed., Oxford UP 2007) 635-647; McLachlan et al., *supra* n. 83, 226-247; Dolzer & Schreuer, *supra* n. 32, 124-128; Tudor, *supra* n. 8, 53-104; Diehl, *supra* n. 8, 151-152; C. Schreuer, *Fair and Equitable Standard: FET: Interaction with Other Standards*, 4(5) TDM (2007); R. Dolzer, *Fair and Equitable Treatment: A Key Standard in Investment Treaties*, 39(1) Int'l Law, 360 (2005); Haeri, *supra* n. 23, 34; Kinnear, *supra* n. 37, 7; M.C. Ryan, *Glamis Gold, Ltd. v. The United States and the Fair and Equitable Treatment Standard*, 56(4) McGill LJ 932-934 (2011); Salacuse, *supra* n. 8, 226-227: R. Preiswerk, *New Developments in Bilateral Investment Protection: With Special Reference to Belgian Practice*, 3 RBDI 173, 186 (1967); N. Blackaby, et al., *Redfern and Hunter on International Arbitration* (Oxford UP 2009), 494 DOI: 10.1093/law:iic/9780199557189.001.1; Islam, *supra* n. 13, 72.

153. Picherack, *supra* n. 8, 260-262, 265, 291; Thomas, *supra* n. 8, 50; Mayeda, *supra* n. 8, 273-291; Orellana, *supra* n. 8, 7; B. Choudhury, *Evolution or Devolution? Defining Fair and Equitable Treatment in International Investment Law*, 6(2) J. World Invest. & Trade 317-320 (2005) DOI: 10.1163/221190005x00091; Sornarajah, *supra* n. 9, 170ff; Ch. Leben, *L'évolution du Droit International des Investissements*, in: SFDI, *Un accord multilatéral sur l'investissement: d'un forum de négociation à l'autre?* (1999) 7-28; M.R. Jiménez, *Considerations of NAFTA Chapter II*, 2 Chicago JIL 243, 244 (2001); Paparinskis, *supra* n. 8, 163; Montt, *supra* n. 117, 302-310.

154. Kläger, *supra* n. 44, 61; Haeri, *supra* n. 23, 33 ('Thus, absent specific treaty wording linking the fair and equitable treatment standard with the international minimum standard in customary international law, the better view is that the fair and equitable treatment standard is an autonomous standard. In such circumstances, the fair and equitable treatment standard cannot be construed as a reference to the international minimum standard in customary international law'); C. Schreuer, *Fair and Equitable Treatment in Arbitral Practice*, 6 J. World Invest. & Trade, 363-366, 365, 385 (2005) DOI: 10.1163/221190005x00118 ('in the context of the NAFTA, it is now established that the term as used in Article 1105(1 therein is no more than a reference to established principles of international law. In other contexts, notably that of BITs, the answer depends on the wording of the particular clause. In the absence of indications to the contrary, the better view is to give it an autonomous meaning'); Islam, *supra* n. 13, 68-70.

155. The technique of reference (*renvoi*) is often used in treaties: Paparinskis, *supra* n. 8, 160.

156. Dumberry, *supra* n. 2, 44-46.

157. *Ibid.*, 44, referring to many cases, including *United Parcel Service of America Inc. v. Canada*, UNCITRAL, Award on Jurisdiction, 22 Nov. 2002, para. 97 ('the obligation to accord fair and equitable treatment is not in addition to or beyond the minimum standard. Our reasons in brief are, first, that that reading accords with the ordinary meaning of article 1105. That obligation

stated that their intention was, in fact, that the FET standard refers to the MST under custom.[158] The same conclusion was reached by the CAFTA *Lopez* Tribunal, indicating that 'the starting point of any analysis of the content of the MST and its relationship with FET is the language of the applicable instrument and, in particular, the degree of linkage it establishes between FET, on the one hand, and customary international law and MST on the other'.[159] For the Tribunal, 'by stating that the Parties must accord investments "treatment in accordance with customary law, including fair and equitable treatment", Article 10.5.1 of the Treaty indicates that FET is considered part of customary international law'.[160] I have also found other awards where tribunals assessing other treaties have indicated that the FET is part of customary international law.[161]

III THE 'RETURN' OF THE MST

Chapter III examines the phenomenon of the 'return' of the MST.[162] As mentioned before, by the year 2000, the majority of BITs contained a stand-alone (or autonomous) reference to the FET standard without any reference to the MST. By then, the concept of the MST had clearly lost its once prevailing importance as a source of investment protection for foreign investors. One could have assumed at the time that the MST's role would become limited to the traditional function played by customary rules under international law in the context of the proliferation of treaty norms. The MST would,

is "included" within the minimum standard'); *Cargill, supra* n. 4, para. 296 ('In summation, the Tribunal finds that the obligations in Article 1105(1) of the NAFTA are to be understood by reference to the customary international law minimum standard of treatment of aliens. The requirement of fair and equitable treatment is one aspect of this minimum standard').

158. *See*, FTC Note of Interpretation of 2001, *supra* n. 9.
159. *Lopez, supra* n. 7, para. 407, referring to R. Dolzer, U. Kriebaum & C. Schreuer, *Principles of International Investment Law* (Oxford UP 2022) 200.
160. *Lopez, supra* n. 7, para. 408.
161. *Blusun S.A., Jean-Pierre Lecorcier and Michael Stein v. Italy*, ICSID Case No. ARB/14/3, Award, 27 Dec. 2016, 319, indicating that 'the core commitment' under Art. 10 of the ECT is to accord FET, adding that 'This incorporates the fair and equitable treatment standard under customary international law and as applied by tribunals.' The award is cited and approved in: *RWE Innogy GmbH and RWE Innogy Aersa S.A.U. v. Spain*, ICSID Case No. ARB/14/34, Decision on Jurisdiction, Liability and Certain Issues of Quantum, 30 Dec. 2019, 443. *See also*, *Elliott, supra* n. 43, para. 568 ('The Tribunal must thus interpret the terms "fair and equitable treatment" and "full protection and security" in the context of, and as an element of, the MST obligation'); *Kenon Holdings Ltd and IC Power Ltd v. Peru*, ICSID Case No. ARB/19/19, Award, 3 Oct. 2023, rep. in: IARep, 11 Oct. 2023. A different position seems to have been adopted in: *RREEF Infrastructure (G.P.) Limited and RREEF Pan-European Infrastructure Two Lux S.à.r.l. v. Spain*, ICSID Case No. ARB/13/30, Decision on Responsibility and on the Principles of Quantum, 30 Nov. 2018, 258 ('the minimum standard as applied traditionally in international law is included in the FET which adds to it in favour of the investor').
162. For a recent analysis on this question, *see*: P. Dumberry, *The 'Minimum Standard of Treatment' in International Investment Law: The Fascinating Story of the Emergence, the Decline and the Recent Resurrection of a Concept*, in: P. Merkouris, A. Kulick, J.M. Álvarez-Zarate & M. Żenkiewicz (eds), *Custom and Its Interpretation in International Investment Law* (Cambridge UP 2023) (*see also* in: L. Pasquet, K.P. Van der Ploeg & L.C. Jankiewicz (eds), *International Law and Time: Narratives and Techniques: Proceedings of the Conference 'International Law and Time'* (Springer 2022) 381-404).

for instance, remain the applicable legal regime of protection in the absence of any BIT and could also play a gap-filling role whenever a treaty, contract, or domestic legislation is silent on a given issue.[163] In any event, it was clear that the MST's role in the realm of investment treaty protection was becoming more negligible than ever before in its long history. The MST's glory days were long gone.

Yet, instead of slowly disappearing and becoming somewhat irrelevant, the MST unexpectedly made a comeback as a result of the broad interpretation of FET clauses that was given by arbitral tribunals. The following sections will examine how States have reacted to these controversial awards: they began to refer explicitly to the MST in FET clauses contained in their investment treaties with the clear aim of limiting the scope of investors' rights under these clauses (sections 3.1, 3.2 and 3.3). Finally, I will analyse the FET clause contained in the CETA, which includes a detailed list of the elements considered to be in breach of the standard (section 3.4).

3.1 The NAFTA Odyssey and Its Impact on the Evolution of the FET Standard

This section briefly analyses how the FET standard evolved in the North American context from a simply worded three-line provision[164] to a full-page clause containing numerous specifications and clarifications.

The controversy regarding the interpretation of NAFTA Article 1105(1) began in 2000 when three NAFTA tribunals rendered awards that defined different aspects of its scope.[165] These three NAFTA tribunals interpreted the FET clause as providing investors with treatment of protections *above and beyond* the MST (*Metalclad*,[166] *S.D. Myers*,[167] and *Pope and Talbot*).[168] In other words, under this approach, the FET standard imposes on the host State a greater level of protection for foreign investors than under custom. This approach provided *more rights* to investors than under the MST. Most importantly, these three tribunals adopted this interpretation notwithstanding the important fact that the FET under Article 1105 (entitled 'MST') is clearly linked to the standard existing under 'international law'.

The broad interpretations of FET clauses adopted by some tribunals led many States to take concrete measures to effectively reduce tribunals' margin of appreciation when assessing the conformity of States' conduct with the FET standard. The most virulent and comprehensive reaction came from the NAFTA parties. Under the aegis of the FTC, they responded by issuing a binding 'Note of Interpretation' which interpreted

163. International Law Commission, 'First Report on Formation and Evidence of Customary International Law', by Michael Wood, Special Rapporteur, ILC Sixty-fifth session, Geneva, 6 May-7 Jun. and 8 Jul.-9 Aug. 2013 UN doc. A/CN.4/663. More generally on the question of customary rules in international investment law, *see*: Dumberry, *supra* n. 74.
164. NAFTA Art. 1105(1), entitled 'Minimum Standard of Treatment,' indicates that 'Each Party shall accord to investments of investors of another Party treatment in accordance with international law, including fair and equitable treatment and full protection and security.'
165. On this debate, *see* Dumberry, *supra* n. 2.
166. *Metalclad Corporation v. Mexico*, ICSID No. ARB/AF/97/1, Award, 30 Aug. 2000, paras 70, 76.
167. *S.D. Myers*, *supra* n. 35, para. 266.
168. *Pope and Talbot Inc. v. Canada*, UNCITRAL, Award on the Merits of Phase II, 10 Apr. 2001.

the FET standard *restrictively* by expressly limiting the level of protection to be accorded to foreign investors to that existing under the MST under custom.[169] Part B of the Note reads as follows:

> 1. Article 1105(1) prescribes the customary international law minimum standard of treatment of aliens as the minimum standard of treatment to be afforded to investments of investors of another Party.
> 2. The concepts of 'fair and equitable treatment' and 'full protection and security' do not require treatment in addition to or beyond that which is required by the customary international law minimum standard of treatment of aliens.
> 3. A determination that there has been a breach of another provision of the NAFTA, or of a separate international agreement, does not establish that there has been a breach of Article 1105(1).

The Note itself rapidly became the centre of an important controversy among parties to NAFTA arbitration proceedings, arbitrators and scholars.

Thus, faced with the binding FTC Notes of Interpretation of 31 July 2001 (linking the FET to the MST), several tribunals (*Pope & Talbot, Mondev, ADF* and others) have simply 'moved the goal post'.[170] They have thus interpreted customary international law broadly by emphasising its evolutionary character. In doing so, these awards have (at least implicitly) challenged the FTC Note. The *Merrill & Ring* Tribunal later took this 'evolutionary' approach to the extreme by adopting the theory of 'convergence'. It held that the MST had evolved so rapidly in recent years that it now (apparently) protects foreign investors 'against all such acts or behaviour that might infringe on a sense of fairness, equity and reasonableness'.[171] The adoption of this approach by the *Merrill & Ring* Tribunal is a direct challenge to the FTC Note.[172] Other tribunals (*Glamis, Cargill*) have taken a different approach. The *Glamis* Tribunal first noted that the 'fundamentals' of the *Neer* standard still apply today, and that therefore, in order to prove a violation of the MST, an investor must show that the conduct was 'egregious' and 'shocking'.[173] Yet, the Tribunal was quick to add that it was 'entirely possible, however that, as an international community, we may be shocked by State actions now that did not offend us previously'.[174] In other words, while the *'test'* may not have changed, it nevertheless remains that the *perception* regarding what is 'egregious' and 'shocking' has evolved over time. The type of State conduct that would have not been considered a breach of the MST in the past may be deemed so today. Whether or not this is the case is for each tribunal to determine. Nothing prevents a tribunal from adopting a very liberal interpretation of what it considers to be 'egregious' and 'shocking' State

169. FTC, 'Note of Interpretation', *supra* n. 6.
170. Dumberry, *supra* n. 2, 89-124; P. Dumberry, *Moving the Goal Post! How Some NAFTA Tribunals have Challenged the FTC Note of Interpretation on the Fair and Equitable Treatment Standard under NAFTA Article 1105*, 8(2) World Arb. & Med. Rev, 86 (2014).
171. *Merrill & Ring, supra* n. 4, 210.
172. Dumberry, *supra* n. 2, 117-122.
173. Glamis, *supra* n. 4, para. 616.
174. *Ibid.*, para. 616.

conduct.[175] For that reason, I have argued elsewhere that the practical differences between the reasoning adopted by the *Glamis* Tribunal and that of the *Mondev* and *ADF* tribunals may be more apparent than real.[176]

3.2 The Elements of 'Clarification' Contained in the US Model BIT

Around the same time, States also started *explicitly* mentioning in their BITs that the FET standard was not only linked to 'international law', but that it was also, in fact, a reference to the MST under customary international law.[177] In 2004, two of the NAFTA Parties (US and Canada) started this trend when they adopted their respective Model BITs. For instance, Article 5(1) of the US Model BIT provides that '[e]ach Party shall accord to covered investments treatment in accordance with *customary* international law, including fair and equitable treatment and full protection and security'.[178] Most importantly, the provision further contains three elements of clarification. The *first* clarification in Article 5(2), which was copied almost verbatim from the FTC's 2001 Note, identifies the customary rule at stake:

> For greater certainty, paragraph 1 prescribes the customary international law minimum standard of treatment of aliens as the minimum standard of treatment to be afforded to covered investments. The concepts of 'fair and equitable treatment' and 'full protection and security' do not require treatment in addition to or beyond that which is required by that standard, and do not create additional substantive rights ... .[179]

Article 5 of the US Model BIT also contains a *second* clarification about the definition of custom. A footnote attached to the title of the provision indicates that 'Article 5 shall be interpreted in accordance with Annex A,' entitled 'Customary International Law,' where 'the Parties confirm their shared understanding' that the concept 'generally and as specifically referenced' in the BIT 'results from a general and consistent practice of States that they follow from a sense of legal obligation'.[180] Clearly, Canada and the US decided to adopt such language, and these two clarifications, in order to refute the expanding interpretation applied by some NAFTA tribunals and to incorporate the content of the FTC Note of 2001.[181] As explained by Sharp, an

175. *See*, C. Lévesque, *Chronique de Droit international économique en 2010-2011 – Investissement*, 48 Can YIL 311-313 (2010).
176. Dumberry, *supra* n. 2, 106ff.
177. UNCTAD, *supra* n. 14, 29.
178. USTR, '2004 Model Bilateral Investment Treaty' (hereinafter 'US Model BIT'), emphasis added.
179. US Model BIT (2004) and (2012).
180. Annex A further adds that 'With regard to Article 10.5, the customary international law minimum standard of treatment of aliens refers to all customary international law principles that protect the economic rights and interests of aliens.'
181. C. Lévesque, *Influences on the Canadian Model FIPA and US Model BIT: NAFTA Chapter 11 and Beyond*, 44 Can YIL 255 (2006); K. Vandevelde, *A Comparison of the 2004 and 1994 US Model BITs*, 1 Yb Int'l Invest. L. & Pol., 291 (2008-2009) DOI: 10.1093/oso/9780195371376.005.0007; C. Lévesque & A. Newcombe, *Commentary on the Canadian Model Foreign Promotion and Protection Agreement*, in: C. Brown (ed.), *Commentaries on Selected Model Investment Treaties* (Oxford UP 2013) 78-80.

increasing number of States are linking substantive protections, including FET, to customary international law, such as in the Model BIT, and that 'at least three reasons explain this trend':

- *Experience*: Most States today have firsthand experience acting as a respondent in investment arbitration, as more than 600 investment disputes have been brought against more than 100 States.
- *Visibility*: Arbitration pleadings and awards increasingly are made public and are readily accessible, giving States greater insight into how substantive standards and procedural rules have been pleaded and decided under their own, and other States' international investment agreements.
- *Interests*: Many more States today import and export significant capital, giving them both foreign investors *and* domestic prerogatives to protect.[182]

As further explained below in section 3.3, many BITs and Free Trade Agreements (FTAs) that the US, Canada and Mexico have entered into after 2004 with other States also contain the same clause referring specifically to the MST under custom. While such specific language is clearly the result of the NAFTA experience, the phenomenon is not limited to the North American context, as many States elsewhere have recently adopted the same types of FET clauses referring to the MST.[183]

The 2004 US Model BIT also added a *third* clarification. It indicates, in relevant part, that the FET obligation under Article 5(1) 'includes the obligation not to deny justice in criminal, civil, or administrative adjudicatory proceedings in accordance with the principle of due process embodied in the principal legal systems of the world'.[184] This third clarification is also featured in the US' most recent BITs and FTAs, as well as some of Canada's investment treaties.[185] The same approach was adopted in the recently signed Canada-United States-Mexico Agreement (CUSMA, which has replaced NAFTA)[186] as well as by other States in the context of, *inter alia*, Association of

182. J. Sharp, *The Minimum Standard of Treatment, Glamis Gold, and Neer's Enduring Influence*, in: M. Kinnear et al. (eds), *Building International Investment Law: The First 50 Years of ICSID* (Kluwer 2015), 281, emphasis in the original.
183. UNCTAD, *supra* n. 14, 25, referring to several treaties involving Asian countries (Australia, New Zealand, Japan, Philippines, China, Malaysia, India, South Korea, Singapore, etc.) and from South America (Peru, Chile).
184. It also contains a clarification about the 'full protection and security' obligation.
185. D.A. Gantz, *The Evolution of FTA Investment Provisions: From NAFTA to the United States – Chile Free Trade Agreement*, 19(4) Am Univ Int L Rev 679, 724ff (2003) DOI: 10.1163/9789004481367_031.
186. Agreement Between the United States of America, the United Mexican States, and Canada (CUSMA, adopted on 10 Dec. 2019, entered into force on 1 Jul. 2020). *See*, Art. 14.6(1). Importantly, Annex 14-D of Ch. 14 on investor-State dispute settlement does not apply between Canada and the US and between Canada and Mexico. It should be added that investors from Canada and Mexico will still be able to sue both States under the ISDS mechanism contained in another multilateral treaty: the Comprehensive and Progressive Agreement for Trans-Pacific Partnership (CPTPP). The implication of this important change from NAFTA is that Art. 14.6(1) on the FET only finds application in disputes involving an US or a Mexican investor against either the US or Mexico. Yet, under Art. 14-D.3 of Annex 14.D (applicable between these two countries), only claims for breach of national treatment, most-favoured nation, and 'direct', not indirect expropriation, can be submitted to arbitration. FET claims are therefore excluded.

Southeast Asian Nations (ASEAN),[187] and Common Market for Eastern and Southern Africa (COMESA).[188] One interesting recent treaty which combines some of the elements of clarification contained in the US Model BIT is the Protocol on Investment to the Agreement Establishing the African Continental Free Trade Area.[189]

Article 10.5 of the CAFTA, signed in 2004, is a perfect illustration of this evolution in the language contained in FET clauses. Its content is the same as the first three paragraphs of Article 5 of the 2004 (and 2012) US Model BITs.[190] The provision contains the same three clarifications mentioned above.[191] Given that these three

---

However, this exclusion does not apply to contracts which qualify as 'covered government contracts' (mentioned at Annex 14-E), which includes oil and gas production, power generation, transportation, telecoms and certain other infrastructure investments. It should be added that under the CUSMA, investors from all three States can still raise NAFTA Ch. 11 claims with respect to legacy investments within three years after the termination of NAFTA.

187. ASEAN Comprehensive Investment Agreement, adopted on 26 Feb. 2009, entered into force on 24 Feb. 2012, Art. 11. It should be added that the provision does not refer to MST or custom. The same is true for the ASEAN-China Investment Agreement (2010), Art. 7. On the contrary, custom is mentioned in these 'Investment Agreements': ASEAN-Korea (2009), Art. 5; ASEAN-India (signed on 2014, not yet in force), Art. 5; ASEAN-Hong Kong, China SAR (2019), Art. 5.

188. Investment Agreement for the COMESA Common Investment Area, adopted on 23 May 2007, not yet in force, Art. 14.

189. The Agreement was signed on 21 Mar. 2018 and the Protocol adopted on 19 Feb. 2023. Article 17 reads as follows:

> 1. Each State Party shall ensure that, in administrative and judicial matters, investors and investments of another State Party are not subject to treatment which constitutes a fundamental denial of justice in criminal, civil and administrative adjudicative proceedings, an evident denial of due process, a manifest arbitrariness, a discrimination based on gender, race or religious beliefs, or an abusive treatment in administrative and judicial proceedings.
> 2. For greater certainty, Paragraph 1 shall not be interpreted as equivalent to fair and equitable treatment. For further certainty, Paragraph 1 includes the minimum standard of treatment under customary international law and does not allow for an interpretation and application of such a standard that would go beyond the elements contained in Paragraph 1.

190. The third paragraph in both instruments indicates that 'A determination that there has been a breach of another provision of this Agreement, or of a separate international agreement, does not establish that there has been a breach of this Article.' *See*, K. Leite, *The Fair and Equitable Treatment Standard: A Search for a Better Balance in International Investment Agreements*, 32(1) American Univ. Int. L. Rev. 379ff. (2016).

191. Article 10.5 ('Minimum Standard of Treatment') reads as follows:

> 1. Each Party shall accord to covered investments treatment in accordance with customary international law, including fair and equitable treatment and full protection and security.
> 2. For greater certainty, paragraph 1 prescribes the customary international law minimum standard of treatment of aliens as the minimum standard of treatment to be afforded to covered investments. The concepts of 'fair and equitable treatment' and 'full protection and security' do not require treatment in addition to or beyond that which is required by that standard, and do not create additional substantive rights. The obligation in paragraph 1 to provide:
>   (a) 'fair and equitable treatment' includes the obligation not to deny justice in criminal, civil, or administrative adjudicatory proceedings in accordance with the principle of due process embodied in the principal legal systems of the world; and (...).

clarifications were clearly the result of the NAFTA experience, it is not surprising that CAFTA tribunals have systematically followed NAFTA case law.[192]

These recent treaties are far from being isolated instruments, as further explained in the next section.

3.3 The Proliferation of Very Detailed FET Clauses in Recent Years

Not surprisingly, numerous BITs[193] and FTAs[194] signed by the US with other States after 2004 contain the exact same FET clause as the US model BIT. Several BITs[195] and FTAs[196] of Canada contain a similar MST clause, although without the third clarification found in the US Model BIT (i.e., the explicit reference to the obligation not to deny justice and to provide due process) and without any definition of custom. A few other Canadian FTAs contain this third clarification, as well as a definition of custom in a footnote.[197] The US Model BIT was also copied in several (but not all)[198] of Mexico's post-2004 BITs. While some instruments (as well as the Model BIT)[199] do not contain the third clarification (nor the footnote),[200] others do.[201]

192. P. Dumberry, *'Cross Treaty Interpretation' en Bloc or How CAFTA Tribunals are Systematically Interpreting the FET Standard Based NAFTA Case Law*, 22(2) LPICT 384-418 (2023) DOI: 10.1163/15718034-bja10093.
193. US-Uruguay BIT (2006), Art. 5; US-Rwanda BIT (2012), Art. 5.
194. *See*, A.P. Tuck, *The "Fair and Equitable Treatment" Standard Pursuant to the Investment Provisions of the U.S. Free Trade Agreements with Peru, Colombia and Panama*, 16 L. & Bus. Rev. Am. 385 (2010). *See*, FTAs with Australia (2005), Art. 11.5; Chile (2003), Art. 10.4; Morocco (2006), Art. 10.5; Singapore (2003), side letter of 6 May 2003; Oman (2009), Art. 10.5; Peru (2009), Art. 10.5; Colombia TPA (2012), Art. 10.5; Korea (2012), Art. 11.5; Panama (2012), Art. 10.5.
195. *See*, BITs entered into with the Czech Rep. (2012), Art. III; Jordan (2009), Art. 5; Latvia (2011), Art. II; Peru (2006), Art. 5; Romania (2009), Art. 2; Slovakia (2012), Art. 3; Kuwait (2014), Art. 6; China (2012) Art. 5 (not referring to custom, but rather to the MST 'as evidenced by general State practice accepted as law'); Benin (2014), Art. 7; Tanzania (2013), Art. 7; Cameroon (2016), Art. 6; Nigeria (signed in 2014, not yet in force), Art. 6; Serbia (2015), Art. 6; Senegal (2016), Art. 6; Mali (2016), Art. 6; Côte d'Ivoire (2015), Art. 6; Burkina Faso (2017), Art. 6; Guinea (2017), Art. 6; Hong Kong (2016), Art. 6; Mongolia (2017), Art. 6; Moldova (2019), Art. 6.
196. *See*, FTAs with Peru (2009), Art. 805; Panama (2013), Art. 906; Honduras (2014), Art. 10.6.
197. *See*, FTAs entered into with Colombia (2011), Art. 805; Korea (2015), Art. 805.
198. *See*, BITs with Spain (2007), Art. IV; Belarus (2009), Art. 5.
199. Mexico Model BIT 2008, Art. 4.
200. BITs with Iceland (2006), Art. 3 with Protocol; Panama (2006, but terminated in 2015), Art. 6; United Kingdom (2007), Art. 3; Trinidad and Tobago (2007), Art. 5; India (2008, but terminated in 2019), Art. 5; Slovakia (2009), Art. 5; China (2009), Art. 5 (with no reference to custom but rather to the 'international law' MST 'as evidence of State practice and opinio juris'); Singapore (2011), Art. 4; Bahrain (2014), Art. 4; Kuwait (2016), Art. 4; Turkey (2017), Art. 4; United Arab Emirates (2018), Art. 4; Australia (2005) Protocol, clause 1; Czech Rep. (2002), Protocol. *See also*, FTAs with Peru (2012), Art. 11.6; Japan EPA (2004), Art. 60.
201. *See*, BIT with Hong Kong (2020), Art. 5 and FTAs with Central America (2012), Art. 11.3 (without the footnote) and Panama (2015), Art. 10.5.

The US Model BIT has since then been followed by many States in Latin America. Several of Peru's BITs contain all three clarifications,[202] some of them without the definition footnote.[203] The same is true for several BITs of Chile,[204] although some of them contain slightly different languages.[205] Several (but not all)[206] BITs and FTAs of Colombia are identical to the US Model BIT.[207] While some Colombian treaties refer to the third clarification (but do not include the footnote defining custom),[208] others do not.[209] Interestingly, Colombia's more recent BITs have followed the new Model BIT[210] and adopted instead of a CETA-style FET clause.[211]

A few States in the Asia Pacific region have followed the same trend. Thus, instruments signed by Australia contain the same structure as the US Model BIT, including the third clarification,[212] some of them with[213] or without[214] the definition footnote. Several instruments of New Zealand also contain the same[215] (or similar)[216]

202. *See*, BIT with Colombia (2010), Art. 4. *See*, FTAs with Chile (2009), Art. 11.4; Singapore (2009), Art. 10.5 (without a reference to due process); Korea (2011), Art. 9.5; Costa Rica (2013), Art. 12.4; Panama (2012), Art. 12.4; Guatemala (signed in 2011, not yet in force), Art. 12.4; Honduras (2017), Art. 10.4.
203. Peru-Japan BIT (2009), Art. 5; China-Peru FTA (2009), Art. 132 (without a reference to due process).
204. *See*, BITs with Uruguay (2012), Art. 5; Hong Kong (2016), Art. 6 (however not defining custom). *See also*, Chile-Colombia FTA (2009), Art. 9.4.
205. Chile-Japan EPA (2007), Art. 75, not containing the third clarification and not defining custom.
206. One recent example is Colombia-Israel FTA (2020), Art. 10.3.
207. *See*, Colombia-Singapore BIT (signed in 2013, not yet in force), Art. 4. *See*, FTAs with the Rep. of Korea (2016), Art. 8.5; Costa Rica (2016), Art. 12.4; Panama (signed in 2013, not yet in force), Art. 14.5.
208. *See*, BITs with BLEU (Belgium-Luxembourg Economic Union) (signed in 2009, not yet in force), Art. III (referring to the MST in accordance with custom 'and general principles of law embodied in the main legal systems of the world'); India (signed in 2009, not in force), Art. 3 (not referring to MST or custom); United Kingdom (2014), Art. II (not referring to MST or custom, but to 'international law'); Korea (signed in 2010, not yet in force), Art. 2; Japan (2015), Art. 4; France (2020), Art. 4 (not referring to custom specifically, but to the MST under 'applicable international law' and adding that the FET includes also the obligation to act in a transparent, non-discriminatory and non-arbitrary manner).
209. *See*, BITs with China (2013), Art. 2; Turkey (signed in 2014, not yet in force), Art. 4 (only referring to the MST under 'international law').
210. Colombia Model BIT 2017.
211. *See*, BITs with the United Arab Emirates (signed in 2017, not yet in force), Art. 5 (not referring to the MST per se but instead to 'the customary or international law standard of treatment and protection'); Spain (signed in 2021, not yet in force), Art. 7 (not referring to the MST or custom).
212. One exception is the Australia-Japan EPA (2014), Art. 14.5, not containing the third clarification.
213. *See*, FTAs with Chile (2009), Art. 10.5; Rep of Korea (2014), Art. 11.5; Peru (2020), Art. 8.6; Hong Kong Investment Agreement (2020), Art. 8; United Kingdom (signed in 2021, not in force), Art. 13.7; Australia-Indonesia CEPA (2020), Art. 14.7; Australia-New Zealand Investment Protocol (2012), Art. 12; Australia-Malaysia FTA (2013), Art. 12.7 (referring to denial of justice, but not to due process).
214. *See*, Australia-Indonesia CEPA (2020), Arts. 14.7, 4; Australia-New Zealand Investment Protocol (2012); Art. 12; Australia-Malaysia FTA (2013), Art. 12.7 (referring to denial of justice, but not to due process).
215. *See*, FTAs with Rep. Korea (2015), Art. 10.7; United Kingdom (signed in 2022, not in force), Art. 14.1.
216. *See*, ECA with Taiwan (2013), Art. 10 (without the footnote). Other instruments contain slightly different language and structure: China-New Zealand FTA (2008), Art. 143 (not containing the

MST clause based on the US Model BIT. Some of the more recent BITs and FTAs of Singapore have the same content as the US Model BIT[217] (but some do not contain the footnote defining custom).[218] Similarly, a few of Malaysia's more recent BITs and FTAs also have the same content, but without the third clarification and the footnote.[219] Several instruments recently entered into by Japan also contain the same element as the US Model BIT (but often using a different and rather unique structure), with[220] or without[221] the third clarification (and the footnote).

Several instruments entered into by South Korea after 2009 also contain the same element as the US Model BIT (sometimes with,[222] but often without the footnote).[223] Some of them do not contain the third clarification.[224] Similar clauses have also been found in a number of other BITs by States[225] as well as in the Model BIT of Azerbaijan.[226] Finally, it should be added that a number of recent regional instruments also contain the exact same clause as the US Model BIT: The Regional Comprehensive Economic Partnership,[227] the Pacific Alliance-Singapore FTA,[228] the Pacific Agreement

first clarification and referring to 'commonly accepted rules of international law' rather than MST under custom); Malaysia-New Zealand FTA (2010), Art. 10.10.

217. *See*, BITs with Burkina Faso (signed in 2014, not yet in force), Art. 4; Nigeria (signed in 2016, not yet in force), Art. 3; Rwanda (signed in 2018, not yet in force), Art. 3; Myanmar (signed in 2019, not yet in force), Art. 3. *See also*, FTAs with Panama (2006), Art. 9.5; Costa Rica (2013), Art. 11.6; Taiwan EPA (2014), Art. 9.7; Turkey (2017), Art. 12.3; Sri Lanka (2018), Art. 10.4; Armenia-Singapore Agreement on Trade in Services and Investment (2019), Art. 3.4.
218. *See*, BITs with Indonesia (2018), Art. 3 (referring to custom, but not the MST); Kazakhstan (signed in 2018, not yet in force), Art. 3 (referring to custom, but not the MST); Korea-Singapore FTA (2006), Art. 10.5.
219. *See*, Malaysia-San Marino BIT (2013), Art. 5; India-Malaysia FTA (2011), Art. 10.5.
220. *See*, BITs with Uruguay (2017), Art. 5; Argentina (signed in 2018, not yet in force), Art. 5; Morocco (2022), Art. 4 (not referring to the first clarification, but including a definition of custom).
221. *See*, BITs with Laos (2008), Art. 5; Iran (2017), Art. 5; Kenya (2017), Art. 5; United Arab Emirates (2020), Art. 5. *See also*, EPAs with Brunei (2008), Art. 59; Thailand (2007), Art. 95; India (2011), Art. 87; Mongolia (2016), Art. 10.5. *See also*, China-Japan-Rep. Korea Trilateral Investment Agreement (2014), Art. 5 (not referring to the MST or custom, but rather to the 'appropriate standard of treatment accorded in accordance with generally accepted rules of international law'). *See also*, other BITs (mentioned in the previous footnotes entered into by Japan with Latin American States).
222. *See*, FTAs with Turkey (2018), Art. 1.6; Viet Nam (2015), Art. 9.5; China (2015), Art. 12.5; Central America (2021), Art. 9.5.
223. *See*, BITs with Rwanda (2013), Art. 3; Uruguay (2011), Art. 2; Cameroon (2018), Art. 2; Myanmar (2018), Art. 2; Kenya (2017), Art. 2; Armenia (2019), Art. 2. *See also*, CEPA with India (2010), Art. 10.4; FTA with Israel (signed in 2021, not yet in force), Art. 9.5 (not referring to MST, but instead to 'applicable rules of customary international law').
224. China-Japan-Korea, Republic of Trilateral Investment Agreement (2014), Art. 5.
225. *See, inter alia*, Morocco-Nigeria BIT (signed in 2016, not in force), Art. 7. Other BITs do not include the definition of custom: Morocco-Viet Nam BIT (signed in 2012, not yet in force), Art. 2 (not referring to the MST, but to custom, and with no reference to due process); Egypt-Mauritius BIT (2014), Art. 4. The list is not exhaustive.
226. Azerbaijan Model BIT 2016, Art. 2.
227. The Regional Comprehensive Economic Partnership, a free trade agreement among these Asia-Pacific nations: Australia, Brunei, Cambodia, China, Indonesia, Japan, South Korea, Laos, Malaysia, Myanmar, New Zealand, Philippines, Singapore, Thailand, and Vietnam. The instrument was signed on 15 Nov. 2020 and entered into force on 1 Jan. 2022. *See*, Art. 10.5.
228. Signed on 26 Jan. 2022, not yet in force. *See*, Art. 8.7. The Pacific Alliance Member States are Chile, Colombia, Mexico and Peru.

on Closer Economic Relations Plus – PACER Plus,[229] the Transpacific Partnership agreement (without the US),[230] and CUSMA, which has replaced NAFTA.

In my view, States that have copied or used language very similar to the US Model BIT (including the three above-mentioned elements of clarification) in their post-2004 instruments were undoubtedly inspired by the NAFTA experience. Their aim was clearly to limit the scope of the FET standard. This is indeed how some tribunals have recently interpreted these clauses. One example is the *Al Tamimi v. Oman* case,[231] which is further examined in Part II.

3.4 CETA: The Ultimate Detailed FET Clause

The final text of Article 8.10 (entitled 'Treatment of Investors and of Covered Investments'), contained in the CETA,[232] reads as follows:

> 1. Each Party shall accord in its territory to covered investments of the other Party and to investors with respect to their covered investments fair and equitable treatment and full protection and security in accordance with paragraphs 2 through 6.
> 2. A Party breaches the obligation of fair and equitable treatment referenced in paragraph 1 if a measure or series of measures constitutes:
>   (a) denial of justice in criminal, civil or administrative proceedings;
>   (b) fundamental breach of due process, including a fundamental breach of transparency, in judicial and administrative proceedings.
>   (c) Manifest arbitrariness;
>   (d) Targeted discrimination on manifestly wrongful grounds, such as gender, race or religious belief;
>   (e) Abusive treatment of investors, such as coercion, duress and harassment; or
>   (f) A breach of any further elements of the fair and equitable treatment obligation adopted by the Parties in accordance with paragraph 3 of this Article.
> 3. The Parties shall regularly, or upon request of a Party, review the content of the obligation to provide fair and equitable treatment. The Committee on Services and Investment, established under Article 26.2.1(b) (Specialized Committee), may develop recommendations in this regard and submit them to the CETA Joint Committee for decision.
> 4. When applying the above fair and equitable treatment obligation, a tribunal may take into account whether a Party made a specific representation to an investor to induce a covered investment, that created a legitimate expectation,

229. Pacific Agreement on Closer Economic Relations Plus – PACER Plus, signed on 14 Jun. 2017 and entered into force on 20 Dec. 2020. *See* Art. 9. The parties are Australia, Cook Islands, Micronesia, Kiribati, Nauru, New Zealand, Niue, Palau, Marshall Islands, Samoa, Solomon Islands, Tonga, Tuvalu and Vanuatu.
230. Comprehensive and Progressive Agreement for Trans-Pacific Partnership (CPTPP), adopted on 8 Mar. 2018, entered into force on 30 Dec. 2018, Art. 9.6. The parties are Canada, Australia, Brunei, Chile, Japan, Malaysia, Mexico, New Zealand, Peru, Singapore, and Vietnam.
231. *Hamadi, supra* n. 7.
232. The final text of the agreement was released, following legal review, on 29 Feb. 2016: http://www.international.gc.ca/trade-commerce/trade-agreements-accords-commerciaux/agr-acc/ceta-aecg/index.aspx?lang=eng.

and upon which the investor relied in deciding to make or maintain the covered investment, but that the Party subsequently frustrated.

5. For greater certainty, 'full protection and security' refers to the Party's obligations relating to physical security of investors and covered investments.
6. For greater certainty, a breach of another provision of this Agreement, or of a separate international agreement does not establish a breach of this Article.
7. For greater certainty, the fact that a measure breaches domestic law does not, in and of itself, establish a breach of this Article. In order to ascertain whether the measure breaches this Article, the Tribunal must consider whether a Party has acted inconsistently with the obligations in paragraph 1.[233]

When drafting Article 8.10, the parties had in mind the 'alternative way to qualify, clarify and/or narrow down the FET standard' which had been put forward in a 2012 UNCTAD report to 'replace the general FET provision'.[234] Yet, what is probably the most striking feature of Article 8.10 is the undeniable fact that the final list of elements it contains (and their actual contours) is, to a very large extent, based on how NAFTA tribunals have interpreted Article 1105 over the last 20 years.[235]

Article 8.10 is the first FET clause contained in an IIA that specifically enumerates the different situations resulting in a breach of the obligation. This is a *closed list*[236] that specifically defines what the parties consider to be the standard. Canada had never before adopted such an FET clause. This is also a first in the European context since the CETA is the first trade agreement containing a comprehensive investment chapter concluded by the EU. The same CETA-style approach has been recently adopted by the EU in agreements subsequently concluded with three States.[237] The new Model BITs

233. *See*: P. Dumberry, *Fair and Equitable Treatment*, in: S. Schacherer & M.M. Mbengue (eds), *Foreign Investment under the Comprehensive Economic and Trade Agreement (CETA)* (Springer 2018); P. Dumberry, *Article 8.10: Treatment of Investors and of Covered Investments*, in: M. Bungenberg & A. Reinisch (eds), *CETA Investment Law: Article-by-Article Commentary* (Nomos-Hart 2021) 249-269.
234. UNCTAD, *supra* n. 14, 108, listing the following specific obligations: '(a) Denial of justice and flagrant violations of due process; (b) Manifestly arbitrary treatment; (c) Evident discrimination; (d) Manifestly abusive treatment involving continuous, unjustified coercion or harassment; (e) Infringement of legitimate expectations based on investment-inducing representations or measures, on which the investor has relied.'
235. *See*, Dumberry, *supra* n. 192. My analysis of NAFTA case law (Dumberry, *supra* n. 2, 125-275) suggests that only the prohibition of manifest arbitrary conduct, denial of justice and the obligation of due process are unambiguously stand-alone elements of the FET obligation under Art. 1105.
236. Whether or not this is the case has been debated since the word 'only' does not appear before the enumeration of obligations. *See*, G. Van Harten, *The EU-Canada Joint Interpretive Declaration/Instrument on the CETA*, Osgoode Legal Studies Research Paper No. 6/2017. In any event, what is clear is that the parties initially intended the list to be non-exhaustive. Thus, the February 2013 draft refers to the EU proposal using the words 'notably' and 'not exclusively' before the list of obligations. Canada's proposal mentioned that it 'includes' such obligations. Such language was not kept in the final text. See, however, CETA, 4th Joint Committee, 'Joint Statement: Sustainable economic growth in the EU and Canada through the Comprehensive Economic and Trade Agreement', 4 Feb. 2024, indicating that list of elements is exhaustive.
237. EU-Singapore FTA and Investment Protection Agreement, signed on 18 Oct. 2018, and not yet in force; EU-Vietnam FTA, signed on 30 Jun. 2019, not yet in force; Modernisation of the Trade part of the EU-Mexico Global Agreement, text agreed on 21 Apr. 2018, not yet in force.

adopted by Belgium-Luxembourg,[238] the Netherlands,[239] Canada,[240] Italy,[241] Morocco,[242] Slovakia,[243] and Colombia[244] also contain a very similar closed list of FET elements. The same is true for the latest Indian Model BIT.[245] It should be added that the proposed text of the (now doomed) Transatlantic Trade and Investment Partnership (TTIP) between the EU and the US also contained an FET clause with similar language to Article 8.10.[246]

One of the most notable features of Article 8.10 is the important fact that it does *not* refer to the terms MST or custom.[247] This is quite a novel approach for Canada because all of its recent investment treaties contain such a reference. The parties certainly believed that there was no need to expressly link the FET to the standard existing under the MST precisely because the clause contains a comprehensive enumeration of the elements they considered to be comprised in the FET 'box'. In my view, such an omission of the term MST should not be interpreted as a possible setback to the phenomenon of the 'return' of the MST. This is because the list of obligations contained in Article 8.10 is, in fact, the same as those generally considered to be comprised within the umbrella concept of the MST.[248] One writer has recently referred to Article 8.10 as an MST clause with another name.[249]

Another writer has recently noted that 'tying the FET to customary international law has done little to reduce the uncertainty' about the content and the scope of the standard.[250] There is indeed some truth to this in the NAFTA context.[251] For that

238. Belgium and Luxembourg Model BIT 2018, Art. 4, referring to FET, but not to the MST or custom.
239. The Netherlands Model BIT 2018, Art. 9, referring to FET, but not to the MST or custom.
240. Canadian Model BIT 2021, Art. 8, entitled MST and mentioning custom, but not the term FET.
241. Italy Model BIT 2022, Art. 4, referring to FET, but not to the MST or custom.
242. Morocco Model BIT 2019, Art. 6, referring to FET, but not to the MST or custom.
243. Slovakia Model BIT 2019, Art. 5, referring to FET, but not to the MST or custom.
244. Colombia Model BIT 2017, unnumbered clause, referring to FET, but not to the MST or custom.
245. India's Model BIT 2016, Art. 3.1. The provision does not use the terms FET or MST, but instead refers to the expression 'violation of customary international law'. This type of clause is found in these subsequent BITs signed with Belarus (2018, not yet in force), Art. 3; Kyrgyzstan (2019, not yet in force), Art. 3; Brazil (2020, not yet in force), Art. 4 (not referring to FET or the MST, but to 'applicable rules and customs of international law').
246. Commission Draft Text TTIP – Investment, online: https://www.astrid-online.it/static/upload/protected/comm/comm-ue_draft-text-ttip---investment_16_09_15.pdf, *see* Art. 3.
247. Interestingly, in a previous draft, the parties had included another paragraph indicating that the FET protection could also cover treatment other than those specifically enumerated in the second paragraph if they were 'contrary to the fair and equitable treatment obligation recognized in the general practice of States accepted as law'. This was a clear reference to the concept of custom under international law. This addition essentially acknowledged the evolving nature of the FET standard and the fact that new situations could eventually become contrary to custom in the future. This feature was, however, not kept in the final text. This is most likely because the parties felt that any such evolution could be taken into account by the periodic review mechanism (provided for in paras 2(f) and 3) whereby they may add new situations that they consider to be in breach of the standard. On this point, *see*: U. Kriebaum, *FET and Expropriation in the Comprehensive Economic Trade Agreement between the European Union and Canada (CETA)* TDM 21-22 (2016).
248. Dumberry, *supra* n. 2, 104ff.
249. E.B. Barrera, *The Case for Removing the Fair and Equitable Treatment Standard from NAFTA*, CIGI Papers No. 128, 10 (2017).
250. *Ibid.*, 9.

reason, the degree of specificity of the CETA FET clause is a welcome development. The reference to the MST in BITs (and the FTC Note) has not been entirely successful in harmonising the interpretation of the standard and limiting its scope.[252] Under the CETA FET clause, a tribunal would no longer have the freedom to simply 'move the goal post' by broadly interpreting how the MST has evolved in recent years. In CETA, the 'evolution' has effectively been *stopped* with the specific enumeration of elements contained in the FET clause.[253] In my view, this clause contains the most appropriate language to limit the discretion of tribunals in defining FET widely.

In theory, one could argue that it is still possible for a tribunal (following the *Glamis* example) to give a wide interpretation to any of the specific elements contained in the enumeration set out in Article 8.10. As such, even a closed list of what constitutes an FET breach would not prevent a tribunal like *Merrill & Ring* from interpreting the concept of arbitrariness or due process in a very broad manner.[254] Indeed, nothing can prevent a *Bilcon* like-minded tribunal from coming up with its own particular view of what it considers to be a 'manifest' or a 'fundamental' breach of the FET standard.[255] Yet, in my view, the possibility of such an outcome is rather unlikely since the CETA has established a permanent Tribunal of first instance and the Appellate Tribunal.[256] This will ensure that the same adjudicators decide on every case, thereby allowing for a more consistent and coherent jurisprudence with regard to the FET standard.[257] This is the best safeguard against any future attempts by arbitral tribunals to adopt a broad interpretation of the FET standard.[258]

251. F. Jadeau & F. Gélinas, *CETA's Definition of the Fair and Equitable Treatment Standard: Toward a Guided and Constrained Interpretation*, 13(1) TDM 10 (2016) DOI: 10.2139/ssrn.29 31503.
252. *Ibid.*, 11-12; G. Ünüvar, *The Vague Meaning of Fair and Equitable Treatment Principle in Investment Arbitration and New Generation Clarifications*, iCourts Working Paper Series, No. 55(2), 22 (2016); G. Ünüvar, *Is CETA the Promised Breakthrough? Interpretation and Evolution of Fair and Equitable Treatment and Indirect Expropriation Provisions*, in: M. Andenas & L. Pantaleo (eds), *The EU as an Actor in International Economic Law* (TMC Asser Press 2019).
253. There remains, of course, the possibility under Art. 8.10.3 for the parties to review and update the content of the standard.
254. *See*, comments in: C. Henckels, *Protecting Regulatory Autonomy Through Greater Precision in Investment Treaties: The TPP, CETA and TTIP*, 19(1) JIEL (2017).
255. E. De Brabandere, *States' Reassertion of Control Over International Investment Law: Redefining 'Fair and Equitable Treatment' and 'Indirect Expropriation'*, in: A. Kulick (ed.), *States' Reassertion of Control over International Investment Agreements and International Investment Treaty Dispute Settlement* (Cambridge UP 2016), 298.
256. Article 8.27, 8.28. *See*, S. Schacherer, *TPP, CETA and TTIP Between Innovation and Consolidation: Resolving Investor-State Disputes under Mega-Regionals*, 7 J. Int. Disp. Settl. 631 (2016) DOI: 10.1093/jnlids/idw022; G. Van Harten, *ISDS in the Revised CETA: Positive Steps, But Is It a 'Gold Standard'?*, CIGI Investor-State Arbitration Commentary Series No. 6 (2016); A. VanDuzer, *Investor-State Dispute Settlement in CETA: Is It the Gold Standard?*, C.D. Howe Institute Commentary No. 459 (2016); Ottawa Faculty of Law Working Paper No. 2016-44.
257. *See*, Schacherer, *supra* n. 256, 642.
258. Moreover, CETA Art. 8.31(3) provides the possibility for the CETA Joint Committee to adopt a binding interpretation 'where serious concerns arise as regards matters of interpretation that may affect investment'.

PART II 'Analysis of Case Law'

Introduction and a Few Words on Methodology

As mentioned in the Introduction, this comprehensive empirical research project examines how investment tribunals have assessed the status, scope and content of the 'Fair and Equitable Treatment' (FET) standard clause found in the vast majority of bilateral and multilateral investment treaties in the last 25 years.[1] To the best of my knowledge, this is the first comprehensive survey on the issue since the 2012 United Nations Conference on Trade and Development (UNCTAD) Report.[2] Allegations of breach of the FET clause are mentioned in the vast majority of claims filed by foreign investors. According to one estimate, this is the case for 80% of claims.[3]

I have examined all publicly available awards/decisions rendered by arbitral tribunals dealing with FET clauses. I have used the search engines on the IAReporter and ITA Law websites and found over 400 results of awards rendered until the end of 2023 (including more than 100 awards on jurisdiction) containing the terms 'fair and equitable' in English, French and Spanish. I limited my research to cases involving FET clauses contained in investment treaties. Cases involving allegations of breach of FET clauses in domestic law,[4] or in

1. Tribunals have considered that expressions such as 'just and fair treatment' have the same meaning as FET. For instance, *see*: *Luigiterzo Bosca v. Lithuania*, UNCITRAL, Award, 17 May 2013, para. 196; *Helnan International Hotels v. Egypt*, ICSID Case No. ARB/05/19, Award, 3 Jul. 2008, para. 106; *Parkerings-Compagniet AS v. Lithuania*, ICSID Case No. ARB/05/8, Award, 7 Sep. 2011, paras 271-278.
2. UNCTAD, *Fair and Equitable Treatment*, UNCTAD Series on Issues in International Investment Agreements II (2012).
3. UNCTAD, 'Special Update on Investor-State Dispute Settlement: Facts and Figures,' IIA Issues Note, No. 3, November 2017.
4. *See*, for instance, the following cases: *Bedri Selmani v. Kosovo*, ICC Case No. 24443/MHM/HBH, Award, 6 Dec. 2022, paras 528ff.; *Interocean Oil Development Company and Interocean Oil Exploration Company v. Nigeria*, ICSID Case No. ARB/13/20, Award, 6 Oct. 2020, paras 333ff.; *Stans Energy Corp. and Kutisay Mining LLC v. Kyrgyz Republic (II)*, PCA Case No. 2015-32, Award, 20 Aug. 2019, paras 629ff.; *Antoine Abou Lahoud and Leila Bounafeh-Abou Lahoud v. D.R. Congo*, ICSID Case No. ARB/10/4, Award, 7 Feb. 2014, paras 425ff.; *Duke Energy International Peru Investments No. 1 Ltd. v. Peru*, ICSID Case No. ARB/03/28, Award, 18 Aug. 2008, paras 280ff.; *Tradex Hellas S.A. v. Albania*, ICSID Case No. ARB/94/2, Award, 29 Apr. 1999.

contracts,[5] were not part of my analysis.[6] Furthermore, my research focused on awards where tribunals have actually provided analysis regarding the content and the scope of FET clauses contained in treaties. Accordingly, many awards/decisions were excluded from the scope of my research. For instance, cases where the FET clause was mentioned by the parties during the proceedings, but the tribunal did not provide any analysis on the issue because it focused instead on other provisions, were excluded from my research.[7] Other awards were also excluded because the tribunal denied jurisdiction over the claim, or it was held to be inadmissible, and therefore said nothing about the FET clause. Many other awards were excluded because while the tribunal held that it had jurisdiction over the dispute, and mentioned briefly the FET allegations, it nevertheless decided that the issue would have to be examined at a later phase of the proceedings. Ultimately, I have only considered awards where the tribunal examined allegations of FET breaches in a distinct section of its award after having set out the parties' arguments.[8] In total, I have found 279 relevant awards. They are examined in this part.

In Part I, I explained that while the vast majority of BITs (95% of them) include an FET clause,[9] a considerable degree of variation in the actual content of the clause still exists. The most significant distinction is between three different types of clauses. On the one hand, many treaties contain 'stand-alone' clauses containing an 'unqualified' reference to the obligation to accord a FET. On the other hand, BITs often contain clauses referring to an FET obligation linked to 'international law'. Finally, there are an increasing number of treaties that contain FET clauses specifically referring to the MST or custom. Previous studies have shown that these different formulations matter. The distinction in the type of clause is pivotal in the determination of the actual scope of the

5. *See*, for instance: *WalAm Energy LLC v. Kenya*, ICSID Case No. ARB/15/7, Award, 10 Jul. 2020, paras 543ff., 551ff.
6. It should be added that I have found no award supporting the existence of an FET obligation under custom, which could be invoked by an investor in the absence of a treaty, a domestic law or a contract expressly providing for that protection. The argument was rejected in *İçkale İnşaat Limited Şirketi v. Turkmenistan*, ICSID Case No. ARB/10/24, Award, 8 Mar. 2016, para. 341: 'The Tribunal finds no merit, legal or otherwise, in the Claimant's argument that it is entitled to invoke the FET, FPS, non-discrimination, and umbrella clause protections on the basis that they have become "an international customary norm for Turkmenistan". In any event, even assuming the FET, FPS, non-discrimination, and umbrella clause standards were to be considered as part of customary international law (and not only the customary international law of, or applicable to, Turkmenistan), which is an argument neither Party has made, there is no basis in the BIT for the Tribunal to apply any investment protection standards other than those specifically included in the BIT.' In *Getma International and others v. Guinea [II]*, ICSID Case No. ARB/11/29, Award, 16 Aug. 2016, para. 358, the argument was raised by the claimant since the Code of Investments did not contain a reference to FET.
7. *See*, *inter alia*, *Casinos Austria International GmbH and Casinos Austria Aktiengesellschaft v. Argentina*, ICSID Case No. ARB/14/32, Award, 5 Nov. 2021, paras 433ff.; *Bank Melli Iran and Bank Saderat Iran v. Bahrain*, PCA Case No. 2017-25, Award, 9 Nov. 2021, paras 698ff.
8. I have decided not to examine awards which referred to FET, but where the text of the clause was not available. *See*, *M. Meerapfel Sohne AG v. Central African Republic*, ICSID Case No. ARB/07/10, Award, 12 May 2012, based on the Memorandum of Understanding (MoU) but the text of the FET clause is not available.
9. OECD, *'Fair' and 'Equitable' Treatment Provisions in Investment Treaties; A Large-Sample Survey of Treaty Provisions* (2023) 4.

FET obligation. Thus, arbitral tribunals have adopted a different approach depending on the actual drafting of the FET clause.[10] This is also the conclusion reached by a 2004 Organisation for Economic Co-operation and Development (OECD) paper:

> Because of the differences in its formulation, the proper interpretation of the 'fair and equitable treatment' standard depends on the specific wording of the particular treaty, its context, the object and purpose of the treaty, as well as on negotiating history or other indications of the parties' intent. For example, some treaties include explicit language linking or, in some cases limiting, fair and equitable treatment to the minimum standard of international customary law. Other treaties which either link the standard to international law without specifying custom, or lack any reference to international law, could, depending on the context of the parties' intent, for example, be read as giving the standard a scope of application that is broader than the minimum standard as defined by international customary law.[11]

Almost 10 years later, a 2012 UNCTAD report indicated that the drafting variations in FET clauses have in fact been interpreted by tribunals as meaning *different content* as well as *different thresholds* to find a violation:

> [The] identification of the correct source of the FET standard – whether it is grounded in customary international law or is a self-standing obligation – can have important consequences in terms of the standard's content and, more precisely, of the types of State measures that can be challenged as well as the required threshold for finding a violation, that is, the required degree of seriousness of the breach.[12]

While this reading of case law has been contested by some,[13] it is generally accepted by authors.[14] In an influential book, Paparinskis summarised case law as follows:

10. UNCTAD, *supra* n. 2, at xiv; A. Newcombe & L. Paradell, *Law and Practice of Investment Treaties: Standards of Treatment* (Kluwer 2009) 263-264; M. Paparinskis, *The International Minimum Standard and Fair and Equitable Treatment* (Oxford UP 2013) 94.
11. OECD, *Fair and Equitable Treatment Standard in International Investment Law*, Working Papers on International Investment Law, No. 2004/3 (2004), 40. *See also*: K. Yannaca-Small, *Fair and Equitable Treatment Standard: Recent Developments*, in: A. Reinisch (ed.), *Standards of Investment Protection* (Oxford UP 2008) 113-114.
12. UNCTAD, *supra* n. 2, 8.
13. A. Diehl, *The Core Standard of International Investment Protection: Fair and Equitable Treatment* (Wolters Kluwer 2012) 135.
14. For a recent analysis, *see*: M. Emami & R. Gul, *Diversity in the Formulation of Fair and Equitable Treatment in International Investment Agreements*, 14(1) J. E. Asia & Int'l L. (2021) 79-100 DOI: 10.14330/jeail.2021.14.1.04, examining many cases and concluding that 'tribunals have had different interpretations of the FET based on various formulations of the standard' (at 93). *See also*, R. Islam, *The Fair and Equitable Treatment (FET) Standard in International Investment Arbitration: Developing Countries in Context* (Springer 2018) 53: 'The standard has been expressed in number of different ways in different investment treaties. It has been hotly debated whether these different constructions are merely a matter of stylistic approach or difference in constructions also lead to variations in the substance of the content of the standard. The different wordings used in different treaties in relation to FET therefore have complicated the issue, and the tribunals have varied their interpretation in accordance with the construction of the treaty language. Thereby due to different treaty language the interpretation of the tribunals determining its scope and extend under different circumstances of the host country impacts the outcome of particular disputes.' But she nevertheless believes that 'despite differences in construction,

> As the CMS Gas Transmission Company v. Argentina annulment committee observed in a piece of well-put understatement, 'the fair and equitable standard has been invoked in a great number of cases brought to ICSID arbitration and ... there is some variation in the practice of arbitral tribunals in this respect'. At one end of the spectrum, Tribunals take the view that fair and equitable treatment refers to a customary minimum standard. At the other end of the spectrum, Tribunals take the view the fair and equitable treatment is a treaty standard that does not refer to customary law, and that goes further than it. As between the two extremes, Tribunals do not consider it necessary to make a clear distinction, or indeed even recognize the distinction, but consider the rules to be substantively similar, or at least similar in the particular cases.[15]

The goal of this research project is to assess whether the conclusions reached by both the OECD and the UNCTAD reports are still valid 10 years later.

I have focused my attention on the following three questions:

(1) Based on the language of the FET clause in the treaty, what is the tribunal's reasoning regarding the relationship between the standard of treatment it provides to foreign investors and the standard under 'international law', the 'minimum standard of treatment' (MST) under custom, or, more generally, customary international law? In other words, do they constitute an equivalent treatment or does one offer a better level of protection than the other(s)?

(2) In relation to how the tribunal analysed the first question, what did it say about the content of the FET standard? In other words, what are the different elements of treatment that the host State must accord to foreign investors? More specifically, does the tribunal consider that the standard includes the protection of the investor's legitimate expectations?

(3) Does the answer to these two questions have any consequences or impact on a tribunal's finding in terms of liability and awarding compensation?

One additional clarification should be made at this juncture regarding the second question. As noted by Bondy, the protection of investors' 'legitimate expectations' has become a central feature of FET jurisprudence when interpreting the clause as a 'bare' treaty standard.[16] While the concept has been narrowly defined by tribunals in the last decades, it remains 'arguably the most controversial doctrine arising out of arbitral interpretations of FET'.[17] In its 2012 Report, UNCTAD noted that elements of protection such as 'transparency, consistency, legality and stability of regulatory framework, have featured in a number of arbitral awards, but it appears premature to speak about a consensus in relation to those, given the concern and criticism they have raised and the fact that some of them were drawn from the preamble of the applicable treaty and not

there remains sufficient similarity across different treaties to support the claim that there is an overarching and singular concept of FET that can be the subject of detailed analysis' (at 54).

15. Paparinskis, *supra* n. 10, 93.
16. C. Bondy, *Fair and Equitable Treatment: Ten Years On*, in: J.E. Kalicki & M.A. Raouf (eds), *Evolution and Adaptation: The Future of International Arbitration* (ICCA Congress Series 2019) 198-225, 209.
17. *Ibid.*, 210.

from the FET obligation itself'.[18] In a recent case, the International Court of Justice (ICJ) first noted that 'references to legitimate expectations may be found in arbitral awards concerning disputes between a foreign investor and the host State that apply treaty clauses providing for fair and equitable treatment'.[19] However, it also added that 'it does not follow from such references that there exists in general international law a principle that would give rise to an obligation on the basis of what could be considered a legitimate expectation. Bolivia's argument based on legitimate expectations thus cannot be sustained'.[20] In other words, the Court did not believe that there exists an obligation to protect legitimate expectations under 'general international law'. The question of the implication of that dictum in the specific context of investment arbitration has been raised in a recent CAFTA award.[21] In any case, it shows that the existence of the concept of legitimate expectations in international law is still a controversial question.

In fact, as further examined below, many tribunals interpreting FET clauses linked to the MST have held that there is no such general obligation under international law. In the context of the North American Free Trade Agreement (NAFTA), the vast majority of tribunals have not considered the concept of legitimate expectations as a stand-alone element of the FET standard under Article 1105; it is rather a 'factor' to be taken into account when assessing whether or not *other well-established* elements of the standard have been breached (for instance, due process, arbitrary conduct, etc.). NAFTA awards have also repeatedly defined the concept of legitimate expectations narrowly in order to significantly reduce its scope of application.[22] A good example is the four-elements definition adopted by the *Thunderbird* Tribunal: (1) conduct or representations must have been made by the host State; (2) the claimant must have

18. UNCTAD, *supra* n. 2, 90.
19. *Obligation to Negotiate Access to the Pacific Ocean (Bolivia v. Chile)*, Judgment, ICJ Rep. 2018, para. 162.
20. *Ibid.*
21. *The Lopez-Goyne Family Trust and Others v. Nicaragua*, ICSID Case No. ARB/17/44, Award, 1 Mar. 2023, para. 419: 'In this Tribunal's view, that judgment is not apposite for the question under consideration here. That is because Bolivia v. Chile was a State-to-State dispute concerning Chile's alleged obligation to negotiate Bolivia's sovereign access to the sea and the Court had to determine, on the basis of customary international law applicable to relations between States, what types of expectations could acquire relevance in that context. It is impossible to extrapolate anything from that finding of the Court as to the type of expectations that can arise and be protected in the completely different context of relations between a State and aliens governed by a treaty on the protection of investments. The Court's dictum dismissing the relevance of investor-State jurisprudence is to be understood simply as denying that such awards can be invoked as evidence of the existence of a rule of customary international law on legitimate expectations applicable to the relations between States. In this Tribunal's opinion, it is not dispositive in a completely different context to infer the existence of a rule of customary international rule specifically on the treatment of aliens denying effects to legitimate expectations engendered by States in the specific context of their relations with foreign investors.'
22. P. Dumberry, *The Protection of Investors' Legitimate Expectations and the Fair and Equitable Treatment Standard under NAFTA Article 1105*, 31(1) J. Int. Arb. (2014) 47-74. One exception is *William Ralph Clayton, William Richard Clayton, Douglas Clayton, Daniel Clayton and Bilcon of Delaware, Inc. v. Canada*, UNCITRAL PCA Case No. 2009-04, Award on Jurisdiction and Liability, 17 Mar. 2015, paras 444-445, 448-449, 455ff., 470, 589.

relied on such conduct or representations to make its investment; (3) such reliance by the claimant on these representations was 'reasonable'; and (4) the host State subsequently repudiated these representations therefore causing damage to the investor.[23] In subsequent awards, NAFTA tribunals have further restrictively *qualified* these four requirements. For instance, the *Glamis* award required that an investor's expectations be based on 'definitive, unambiguous and repeated'[24] specific 'commitments'[25] (or 'assurances')[26] made by the host State to have 'purposely and specifically induced the investment'[27] by the investor. In this book, I have considered that tribunals which have adopted a similar reasoning have adopted a 'restrictive', or narrow, interpretation of the concept of legitimate expectations and the content of the FET standard.

On the contrary, I have found many awards where tribunals have considered that the FET standard includes the protection of investors' legitimate expectations and an obligation of transparency. This is the case of the vast majority of awards assessing stand-alone FET clauses and provisions referring to 'international law'. Tribunals have often referred to these concepts very broadly without qualifying them or setting any limits to the type of protection they offer to investors. One classic example is the *Tecmed* award, further discussed below.[28] In this book, I have considered that these tribunals have adopted a 'broad' interpretation of the concept of legitimate expectations and the content of the FET standard. In a recent article Grisel noted the *Tecmed* award 'is undoubtedly the landmark FET case as it might have prompted other tribunals, including the Waste Management and Occidental tribunals, to position themselves vis-à-vis Tecmed's interpretation of FET'.[29] Thus, it was the case most often referred to by subsequent awards dealing with FET.[30] Even if it is the most cited case, it is not always cited in agreement. Some awards have been very critical of its wide interpretation.[31] It has also been noted by the NAFTA *Glamis* Tribunal that the reasoning of the *Tecmed* award does not '[define] anything other than an autonomous standard' and that it offered no guidance to tribunals having to assess an FET clause linked to the MST.[32]

23. *International Thunderbird Gaming Corporation v. Mexico,* UNCITRAL, Award, 26 Jan. 2006, para. 147.
24. *Glamis Gold Ltd v. United States*, UNCITRAL, Award, 8 Jun. 2009, para. 802.
25. *Ibid.*, para. 767.
26. *Ibid.*, paras 800-801.
27. *Ibid.*, para. 766. *See also*, para. 767.
28. *Técnicas Medioambientales Tecmed, S.A. v. Mexico,* ICSID No. ARB(AF)/00/2, Award, 29 May 2003.
29. F. Grisel, *Fair and Equitable Treatment: Ordering Chaos through Precedent?,* in: D. Behn, O.K. Fauchald & M. Langford (eds), *The Legitimacy of Investment Arbitration: Empirical Perspectives* (Cambridge UP 2022) 268.
30. *Ibid.*: 'it was unquestionably the dominant reference for the FET: before 2010, 21 out of 37 tribunals interpreting the FET cited Tecmed. Adding the cases after 2010 shows that Tecmed's influence may have waned somewhat but remains significant: it has been cited by 36 of the 114 tribunals that have analysed the FET standard until 2014'.
31. *MTD Equity Sdn. Bhd. and MTD Chile S.A. v. Chile,* ICSID Case No. ARB/01/7, Decision on Annulment, 21 Mar. 2007, para. 67.
32. *Glamis, supra* n. 24, para. 610.

In the following chapters, I will examine the reasoning of tribunals dealing with the following three different types of FET clauses:[33]

- Clauses containing an unqualified formulation of the FET obligation, i.e., a stand-alone obligation to provide FET without any reference to international law or any other standards (found in 174 awards, Chapter I).
- Clauses containing an explicit reference to the standard existing under 'international law'. In this category, there are two distinct types of clauses:
  - those providing for treatment 'in accordance with international law'; and
  - those indicating that the treatment should be 'no less than that required under international law' (found in a total of 63 awards, Chapter II).
- Clauses where the FET obligation is expressly linked to the MST or custom (found in 42 awards, Chapter III).

I STAND-ALONE FET CLAUSES

Introduction

A stand-alone clause simply refers to the obligation to offer investors a FET, without any mention of any other standard of treatment or any reference to 'international law' or the MST. This is a typical example of this type of clause:

> Investments of investors of either Contracting Party shall at all times be accorded fair and equitable treatment and shall enjoy full protection and security in the territory of the other Contracting Party (Czech Republic-Bahrain BIT, 2007, Art. 2(2)).

In a recent 2023 Report, the OECD explained that the use of stand-alone FET clauses (i.e., those 'without any interpretative guidance')[34] 'declined in the early 2000s, and the decline accelerated sharply after 2009'.[35] Interestingly, the Report noted that 'no treaty in the sample concluded after 2018 features this design'.[36] In other words, no new treaties signed in the last five years contain a 'stand-alone' FET clause. Notwithstanding these new developments, it remains that this type of clause is the most frequently used FET clause in all investment treaties that are in force. While no

33. A number of recent treaties contain FET clauses with a closed list of specific elements of the FET obligation. One example is the CETA between the European Union (EU), its Member States and Canada. *See*: P. Dumberry, *Fair and Equitable Treatment*, in: S. Schacherer & M.M. Mbengue (eds), *Foreign Investment under the Comprehensive Economic and Trade Agreement (CETA)* (Springer 2018); P. Dumberry, *Article 8.10: Treatment of Investors and of Covered Investments*, in: M. Bungenberg & A. Reinisch (eds), *CETA Investment Law: Article-by-Article Commentary* (Nomos-Hart 2021) 249-269. No award dealing with this type of clause has yet been rendered.
34. OECD, *supra* n. 9, 15.
35. *Ibid.*
36. *Ibid.*

longer used in most recent treaties, they still represent almost 80% of treaties concluded between 1959 and 2023.[37]

As mentioned in Part I, for the majority of authors, the FET standard is *generally* considered an *independent* treaty standard having an autonomous meaning from the MST.[38] This interpretation is correct when the FET clause is unqualified and contains no reference whatsoever to international law or the MST.[39] In other words, there are good reasons to consider that a 'stand-alone', or 'bare', FET clause has an 'autonomous character', i.e., it is not linked to the standard of treatment existing under 'international law' or the MST under custom.[40] To the best of my knowledge, the expression 'autonomous' FET clause was first used by Mann in his famous 1981 article. He noted that 'the terms "fair and equitable treatment" envisage conduct which goes far beyond the minimum standard and afford protection to a greater extent and according to a much more objective standard than any previously employed form of words', adding that 'the terms are to be understood and applied *independently and autonomously*'.[41] The *Tecmed* Tribunal was the first to use the term 'autonomous'.[42] Yet, and importantly, the Tribunal was not assessing a stand-alone FET clause, but an 'in accordance with international law' clause (this category of clauses will be examined below in Chapter II). In any event, the *Tecmed* Tribunal said that the FET clause was 'an expression and part of the bona fide principle recognized in international law' which requires a State to provide treatment 'that does not affect the basic expectations that were taken into account by the foreign investor to make the investment'.[43] These 'expectations' were defined very broadly to include, *inter alia*, that the host State will 'act in a consistent manner, free from ambiguity and totally transparently in its relations with the foreign investor, so that it may know beforehand any and all rules and regulations that will govern its investments, as well as the goals of the relevant policies and administrative practices or directives, to be able to plan its investment and comply with such regulations'.[44]

One question examined in this study is whether or not the fact that a tribunal interprets a 'stand-alone' FET clause to have an autonomous character has any consequences in terms of the interpretation (broad or restrictive) it gives to the

37. *Ibid.*
38. *See*, long list of writers in P. Dumberry, *Fair and Equitable Treatment: Its Interaction with the Minimum Standard and Its Customary Status* (Brill 2018) 28. Also referring to authors taking the opposite view.
39. *Ibid.*, 28-29. *See also*, many writers taking the same position.
40. Yet, as logical and sound as it may be, this interpretation is *not* convincing *in certain particular cases* where a treaty *explicitly* links the FET to the standard existing under 'international law' or the MST. This is clearly the case under NAFTA Art. 1105.
41. F.A. Mann, *British Treaties for the Promotion and Protection of Investments*, 52 British YIL 244 (1981), emphasis added.
42. *Tecmed, supra* n. 28, para. 155, noting that its understanding of the scope of clause is 'resulting from an autonomous interpretation, taking into account the text of Article 4(1) of the Agreement according to its ordinary meaning (Article 31(1) of the Vienna Convention), or from international law and the good faith principle, on the basis of which the scope of the obligation assumed under the Agreement and the actions related to compliance therewith are to be assessed'.
43. *Ibid.*, paras 153-154.
44. *Ibid.*

provision and in matters of finding liability and awarding compensation. According to the 2012 UNCTAD Report, there is such a connection. The Report mentioned that a 'stand-alone' FET clause 'leaves a wide margin of discretion to arbitrators and may lead to an overbroad and surprising extension of the FET standard' which 'may result in a low liability threshold and brings with it a risk for State regulatory action to be found in breach of it'.[45] The Report noted that many arbitral tribunals have interpreted 'stand-alone' FET clauses as 'delinked from customary international law and focused on the plain meaning of the terms "fair" and "equitable"'.[46]

This chapter examines two questions.

First, how have tribunals interpreted stand-alone FET clauses regarding the controversial issue of their relationship with the MST? In other words, have they considered the clause to have an 'autonomous' character? It has been taken for granted in the literature that this is indeed the case.[47] For instance, the UNCTAD Report noted that many arbitral tribunals have interpreted 'stand-alone' FET clauses as 'delinked from customary international law and focused on the plain meaning of the terms "fair" and "equitable"'.[48] My findings show, perhaps surprisingly, that the vast majority of awards actually do not take a position on the issue of the status of a stand-alone FET clause and its relationship with the MST. In fact, in a great number of awards, the question is completely ignored by the tribunal. Yet, it is also true that most tribunals which did examine the question have concluded that the clause has an autonomous character. Only a few tribunals have considered the clause as a reference to international law or the MST under custom.

The second question addressed in this chapter has, to the best of my knowledge, not been empirically examined before. Does the fact that a tribunal interprets a 'stand-alone' FET clause to have an autonomous character have any consequences in terms of the interpretation (broad or restrictive) it gives to the provision and how it addresses matters of liability and compensation? According to the 2012 UNCTAD Report, there is a connection. The Report mentioned that a 'stand-alone' FET clause 'leaves a wide margin of discretion to arbitrators and may lead to an overbroad and surprising extension of the FET standard' which 'may result in a low liability threshold

45. UNCTAD, *supra* n. 2, 22.
46. *Ibid.*, referring to several cases.
47. For instance, Emami & Rehna, *supra* n. 14, 88 ('In arbitral practice, many tribunals have also interpreted an autonomous or unqualified FET provision delinked from MST or CIL. In other words, they have focused on the plain meaning of the terms "fair and equitable," thereby resulting in a low liability threshold and causing a risk that State regulatory measures will be determined to have breached it. (...) These decisions have shown when FET is drafted in a standalone form; tribunals have interpreted them autonomously and delinked from MST under CIL'); D. Gaukrodger, *Addressing the Balance of Interests in Investment Treaties; The Limitation of Fair and Equitable Treatment Provisions to the Minimum Standard of Treatment under Customary International Law*, OECD Working Papers on International Investment (2017) 12 ('it appears that many "bare" FET clauses (...) are today generally interpreted by arbitral tribunals as establishing an autonomous FET standard'), 13 ('where a treaty FET provision is seen as establishing an autonomous obligation of fairness unconnected to customary international law, it may be seen as an invitation to elaborate a series of rules to ensure fairness in different contexts. A number of ISDS commentators have described autonomous FET provisions in these terms').
48. UNCTAD, *supra* n. 2, 22, referring to several cases.

and brings with it a risk for State regulatory action to be found in breach of it'.[49] My analysis of 120 awards confirms that a correlation does exist. The success rate of FET claims is higher for tribunals which have expressly stated that a stand-alone FET clause has an 'autonomous' character compared to others which did not take a position on this question (2\3 versus 50%). These findings suggest that when a tribunal discusses the status of the FET clause and takes a position on the matter, it is more likely to give a broad interpretation of the standard and to conclude that a breach has been committed.

I have examined 120 awards interpreting stand-alone FET clauses. To these awards, 54 other awards should be added which will be examined separately because of the unique features of the FET clause contained in the Energy Charter Treaty (ECT) (section 1.4). These awards can be divided into three different categories:

(1) Awards expressly stating that the clause has an autonomous character (section 1.1).
(2) Awards interpreting the clause as an implicit reference to the MST or international law (section 1.2).
(3) Awards not taking a position on the status of a stand-alone FET clause and its relation to the MST (section 1.3).

1.1 Awards Interpreting the Clause to Have an Autonomous Character

Interestingly, the 2004 OECD paper on FET noted that '[n]o case ha[d] been found that applied the "fair and equitable treatment" standard of a bilateral investment treaty as an autonomous standard'.[50] Things have changed since then. I have found 23 awards expressly stating that the clause has an autonomous character.

In the following sections, I will show that most of these awards have been explicit about why the clause should be considered to have an autonomous character (section 1.1.1). I will also show that their reasoning on this point has had a direct impact on how they have assessed the content of the standard (section 1.1.2) and in terms of finding liability and awarding compensation (section 1.1.3).

1.1.1 Most Awards are Explicit about Why the Clause Should Be Considered to Have an Autonomous Character

The vast majority of awards (18 out of 23 awards) have explained that it is *precisely because* the FET clause is *not* qualified with any standard (in contrast with NAFTA, for instance) that it should *not* be understood as being limited to the customary MST.[51]

49. *Ibid.*
50. OECD, *supra* n. 11, 23.
51. *Saluka Investments BV (The Netherlands) v. Czech Republic*, PCA Case No. 2001-04, Partial Award, 17 Mar. 2006, para. 294; *Indian Metals & Ferro Alloys Ltd v. Indonesia*, PCA Case No. 2015-40, Award, 29 Mar. 2019, para. 225 ('in contrast to NAFTA or other BITs the Treaty does not expressly limit the FET standard to treatment "in accordance with international law" or

They have concluded that such an omission was not accidental. For these tribunals, the contracting parties made a conscious decision not to link the FET to the MST or to 'international law'. They wanted the standard to be interpreted broadly, not limiting it to the MST. As noted by the *Addiko* award, the MST 'is a well-established concept in international law and the parties to the treaty could have specifically referred to it, if

analogous formulations. Moreover, the Tribunal also notes that several non-NAFTA tribunals that interpreted clauses with such formulations concluded that these formulations should not be understood as limiting the FET to the customary minimum standard of treatment'); *Gardabani Holdings B.V. and Silk Road Holdings B.V. v. Georgia*, ICSID Case No. ARB/17/29, Award, 27 Oct. 2022, para. 498 ('Unlike other treaties, the BIT makes no reference to the minimum standard of treatment at international law nor to treatment "in accordance with principles of international law" or any similar formulation. As has been found by other arbitral tribunals, the Tribunal believes that the FET standard embodied in the BIT constitutes an autonomous treaty standard which is not limited to the minimum standard of treatment at customary international law'); *Deutsche Telekom v. India*, PCA Case No. 2014-10, Interim Award, 13 Dec. 2017, para. 331; *Cervin Investissements S.A. and Rhone Investissements S.A. v. Costa Rica*, ICSID Case No. ARB/13/2, Award, 7 Mar. 2017, paras 452-453; *Cairn Energy PLC and Cairn UK Holdings Limited (CUHL) v. India*, PCA Case No. 2016-07, Award, 21 Dec. 2020, paras 1701-1703; *Biwater Gauff (Tanzania) Limited v. Tanzania*, ICSID Case No. ARB/05/22, Award, 24 Jul. 2008, paras 591-592 (indicating that 'given the wording of Article 2(2) of the BIT here, the Arbitral Tribunal sees force in the argument that the Contracting States here ought to be taken to have intended the adoption of an autonomous standard', but, at the same time, also adding that this standard was 'not materially different from the content' of the MST under custom); *Inmaris Perestroika Sailing Maritime Services GmbH and others v. Ukraine*, ICSID Case No. ARB/08/8, Award, 1 Mar. 2012, para. 265 ('There is nothing in the BIT that limits Article 2(1) to the standard required by customary international law. In the absence of such a statement, the Tribunal interprets the language as written, i.e., the government is obligated to accord fair and equitable treatment to foreign investments, and therefore there is no need to establish that the government's actions were in breach of customary international law in order to establish a breach of Article 2(1)'); *Teinver S.A., Transportes de Cercanías S.A. and Autobuses Urbanos del Sur S.A. v. Argentina*, ICSID Case No. ARB/09/01, Award, 21 Jul. 2017, para. 666 ('In terms of content, the Tribunal is of the view that fair and equitable treatment is not only the minimum standard of treatment at international law, as that term is not used in the Treaty'); *Deutsche Bank, AG v. Sri Lanka*, ICSID Case No. ARB/09/2, Award, 31 Oct. 2012, para. 418 (indicating that 'the contracting parties ought to be taken to have intended the adoption of an autonomous standard', but, at the same time, also 'recognizing' that the 'actual content' of the FET Treaty standard was 'not materially different from the content' of the MST under custom); *Mobile Telesystems (MTS) v. Turkmenistan (2)*, ICSID Case No. ARB(AF)/18/4, Award, 14 Jun. 2023 (reported in IAReporter, 19 Jun. 2023); *Spoldzielnia Pracy Muszynianka v. Slovakia*, UNCITRAL, PCA Case No. 2017-08, 7 Oct. 2020, para. 459 ('Unlike some other treaties, the BIT does not refer to the "international minimum standard" or similar wording'), para. 461 (speaking of 'autonomous FET provisions, such as Article 3(2) of the BIT'); *Veolia Propreté v. Egypt*, ICSID Case No. ARB/12/15, Award, 25 May 2018, para. 162; *Sociedad Aeroportuaria Kuntur Wasi S.A. and Corporación América S.A. v. Peru*, ICSID Case No. ARB/18/27, Decision on Jurisdiction Liability Certain Aspects of Quantum and Further Directions on Quantum, 11 Aug. 2023, para. 668 ('In the Tribunal's view, the CIL standard does not provide the standard of interpretation for this treaty. The BIT contains no express language to this effect, and no evidence has been provided that, unlike the NAFTA and some other treaties, the parties to the BIT intended for the CIL standard to apply'); *GPF GP S.à.r.l v. Poland*, SCC Case No. V 2014/168, Award, 29 Apr. 2020, para. 538 ('The Tribunal observes that the BIT does not refer to "international minimum standard" or similar formulations, unlike other treaties'); *Abed El Jaouni and Imperial Holding SAL v. Lebanon*, ICSID Case No. ARB/15/3, Decision on Jurisdiction and Liability, 25 Jun. 2018, and Award, 14 Jan. 2021, para. 509 ('in the absence of a reference to the customary minimum standard in Article 2(1) of the Treaty, the FET Standard referred thereunder is an autonomous one, and cannot be equated with the customary minimum standard of treatment').

they wished for the customary international law standard to apply'.[52] As explained by the *Tethyan Copper* Tribunal, the fact that they did not do so has important consequences.[53] In the *Cairn* case, the Tribunal said that 'this suggests that the Contracting Parties did not intend to limit the scope of the FET standard to the minimum standard of treatment under customary international law'.[54] They 'intended to offer more than the already available minimum standard of protection to the qualifying investors and investments'.[55] For the Tribunal, 'in accordance with the principle of effet utile, the use of this different wording must have some meaning'.[56] As mentioned above, this line of argument has been supported by authors in the past.[57] In fact, some of the awards just mentioned[58] have quoted this passage from Schreuer's article on FET:

> It is inherently implausible that a treaty would use an expression such as 'fair and equitable treatment' to denote a well-known concept such as the 'minimum standard of treatment in customary international law'. If the parties to a treaty

52. *Addiko Bank AG v. Montenegro*, ICSID Case No. ARB/17/35, Award, 24 Nov. 2021, paras 543-544: 'interpreting the Treaty in accordance with the canons of treaty interpretation set out in Article 31(1) of the VCLT, the Tribunal is of the view that the reference to "fair and equitable treatment" in Article 2(2) is not a reference to the minimum standard of treatment under customary international law'.
53. *Tethyan Copper Company Pty Limited v. Pakistan*, ICSID Case No. ARB/12/1, Decision on Jurisdiction and Liability, 10 Nov. 2017, paras 804-805 ('First of all, the Tribunal notes that Article 3(2) of the Treaty does not contain any (express) reference to the minimum standard or even to principles of international law. Therefore, Respondent's interpretation would reflect the ordinary meaning of this provision only if it can be established that the Contracting Parties considered that the words "fair and equitable treatment" in themselves imply a reference to the minimum standard. In the Tribunal's view, there is no indication that this was indeed the case, in particular taking into account that there are examples of FET provisions in which the Contracting States expressly included a reference to the minimum standard'), para. 807 ('contracting States that intended to limit the FET standard in their treaty to the minimum standard had means to express such intent through clarifying language. As a result, the Tribunal considers the absence of any reference to international law in Article 3(2) as a strong indication that the Contracting Parties did not intend to limit the FET standard contained therein to the minimum standard') para. 810 ('there is no indication that the Contracting Parties intended to limit the FET standard to the minimum standard under customary international law, but it rather appears that they intended to agree on an autonomous standard'). *See also*, *Addiko*, *supra* n. 52, paras 543-544 (the parties 'intended for the standard therein to be an autonomous one').
54. *Cairn*, *supra* n. 51, para. 1701. *See also*: *Gardabani*, *supra* n. 51, para. 498; *Kuntur Wasi*, *supra* n. 51, para. 668 ('The BIT contains no express language to this effect, and no evidence has been provided that, unlike the NAFTA and some other treaties, the parties to the BIT intended for the CIL standard to apply').
55. *Cairn*, *supra* n. 51, para. 1702.
56. *Ibid.*, also noting that 'the differences between them, is in the present day context somewhat academic given the cross-fertilisation of approaches taken under differently worded treaties' (at fn. 2146).
57. C. Schreuer & R. Dolzer, *Principles of International Investment Law* (OUP 2008), 124, arguing that 'if the parties to a treaty want to refer to CIL, one would assume that they will refer to it as such rather using a different expression', adding that 'as a matter of textual interpretation, it seems implausible that a treaty would refer to a well-known concept like the "minimum standard of treatment in customary international law" by using the expression "fair and equitable treatment"'.
58. *Biwater*, *supra* n. 51, para. 591; *Deutsche Bank*, *supra* n. 51, para. 418.

want to refer to customary international law, it must be presumed that they will refer to it as such rather than using a different expression.[59]

One interesting issue arose in the *Veolia* case where the BIT contained a stand-alone FET clause. The Tribunal noted that '[t]here is no evidence, even in the travaux préparatoires, to support the view advanced by the Respondent that the treaty refers to the minimum standard of treatment under customary international law'.[60] It also mentioned that the 'Exposé des Motifs' of the draft law presented before the French National Assembly for the incorporation of the France-Egypt BIT into French law, mentioned that 'L'Article 3 se réfère aux critères combinés du droit international ainsi que du traitement national (...)'.[61] The Tribunal understood this passage to mean that the FET 'has to be interpreted with reference to international law and applied in conformity with the rules and principles of that law'.[62] Yet, it also noted that 'the manner in which it is formulated in the France-Egypt BIT, as well as its context, indicates its autonomous character and distinguishes it from the classical minimum standard of international law'.[63] The Tribunal mentioned that some BITs concluded by the parties with other States do contain the words 'in conformity with international law'.[64] Given that these words were not found in this BIT, the Tribunal concluded that 'it would not be correct to presume that France and Egypt intended to refer to the minimum standard of customary international law' in this treaty.[65] In other words, the stand-alone FET clause had to be considered as such, i.e., without any reference to any other standards.

The *Cairn* award also dealt with this interesting argument: 'recent State practice confirms that States that agreed to establish an FET obligation in fact meant it to be limited to the MST'.[66] This passage is a reference to recent investment treaties that increasingly include FET clauses that explicitly refer to the MST. The Tribunal was unconvinced: 'Simply because certain States have clarified *their* intent does not mean that all States are bound by that clarification. The Respondent has provided no appropriate evidence that this was the Contracting Parties' shared intent.'[67] It also made this important comment:

> Some States have been careful to expressly link FET to the MST or to customary international law generally. Most States have opted to simply provide for FET. The absence of linkages of FET to customary international law has led many tribunals to hold that an unqualified FET standard is an 'autonomous' one that has a more substantial content than the Minimum Standard of Treatment. The present

59. C. Schreuer, *Fair and Equitable Treatment in Arbitral Practice*, 6 J. World Invest. & Trade (2005) 357, 360 DOI: 10.1163/221190005x00118.
60. *Veolia Propreté, supra* n. 51, para. 163.
61. *Ibid.*
62. *Ibid.*
63. *Ibid.*
64. *Ibid.*, para. 164.
65. *Ibid.* It also noted that the existence of the MFN clause in Art. 3(2) militates in favour of construing Art. 3(1) as an autonomous standard rather than the minimum standard in customary international law (para. 165).
66. *Cairn, supra* n. 51, para. 1703.
67. *Ibid.*, emphasis in the original.

> Tribunal, faced with a large body of admittedly non-binding precedent, agrees that it must give effect to the ordinary meaning of the words 'fair and equitable' unless there is an accepted interpretative basis for doing otherwise. Hence it adopts the view that Article 3 of the Treaty contains an autonomous standard.[68]

The *Cairn* Tribunal also referred to other material put forward by the respondent[69] and summarised its argument as follows: 'although the UK BITs employ the phrase "fair and equitable treatment", in view of the OECD draft Convention's influence on British investment treaty-making practice, and that Convention's essentially equating FET to the minimum standard of treatment (MST), it follows that the Tribunal should be similarly guided in its interpretation of the 1994 India-UK BIT'.[70] The Tribunal held that this evidence could not be considered *travaux préparatoires* and that there were no materials 'which would show that the negotiators expressed a shared understanding (or even exchanged views) that FET, as used in Article 3, was to be understood in the light of the 1967 OECD draft Convention's commentary'.[71]

Other awards have also concluded that a stand-alone FET clause should be considered an autonomous clause without, however, providing much explanation.[72] For instance, some have simply referred to both parties' agreement that the FET clause was 'an autonomous one, different from the international minimum standard' and that it should be interpreted based on Articles 31 and 32 of the Vienna Convention on the Law of Treaties (VCLT).[73] In *National Grid*, the reasoning of the Tribunal also suggests that it considered the provision an autonomous FET clause, without explicitly using that term. Thus, it stated that 'after first observing that there is no reference to the minimum standard of treatment under international law in the Treaty in contrast to the language of NAFTA, the Tribunal will proceed to examine the ordinary meaning of the terms "fair" and "equitable"'.[74] It then referred to the context and the preamble and stated that the FET obligation 'is placed squarely in the context of an obligation to "encourage and create" favourable conditions for investors', adding that 'in this context, it seems a logical consequence that the Contracting Parties would choose not to use limitations to such treatment such as found in the expression "minimum treatment standard under international law"'.[75]

The reasoning behind the *Bayindir* award is rather ambiguous. The case involved a BIT between Turkey and Pakistan that did not contain an FET clause. The Tribunal allowed (via the Most-Favored-Nation (MFN) clause) the importation of an FET clause

68. *Ibid.*, para. 1704, fn. 2146.
69. *Ibid.* The respondent mentioned an article written by two officials involved in the negotiation of UK BITs (E. Denza & S. Brooks, *Investment Protection Treaties: United Kingdom Experience*, 36 ICLQ (1987) 908, 910 DOI: 10.1093/iclqaj/36.4.908) which had mentioned the 1967 OECD Draft Convention's 'influence on the British approach to the development of its own draft BIT'.
70. *Ibid.*
71. *Ibid.*
72. *Mohamed Abdel Raouf Bahgat v. Egypt I*, PCA Case No. 2012-07, Final Award, 23 Dec. 2019, paras 246-247; *Albacora S.A. v. Ecuador*, PCA Case No. 2016-11, Award, 18 Jul. 2019, reported in IAReporter, 26 Jul. 2019.
73. *Ioan Micula, Viorel Micula, S.C. European Food S.A, S.C. Starmill S.R.L. and S.C. Multipack S.R.L. v. Romania*, ICSID Case No. ARB/05/20, Final Award, 11 Dec. 2013, para. 503.
74. *National Grid plc v. Argentina*, UNCITRAL, Award, 3 Nov. 2008, para. 167.
75. *Ibid.*, para. 170.

found in another BIT signed by Pakistan with Switzerland. In one passage it noted that 'the basis for importing an FET obligation into the Treaty is provided by its MFN clause, from which it follows that the applicable FET standard is a self-standing treaty obligation as opposed to the customary international minimum standard to which the Respondent referred'.[76] The passage suggests that the clause should be considered an autonomous FET clause because it was imported via the MFN clause. Yet, later the Tribunal also mentioned that the BIT 'makes no reference to general international law', but that 'customary international law and decisions of other tribunals may assist in the interpretation of this provision'.[77] It also added that this was 'particularly apposite here given that' the provision 'states a general obligation of fair and equitable treatment'.[78] In any event, the Tribunal seems to have adopted a rather broad interpretation by referring to awards which had endorsed the *Tecmed* position on legitimate expectations and the obligation to maintain a stable framework for investment.[79] It concluded that the applicable FET standard had not been breached.

1.1.2 These Tribunals Have Interpreted the Standard Broadly, thus Providing Better Protection than under the MST

Tribunals that have expressly stated that the clause has an autonomous character have considered that it provides investors with a *better* level of protection than under a clause where the standard is linked to the MST. This is clear in the *Cairn* award:

> The BIT is a treaty that protects investments with the aim of 'fostering greater investment by investors of one State in the territory of the Other State'; it acknowledges that 'the encouragement and reciprocal protection under international agreement of such investment will be conducive to the stimulation of individual business initiative and will increase prosperity in both States'. Such purpose is achievable by offering more protection than is already available under customary international law. Given the overarching object and purpose of the BIT, and absent clear limiting language, it can safely be concluded that the Contracting States intended to offer more than the already available minimum standard of protection to the qualifying investors and investments (...).[80]

Another good illustration is the Tribunal's reasoning in *Saluka*. While it noted that the difference between an autonomous FET clause and one linked to the MST 'may well be more apparent than real',[81] it nevertheless affirmed that the FET standard in the

76. *Bayindir Insaat Turizm Ticaret ve Sanayi AS v. Pakistan*, ICSID Case No. ARB/03/29 Award, 27 Aug. 2009, para. 164.
77. *Ibid.*, para. 176.
78. *Ibid.*
79. *Ibid.*, paras 177ff.
80. *Cairn, supra* n. 51, para. 1702.
81. *Saluka, supra* n. 51, para. 291: 'it appears that the difference between the Treaty standard laid down in Article 3.1 and the customary minimum standard, when applied to the specific facts of a case, may well be more apparent than real. To the extent that the case law reveals different formulations of the relevant thresholds, an in-depth analysis may well demonstrate that they could be explained by the contextual and factual differences of the cases to which the standards have been applied'.

BIT at hand had an autonomous character precisely *because* it was *not* linked to international law.[82] The Tribunal also said that it was 'not convinced' that the provision 'at least implicitly incorporates the customary minimum standard'.[83] The Tribunal added that in the context of such an autonomous FET clause, 'in order to violate the standard, it may be sufficient that States' conduct displays a relatively lower degree of inappropriateness'[84] while in contrast, under the minimum standard, 'in order to violate that standard, States' conduct may have to display a relatively higher degree of inappropriateness'.[85] In other words, it is easier for a claimant investor to prove that a breach of an 'autonomous' FET clause has been committed. The Tribunal held that the FET clause had been breached. The parties later reached a settlement.

What are the practical consequences arising from interpreting a stand-alone FET clause to have an autonomous character? Tribunals have considered that the approach is 'in accordance with the methodology prescribed by the Vienna Convention on the Law of Treaties', i.e., 'in the ordinary meaning of the BIT's terms, construed in light of its object and purpose'.[86] For the *Biwater* Tribunal, it gives an arbitral tribunal 'much latitude' as it 'leaves the precise scope' of the standard 'to the determination of the Arbitral Tribunal'.[87] It gives the Tribunal 'the possibility to articulate the range of principles necessary to achieve the treaty's purpose in particular disputes'.[88] It gives the arbitrators significant leeway to determine what they consider to be unfair and unreasonable conduct. The interpretation of an autonomous treaty standard 'can be informed by that which other investment tribunals have given to similarly formulated clauses'.[89] This is indeed what tribunals did. Awards rendered in the last decade typically refer to dozens of decisions dealing with the content and the scope of autonomous FET clauses.

Giving a tribunal a wide margin of appreciation has some very practical consequences in terms of defining the actual content of the FET standard. Tribunals that have considered a stand-alone FET clause to have an autonomous character have also concluded that the standard encompasses elements such as the protection of investor's legitimate expectations.[90] Many of these tribunals have also referred to the so-called

82. *Ibid.*, para. 294: '[Article 3.1 of the Treaty] omits any express reference to the customary minimum standard. The interpretation of Article 3.1 does not therefore share the difficulties that may arise under treaties (such as the NAFTA) which expressly tie the "fair and equitable treatment" standard to the customary minimum standard. Avoidance of these difficulties may even be regarded as the very purpose of the lack of a reference to an international standard in the Treaty. This clearly points to the autonomous character of a "fair and equitable treatment" standard such as the one laid down in Article 3.1 of the Treaty.'
83. *Ibid.*, para. 295.
84. *Ibid.*, para. 293.
85. *Ibid.*, para. 292.
86. *Kuntur Wasi, supra* n. 51, paras 668-669.
87. *Biwater, supra* n. 51, paras 593-595, endorsed by *Addiko, supra* n. 52, paras 548-549.
88. *Ibid.*
89. *Veolia Propreté, supra* n. 51, para. 168.
90. *See*, for instance (the list is not exhaustive): *Indian Metals, supra* n. 51, para. 226; *Gardabani, supra* n. 51, paras 499, 782; *Deutsche Telekom, supra* n. 51, para. 336; *Cairn, supra* n. 51, paras 1715, 1722, 1723 (noting that 'Legitimate expectations might be the relevant analytical tool in some cases, but it is not to be considered the primary tool'), paras 1726, 1788; *Biwater, supra* n. 51, paras 595ff., 602; *Inmaris, supra* n. 51, para. 265; *Addiko, supra* n. 52, paras 553ff.; *Tethyan,*

obligation of transparency as part of the FET standard.[91] While some of them have adopted rather broad definitions of these two concepts,[92] most tribunals have given a narrow definition of the concept of legitimate expectations.[93] This is certainly the case in most recent awards. Other tribunals have also included the principle of proportionality,[94] inconsistency,[95] or 'the principles of reasonable stability or predictability' as part of the FET standard.[96] Some have adopted a narrow definition[97] or have referred to the 'high' threshold required to find a breach.[98]

The broad interpretation adopted by these tribunals is perhaps the most notable feature of these awards. As mentioned above, whether or not the FET standard includes an obligation to protect an investor's legitimate expectations and a general obligation of transparency is a controversial question. As further examined below in Chapter III, most tribunals which have assessed FET clauses expressly linked to the

supra n. 53, paras 811ff.; *Teinver, supra* n. 51, para. 667; *Bahgat, supra* n. 72, para. 246; *Micula, supra* n. 73, paras 520, 527ff., 530ff.; *Deutsche Bank, supra* n. 51, para. 420; *Mobile, supra* n. 51; *Spoldzielnia, supra* n. 51, para. 461; *Veolia Propreté, supra* n. 51, para. 166; *Kuntur Wasi, supra* n. 51, paras 676ff.; *Cervin, supra* n. 51, paras 472ff.

91. *See*, for instance (the list is not exhaustive): *Micula, supra* n. 73, paras 530ff.; *GPF GP, supra* n. 51, para. 543; *Indian Metals, supra* n. 51, para. 226 ('transparent and consistent manner'); *Gardabani, supra* n. 51, paras 499, 501 (speaking of a 'significant threshold such that the respondent state's conduct is sufficiently serious to fall below the required standard of transparency, stability and predictability'); *Deutsche Telekom, supra* n. 51, para. 336; *Cairn, supra* n. 51, paras 1722, 1726; *Addiko, supra* n. 52, para. 553-554.
92. *See*, for instance, *Deutsche Telekom, supra* n. 51, para. 336; *Inmaris, supra* n. 51, para. 265; *Bahgat, supra* n. 72, para. 246; *Deutsche Bank, supra* n. 51, para. 420.
93. *See*, for instance (the list is not exhaustive): *National Grid, supra* n. 74, paras 173ff.; *Spoldzielnia, supra* n. 51, paras 461-462; *Kuntur Wasi, supra* n. 51, paras 676ff., 724ff.; *Micula, supra* n. 73, paras 665ff.; *Teinver, supra* n. 51, paras 667ff.; *GPF GP, supra* n. 51, para. 545 ('To qualify as legitimate, the investor's expectations must be based on assurances (or representations) (i) given by the State in order to encourage the making of the investment;(ii) addressed specifically to the investor;(iii) sufficiently specific in content. In addition, an investor must establish that it placed reliance upon the assurance (or representation)'); *Biwater, supra* n. 51, paras 595ff., 602 ('as long as these expectations are reasonable and legitimate and have been relied upon by the investor to make the investment'); *Gardabani, supra* n. 51, para. 501 ('a state will not breach its obligation to treat investors fairly and equitably if it changes its laws in a legitimate exercise of its regulatory authority, absent a commitment not to do so'), para. 529; *Cairn, supra* n. 51, para. 991; *Addiko, supra* n. 52, paras 553ff., 618ff.; *Tethyan, supra* n. 53, paras 811ff.; *Albacora, supra* n. 72; *El Jaouni, supra* n. 51, paras 510-511, 516, 525ff.; *Indian Metals, supra* n. 51, para. 228 (endorsing the definition in the *Lemire* award); *Cairn, supra* n. 51, paras 1715, 1722, 1723, 1726, 1761ff., 1788; *Veolia Propreté, supra* n. 51, paras 166, 233ff.
94. *Indian Metals, supra* n. 51, paras 226-227.
95. *Kuntur Wasi, supra* n. 51, para. 681, indicating that the 'Tribunal accepts that at least in some circumstances, inconsistency as a legal matter can be a distinct strand of FET independent of arbitrariness,' but not finding any breach.
96. *Cairn, supra* n. 51, paras 1722, 1726; *Addiko, supra* n. 52, paras 553-554.
97. *Cairn, supra* n. 51, paras 1726, 1788 (also indicating that '[T]he principle of legal certainty and predictability cannot be understood in absolute terms and should instead be balanced against the State's power to act in pursuance of the public purpose'); *Micula, supra* n. 73, paras 527ff.
98. *El Jaouni, supra* n. 51, paras 510-511, conduct must be 'manifestly or grossly unfair or unreasonable' 'wilful neglect of duty or a wilful disregard of due process of law, or showed an extreme insufficiency of action falling far below international standards'.

MST (such as in the context of NAFTA[99] and CAFTA)[100] have denied that the standard includes these two elements.

1.1.3 *The Position Adopted by These Tribunals Has Had a Direct Impact in Terms of Finding Liability and Awarding Compensation*

How have awards, which have interpreted stand-alone FET clauses to have an autonomous character, assessed matters of liability and compensation? They can be divided into two categories:[101]

- Some tribunals have not found any breach of the FET standard.[102] This is the case for about one-third of awards (8 out of 23).
- The other two-thirds of the awards concluded that the clause had been breached.

Some tribunals did not award any compensation despite concluding that the FET clause had been violated.[103] Most tribunals have awarded compensation. In some cases, tribunals have awarded compensation for violations of the FET clause together with breaches of other provisions.[104] This global assessment makes it difficult to pin down exactly what portion of the damages was meant to specifically cover the breach of the FET. It should be added that the amount of some damages awarded is very large (for instance, *Tethyan Copper*, USD 4 billion; *Teinver*, USD 320 million). Other tribunals have awarded compensation to cover *only* a breach of the FET clause. The sum awarded in some of these cases is also substantial.[105]

99. *See*, Dumberry, *supra* n. 22. One exception is *Bilcon, supra* n. 22, paras 444-445, 448-449, 455ff., 470, 589.
100. P. Dumberry, *'Cross Treaty Interpretation' en Bloc or How CAFTA Tribunals are Systematically Interpreting the FET Standard Based NAFTA Case Law*, 22(2) LPICT (2023) 384-418 DOI: 10.1163/15718034-bja10093. One recent exception is *Lopez, supra* n. 21, para. 420, indicating that 'many investment treaty tribunals' had 'brought the concept of legitimate expectations within the purview of provisions on the treatment of aliens under the MST'. It added that 'the requirements for a finding of a violation by a State of an investor's legitimate expectation are stringent' (para. 422).
101. In *Saluka, supra* n. 51, a settlement was reached between the parties.
102. *Indian Metals, supra* n. 51, para. 254; *Gardabani, supra* n. 51; *Addiko, supra* n. 52, para. 867; *Mobile, supra* n. 51; *Veolia Propreté, supra* n. 51, para. 431; *GPF GP, supra* n. 51, para. 579; *Albacora, supra* n. 72; *Bayindir, supra* n. 76.
103. *Cervin, supra* n. 51, para. 726; *Biwater, supra* n. 51, para. 814; *Spoldzielnia, supra* n. 51, paras 649-651.
104. *Tethyan, supra* n. 53 (USD 4 billion); *Teinver, supra* n. 51, paras 865, 1147 (USD 320 million); *Bahgat, supra* n. 72, para. 618 (USD 43.77 million); *Deutsche Bank, supra* n. 51 (USD 60 million); *Inmaris, supra* n. 51, para. 438 (the amount of compensation is redacted from the award); *National Grid, supra* n. 74, para. 296 (USD 53.5 million).
105. *Deutsche Telekom, supra* n. 51, *see* Final Award, 27 May 2020, para. 357 (USD 93.3 million); *Kuntur Wasi, supra* n. 51, para. 779 (USD 42 million, in view of its finding on the FET clause, the Tribunal did not examine whether other provisions had been breached). *See also, Cairn, supra* n. 51, para. 2032 (USD 1.2 billion). The award was later set aside by a Dutch court: Hague Court of Appeal, Judgment, 21 Dec. 2021 and the investor did not object to the set aside proceeding given India's 2021 new tax legislation, which provides for a refund of previously-paid retroactive taxes. *See also, Micula, supra* n. 73 (USD 116 million), in view of its finding on

In sum, all tribunals which have explicitly stated that a stand-alone FET clause should be interpreted to have an autonomous character have defined the FET standard broadly by including, for instance, legitimate expectations as an element of protection. The way these tribunals have assessed the status of the clause and its relation to the MST has had a direct impact on their findings in terms of liability and compensation. The 'success rate' of FET claims in this group of awards is two-thirds, which is much higher than for any other categories of awards (further examined in the next sections).

1.2 Awards Interpreting the Clause as an Implicit Reference to International Law or the MST

One of the most striking features of my empirical analysis is that very few tribunals have assessed stand-alone FET clauses as an implicit reference to 'international law', the MST or custom more generally. I have found only six awards, representing 5% of all awards which have examined stand-alone FET clauses.

The first example is probably the *Nagel* award rendered in 2002. The claim of FET breach was rejected. The Tribunal did no say much about the scope and content of the standard; it limited its analysis to this paragraph:

> Article 2(2) of the Investment Treaty requires the signatory countries to treat foreign investments in a 'fair and equitable' way. Under international law, this requirement is generally understood to impose an 'international minimum standard' that is separate from domestic law, but that is indeed a minimum standard. In essence, a breach of this provision may be found only if, based on the totality of the circumstances of the case, the Czech Republic would have acted in such a manner that every reasonable and impartial man would recognise its insufficiency.[106]

The other cases which have considered that a stand-alone FET clause was a reference to the MST (or international law) have been more explicit about the scope and content of the standard. In some of these cases, the tribunals have adopted *restrictive* interpretations of the content of the FET obligation.

One example is *Philip Morris v. Uruguay*. The majority of the Tribunal noted that the absence of any reference in Article 3(2) of the Switzerland-Uruguay BIT to wording such as 'in accordance with international law', custom or the MST 'does not mean that the BIT creates an "autonomous" FET standard'.[107] But, at the same time, the majority of the Tribunal also said that 'in the absence of any additional qualifying language, the reference to FET in Article 3(2) cannot be read as "treatment required by the minimum standard of treatment under international law"'.[108] Born, in his dissenting opinion, also argued that 'there is no indication that Article 3(2) was meant merely to incorporate the

FET clause, the majority of the Tribunal did not examine whether other breaches of the BIT were committed. The award has since been subject to complicated set aside proceedings, that are beyond the scope of this book. *See also*, *El Jaouni*, *supra* n. 51 (awarding only USD 218,000).

106. *William Nagel v. Czech Republic*, SCC Case No. 049/2002, Award, 9 Sep. 2003, para. 193.

107. *Philip Morris Brand Sàrl et al. v. Uruguay*, ICSID Case No. ARB/10/7, Award, 8 Jul. 2016, para. 316.

108. *Ibid.*

international minimum standard'.[109] For the majority of the Tribunal, the clause 'must be interpreted according to the normal canons of treaty interpretation' (Articles 31 and 32 of the VCLT), including 'interpretation in accordance with general international law, as stated in Article 31(3)(c)'.[110] It concluded that '[t]he scope and content of FET under Article 3(2) must therefore be determined by reference to the rules of international law, customary international law being part of such rules'.[111] Having restricted the scope of the clause, the Tribunal nevertheless determined that 'legitimate expectations' and the 'stability of the Uruguay legal system' were components of the FET standard.[112] But it also noted that this 'does not affect the State's rights to exercise its sovereign authority to legislate and to adapt its legal system to changing circumstances'.[113] It also applied a narrow definition of the concept of legitimate expectations.[114] The award found no FET violation.

Similarly, in *Unión Fenosa Gas*, the Tribunal stated that it was 'content to apply under Article 4(1) the *customary international law standard* as prohibiting (inter alia) conduct by the host State which is unjust, arbitrary, unfair, discriminatory or in violation of due process, including conduct that frustrates an investor's "legitimate expectations"'.[115] It adopted a narrow definition of the concept of legitimate expectations[116] and, importantly, stated that it did *not* consider that 'such a representation or undertaking amounts to a free-standing part of the FET standard but, rather that it is "a relevant factor" in assessing whether or not the Respondent violated the FET standard'.[117] In other words, the Tribunal adopted the same type of reasoning as many NAFTA awards.[118] It held that the actions were contrary to the claimant's legitimate expectations and in breach of the FET clause, and awarded USD 2 billion in compensation just for this head of damage.

In *Urbaser*, the Tribunal rejected the view that the FET clause was a reference to the MST under custom. Based on the reference to 'general principles of international law' found in the provision on the law applicable to settle disputes under the treaty (Article X(5)), it stated that this 'makes clear' that FET clauses 'must be understood by reference to general principles of international law' adding that '[t]his includes a reference to the whole of international law and not to a specific part of it'.[119] It applied

109. *Ibid.*, dissenting opinion Born, para. 131.
110. *Ibid.*, majority, para. 317.
111. *Ibid.*
112. *Ibid.*, para. 324.
113. *Ibid.*, para. 422.
114. *Ibid.*, paras 426-427, 434.
115. *Unión Fenosa Gas, S.A. v. Egypt*, ICSID Case No. ARB/14/4, Award, 31 Aug. 2018, para. 9.51, citing *Merrill & Ring v. Canada*, ICSID Case No. UNCT/07/1, Award, 31 Mar. 2010, para. 208, emphasis added.
116. *Unión Fenosa Gas, S.A. v. Egypt*, ICSID Case No. ARB/14/4, Award, 31 Aug. 2018, para. 9.51.
117. *Ibid.*, paras 9.52, 9.53, referring to, *inter alia*, *Mobil Investments Inc. and Murphy Oil Corporation v. Canada*, ICSID Case No. ARB(AF)/07/4, Decision on Liability and on Principles of Quantum, 22 May 2012, para. 152.
118. Dumberry, *supra* n. 22.
119. *Urbaser S.A. et al v. Argentina*, ICSID Case No. ARB/07/26, Award, 8 Dec. 2016, para. 604. The Tribunal also rejected the other 'extreme' position on the other side of the spectrum, i.e., that FET is the same concept as legitimate expectations (para. 606).

a rather narrow definition of the concepts of legitimate expectations and transparency.[120] The Tribunal found an FET violation but awarded no damages.

I have also found other cases where linking the FET clause to the MST led the tribunals to adopt a rather *broad* interpretation of the content of the FET obligation.

One of the first awards was *Siemens*. It noted that the FET clause contains 'no reference to international law or to a minimum standard', but added that 'in applying the Treaty, the Tribunal is bound to find the meaning of these terms under international law bearing in mind their ordinary meaning, the evolution of international law and the specific context in which they are used'.[121] The Tribunal, therefore, concluded that the FET was *not* an autonomous standard and that it had to be examined based on the evolution of customary international law.[122] Interestingly, it stated that 'the current standard includes the frustration of expectations that the investor may have legitimately taken into account when it made the investment'.[123] It concluded that the FET clause (and other provisions) had been breached and awarded USD 217 million in compensation.

In *Suez*, the Tribunal said that the reference to 'the principles of international law' in the Argentina-France BIT 'does not entail a different content' than the other two BITs invoked by the investor.[124] The Tribunal stated that it was bound to 'apply the principles of international law' for all three treaties, even the two containing stand-alone FET clauses.[125] Yet, at the same time, it qualified the FET as 'the *Grundnorm* or basic norm of international investment law'.[126] It assessed the content of the FET guided by Article 31(1) of the VCLT,[127] which included taking into account an investor's legitimate expectations, and defined it rather broadly.[128] It concluded that the FET clause had been breached and awarded USD 405 million.[129]

It is hard to discern any clear patterns within this small pool of awards. While some have interpreted the content of the standard narrowly, others have taken a broad approach. In any event, equalising the FET with the MST (or international law) does not seem to be an insurmountable obstacle for a tribunal to find a breach of the standard and award a large amount of compensation. In half of the awards, the tribunals found liability and awarded compensation (some very large).[130] It therefore

120. *Ibid.*, para. 626.
121. *Siemens A.G. v. Argentina*, ICSID Case No. ARB/02/8, Award, 6 Feb. 2007, para. 291.
122. *Ibid.*, paras 293ff.
123. *Ibid.*, paras 299, 287. It did not take a position on whether the FET requires, as the claimant argued, 'stable investment environments by ensuring transparency and predictable rules and practices' (para. 277).
124. *Suez, Sociedad General de Aguas de Barcelona, S.A. and Vivendi Universal, S.A. v. Argentina (II)*, ICSID Case No. ARB/03/19, Decision on Liability, 30 Jul. 2010, para. 186. The Argentina-Spain BIT and the Argentina-UK BIT both contain stand-alone FET clauses with no specific reference to 'principles of international law'.
125. *Ibid.* In his separate opinion, Nikken stated that this was a 'clear reference to the minimum standard, the only standard on treatment of aliens in general international law at the time when the treaty was concluded' (para. 8).
126. *Ibid.*, para. 188, citing Hans Kelsen, *The Pure Theory of Law* (1934).
127. *Ibid.*, paras 211ff.
128. *Ibid.*, paras 222-223, also at paras 226, 229.
129. *Ibid.*, Award, 9 Apr. 2015.
130. *Unión Fenosa, supra* n. 115 (USD 2 billion); *Siemens, supra* n. 121 (USD 217 million).

appears that equating the FET with the MST (or international law) does not have a significant impact in terms of liability and compensation. The 'success rate' of claimants in this category is lower than for awards expressly stating that the provision has an autonomous character (examined in section 1.1, above). It is not significantly different than for awards which did not take a position on this debate (further examined in the next section).

1.3 Awards Not Taking a Position on the Status of a Stand-Alone FET Clause and Its Relationship with the MST

One perhaps surprising finding about the analysis of awards which have examined stand-alone FET clauses is that the vast majority of them have not taken a position on the debate as to whether the provision should be interpreted to have an autonomous character. In fact, I have found only 29 awards which did (they have been examined in sections 1.1 and 1.2, above). They represent a small percentage (less than 25%) of all awards (120) which have analysed stand-alone FET clauses.

This third group consists of 91 awards. A closer look at the awards shows that the reasoning of tribunals is far from being uniform. The reasoning of some awards suggests that the tribunals considered that the FET treaty standard offers better protection than the MST or that the level of treatment is the same (section 1.3.1). Other awards have mentioned the debate, but they have decided not to take a position (section 1.3.2). Finally, most awards in this category simply did not refer to this question at all (section 1.3.3).

1.3.1 Awards Suggesting That the FET Treaty Standard Offers Better Protection than the MST or that the Level of Protection Is the Same

While many tribunals did not formally take a position regarding the status of an FET clause and its relation to the MST, the reasonings found in 10 awards suggest that the tribunals have considered that the FET treaty standard offers *better* protection compare to that existing under the MST.

A good example is the *Quiborax* Tribunal which considered that it could 'be left open here' whether the BIT's FET obligation 'can be equated with' the MST. It held that the action 'violates international law even under a more demanding standard', i.e., 'if it were to be equated with the customary international law minimum standard of treatment'.[131] In the context of this passage, the expression 'more demanding standard' is a reference to the fact that the claimant would have to show a greater level of severity and gravity under the MST to prove that the provision has been breached. The Tribunal referred to the dictum of the NAFTA *Waste Management* award and said that it had already decided when assessing the Claimants' expropriation claim that the measures were discriminatory and unjustified and that they breached the FET standard 'even if

131. *Quiborax S.A. and Non-Metallic Minerals S.A. v. Bolivia*, ICSID Case No. ARB/06/2, Award, 16 Sep. 2015, paras 291-292.

it were to be equated with the customary international law minimum standard of treatment'.[132] The same conclusion was reached by the *BG Group* Tribunal.[133] Yet, the very fact that the Tribunal in the *Quiborax* case (and the *BG Group* case) referred to the MST as 'a more demanding standard' than the FET standard contained in the BIT suggests that it did *not* consider that they offered the same level of treatment. In other words, as explained in the *Saluka* award (mentioned above), the Tribunal considered that it is easier for a claimant investor to prove that a breach of an autonomous FET clause has been committed compared to when the provision is linked to the MST under custom.

I have also found awards where the tribunals seem to have left the question open, but a closer reading suggests that they endorsed the autonomous approach. For instance, the *Rompetrol* Tribunal considered that there was 'no benefit in engaging in an abstract debate' as to whether the FET clause 'was or was not intended by the Parties simply to incorporate' the MST.[134] But, at the same time, it stated that it had 'no difficulty in following the Claimant's invitation as to the general approach to be taken towards the interpretation'. The claimant considered the clause as an autonomous standard. The passage, therefore, suggests that the Tribunal was of the same view. This is clear considering that the claimant referred to a 'broad and flexible' approach whereby 'its precise application is left to the tribunal in each individual case, in the light of all the circumstances of the case before it'.[135] The broadness of the standard is apparent from this list of elements mentioned by the claimant, and approved by the Tribunal: 'transparency and consistency (including the protection of the investor's basic expectations); freedom from harassment; procedural propriety; and good faith'.[136]

Another example is the *Devas* Tribunal agreeing with the *El Paso* Tribunal that the whole discussion was 'somewhat futile' and that 'the true question is to decide what substantive protection is granted to foreign investors through the FET'.[137] But the Tribunal also stated that the FET clause was not defined and that it 'contains no wording limiting its scope and content to some external standard, whether it be international customary law or something else'.[138] This passage suggests that it considered the provision as an autonomous clause. This is confirmed by the fact that while the Tribunal said that 'it need not enter into a lengthy discussion of the concept and scope' of the standard, it added that 'whatever the scope of the FET standard, the

132. *Ibid.*, para. 292.
133. In *BG Group Plc. v. Argentina*, UNCITRAL, Award, 24 Dec. 2007, para. 291, the Tribunal stated that the respondent had breached the MST and that therefore it was not necessary to determine whether the clause provides a 'more generous independent standard of protection'.
134. *The Rompetrol Group N.V. v. Romania*, ICSID Case No. ARB/06/3, Award, 6 May 2013, para. 197.
135. *Ibid.*, para. 195.
136. *Ibid.*
137. *CC/Devas (Mauritius) Ltd., Devas Employees Mauritius Private Limited and Telcom Devas Mauritius Limited v. India*, PCA Case No. 2013-09, Award, Jurisdiction and Merits, 25 Jul. 2016, para. 456, quoting *El Paso Energy International Co. v. Argentina*, ICSID Case No. ARB/03/15, Award, 31 Oct. 2011, para. 335.
138. *Ibid.*, para. 457.

legitimate expectations of the investors have generally been considered central to its definition'.[139] It also stated that the Claimants 'were entitled to legitimate expectations that, in accordance with the text of the Treaty as well as under a general obligation under international law, the Respondent would deal with them in good faith'.[140] In fact, the 'principle of good faith is not only self-standing, but it also stems from the concept of FET'.[141] The Tribunal therefore defined the standard broadly.

I have also found other awards where the reasoning suggests that the tribunals believe that there is no real difference between the FET treaty standard and the MST. It should be added that some of them have adopted the so-called 'convergence theory'. Under this approach (further discussed below) the level of protection to be accorded to foreign investors under the MST is said to have rapidly evolved in recent decades and is, apparently, believed now to be the same as the one existing under BITs containing an unqualified FET clause. The approach is controversial and has been rejected by many tribunals and authors.[142] In any event, what really matters for the present purposes is that in practice these tribunals have applied the same logic as those which have considered that the FET treaty standard offers better protection for investors than under the MST. The following awards are good illustrations:

- The *Belokon* Tribunal noted 'the absence of qualifying language, such as "in accordance with customary international law"' in the FET clause, but added that 'no point has been taken as to supposed consequences of the particular wording'.[143] This comment suggests that it considered there was no difference in treatment. The Tribunal nevertheless interpreted the clause to have an autonomous character. It stated that the argument that the 'tenets' of the FET standard, which include 'transparency, stability and protection of the investor's legitimate expectations', 'seem broadly well established and have not been disputed by the Respondent'.[144] It held that a breach had been committed.
- The *PAO Tatneft* Tribunal indicated that the FET treaty standard was not 'necessarily different' from the standard existing under the MST.[145] Regarding

139. *Ibid.*, para. 458: 'There is an overwhelming trend to consider the touchstone of fair and equitable treatment to be found in the legitimate and reasonable expectations of the parties, which derive from the obligation of good faith,' citing many cases.
140. *Ibid.*, para. 465.
141. *Ibid.*, para. 467.
142. *See, inter alia*: UNCTAD, *Investor–State Dispute Settlement and Impact on Investment Rule-making* (2007) 75 ('some arbitral decisions had the effect of equating the minimum standard under customary international law with the plain meaning approach to the text. However, it is not self-evident that customary international law has evolved to such a degree'); T. Kill, *Don't Cross the Streams: Past and Present Overstatement of Customary International Law in Connection with Conventional Fair and Equitable Treatment Obligations*, 106 Mich. L. Rev. (2008) 853ff.
143. *Valeri Belokon v. Kyrgyz Republic*, PCA Case No. AA518, Award, 24 Oct. 2014, para. 224.
144. *Ibid.*, para. 227.
145. *PAO Tatneft (formerly OAO Tatneft) v. Ukraine*, PCA Case No. 2008-8, Award on the Merits, 29 Jul. 2014. There is no FET clause in the Russia-Ukraine BIT (1998), so the Tribunal applied (via the MFN clause) Art. 2(2) of the UK-Ukraine. *See* paras 392, 395 ('there is no reason to consider that the situation would need to be different under customary law as presently understood').

the content of the standard, based on the interpretation by 'numerous tribunals', the Tribunal said that it was 'not difficult to ascertain that it encompasses today at least (...) the assurance of a predictable, consistent and stable legal framework'.[146] It held that a breach had been committed.

- The *Rumeli* Tribunal indicated that the distinction between an FET treaty standard and the MST was 'more theoretical than real'[147] and concluded that the treaty standard was 'not materially different' from the MST under custom.[148] But, at the same time, the Tribunal also said that it is 'a concept that depends on the interpretation of specific facts for its content'[149] and that the 'precise scope of the standard is therefore left to the determination of the Tribunal', which 'will have to decide whether in all the circumstances the conduct in issue is fair and equitable or unfair and inequitable'.[150] In other words, the Tribunal used the same type of language as other tribunals (mentioned in section 1.1) which have interpreted the clause to have an autonomous character. In the end, the Tribunal interpreted the clause broadly to include, *inter alia*, transparency, good faith and 'the investor's reasonable and legitimate expectations'.[151] It held that a breach had been committed.
- The *MNSS* Tribunal agreed with the *El Paso* award that the discussion is 'somewhat futile' and explained that 'the futility is confirmed in this case by the Claimants' reliance, among others, on the understanding of the *Waste Management II* tribunal, which places the FET in the context of the minimum standard of treatment'.[152] But at the same time, the Tribunal endorsed the definition adopted the NAFTA *Waste Management* award which referred to a limited list of elements with a high threshold of severity required to find a breach.[153] The Tribunal found no violation of the FET clause.
- The *Gosling* Tribunal questioned 'the relevance of the differentiation' given the evolution of the MST. This passage suggests that it considered that the standard was the same under both the FET treaty standard and under custom. The Tribunal applied a balanced approach regarding legitimate expectations.[154]

146. *Ibid.*, paras 392, 394.
147. *Rumeli Telekom A.S. and Telsim Mobil Telekomunikasyon Hizmetleri A.S. v. Kazakhstan*, ICSID Case No. ARB/05/16, Award, 29 Jul. 2008, para. 611.
148. *Ibid.* There is no FET clause in the Turkey-Kazakhstan BIT so the Tribunal applied via the MFN clause the FET clause in the UK-Kazakhstan BIT.
149. *Ibid.*, para. 610.
150. *Ibid.*
151. *Ibid.*, para. 609, indicating that the parties 'rightly agreed' on this list.
152. *MNSS B.V. and Recupero Credito Acciaio N.V v. Montenegro*, ICSID Case No. ARB(AF)/12/8, Award, 4 May 2016, para. 326.
153. *Ibid.*
154. *Thomas Gosling and others v. Mauritius*, ICSID Case No. ARB/16/32, Award, 18 Feb. 2020, para. 243, indicating that 'the level of the treatment required to breach the standard has evolved' and 'what was considered minimum treatment in the nineteenth century is not the minimum required in the twenty-first, particularly in the context of a treaty specifically providing for fair and equitable treatment'. The Tribunal adopted a narrow definition referring not to the 'subjective expectations of the investors', but that their expectations 'to be protected, must rise to the level of legitimacy and reasonableness in light of the circumstances' (para.

- The *Enkev* Tribunal did not discuss the debate (and the parties do not seem to have raised the issue during the proceedings). It simply indicated that 'there is no cogent evidence of any arbitrary, capricious or discriminatory conduct (...) nor indeed any act or omission amounting to a breach of the FET Standard, whether interpreted as an autonomous standard or as the minimum standard under international law'.[155] This passage could be interpreted as suggesting that, for the Tribunal, both standards provide for the same type of protection.

In sum, while these awards do not take a position on the status of the clause, their reasoning suggests (at least implicitly) that they believe that the FET treaty standard offers better protection than the MST. They have, in practice, adopted broad interpretations that are not truly different from those other awards where stand-alone FET clauses have been considered to have an autonomous character (section 1.1). For instance, they have all considered that the concept of legitimate expectations was part of the FET standard.

In the majority of these cases (7 out of 10), the tribunals have found that there was a breach of the FET clause. The success rate is, therefore, similar to awards which have *expressly* stated that the clause must be interpreted to have an autonomous character (*see*, section 1.1).

1.3.2 Awards Mentioning the Debate, but Leaving the Question Open

Many tribunals have mentioned the existence of the debate, but they have decided that the question could be left open.[156] I have found seven such awards. A good example is the *ECE* award:

> The debate as to the relationship between the fair and equitable treatment standard embodied in the BIT and the standard applicable under customary international law is, in the Tribunal' s view, in the final analysis an essentially academic one with little practical impact. What the Tribunal is called upon to interpret and apply is the fair and equitable standard as embodied in Article 2(1) of the BIT, which corresponds also to the limits of the Tribunal's jurisdiction, namely, whether the Respondent has complied with its obligations under the BIT.

244). It also noted that the FET obligation 'needs to be interpreted in a balanced manner' (para. 245). No FET breach was found.

155. *Enkev Beheer B.V. v. Poland*, PCA Case No. 2013-01, First Partial Award, 29 Apr. 2014, para. 376.

156. *Tokios Tokelés v. Ukraine*, ICSID Case No. ARB/02/18, Award, 26 Jul. 2007, para. 123 ('A sharp doctrinal controversy on the standards of protection demanded by these and similar expressions in investment treaties has created two divergent streams of authority, too well known to require citation here. We do not enter into it now, since in our opinion it does not affect the outcome of the present dispute'. The FET claim was rejected by the majority of the Tribunal); *Joseph Houben v. Burundi*, ICSID Case No. ARB/13/7, Award, 12 Jan. 2016, para. 182 ('La question s'est notamment posée de savoir si ce standard allait au-delà du standard minimum de traitement requis par le droit coutumier international ou s'il s'agissait d'une notion sui generis offrant un niveau de protection plus élevé à l'investisseur. Ces débats n'ayant toutefois pas été abordés par les parties dans le présent arbitrage, le Tribunal estime qu'il n'est pas nécessaire de s'y attarder'); *Consortium RFCC v. Maroc*, ICSID Case No. ARB/00/6, Award, 22 Dec. 2003, para. 33.

> The Respondent argues that the standard should be equated or limited to the minimum standard under customary international law and invokes arbitral decisions adopted in the application of Article 1105 of the North American Free Trade Agreement (NAFTA). The Claimant argues to the contrary that, since Article 2(1) of the BIT makes no reference to international law or the international minimum standard, it must be taken to impose a standard higher than that obtaining under customary international law. The Tribunal finds itself unable to accept either view. It does not find NAFTA Article 1105 (entitled 'Minimum Standard of Treatment'), which explicitly requires the Parties to NAFTA to accord treatment, including fair and equitable treatment, 'in accordance with international law', to be of particular assistance in deriving the proper meaning to be given to a differently formulated provision in an unconnected and free-standing bilateral investment agreement between two European States. Conversely, it can see no logical basis for the Claimants' submission that a failure to mention international law in a treaty provision should be taken to be equivalent to the establishment of a particular relationship to the customary international law standard, either in general or in relation to a specific understanding of what the customary standard is.
>
> Several investment tribunals have held that, when a bilateral treaty adopts a standard of fair and equitable treatment without further qualification, the treaty is to be interpreted and applied in its own right and on its own terms. The present Tribunal shares that view. The applicable principles for the interpretation of Article 2(1) of the BIT are therefore those laid down by Article 31 of the Vienna Convention on the Law of Treaties.[157]

In fact, many of these tribunals have, in practice, applied broad interpretations of the standard. This is indeed the approach taken by the *ECE* Tribunal: 'The language used is simple and straightforward, and appears plainly to lay down a standard that incorporates ample flexibility to determine what should be regarded as "fair and equitable treatment" in relation to the circumstances of particular cases.'[158] These awards have, therefore, interpreted stand-alone FET clauses in a similar manner to other tribunals (mentioned in section 1.1 above) which have explicitly stated that such clauses have an autonomous character. The following awards are good illustrations of this trend:

- In *Binder*, the Tribunal took note of the debate between different interpretations and admitted that the FET was 'generally considered to require at least respect for the international minimum standard of protection (...)'.[159] But faced with a stand-alone clause, it said that the standard needs 'to be given a sufficiently wide interpretation to be consistent with the promotion of investments which is set out' in the provision. For the Tribunal, this includes respect

157. *ECE Projektmanagement v. Czech Republic*, UNCITRAL, PCA Case No. 2010-5, Award, 19 Sep. 2013, paras 4.754-4.757.
158. *Ibid.*, para. 4.758. It also noted that 'The conclusion that the fair and equitable treatment standard under the BIT is not as such limited by reference to the minimum standard of treatment under customary international law (whatever the content of that standard may be), does not mean that the standard is necessarily open-ended or subject to idiosyncratic interpretation by individual tribunals. In particular, there is broad agreement in the decisions as to the core of what is required by the fair and equitable treatment standard' (para. 4.760).
159. *Rupert Joseph Binder v. Czech Republic*, UNCITRAL, Final Award, 15 Jul. 2011, para. 437.

for the investor's legitimate expectations (defined rather narrowly),[160] good faith, transparency and a broad obligation to 'maintain a legal order that is stable and predictable'.[161] No breach was found.

- The *MTD Equity* Tribunal simply noted that 'there is no reference to customary international law in the BIT in relation to fair and equitable treatment' and added that the clause must be interpreted in accordance with the VCLT.[162] Yet, it also stated that it would apply the very broad 'standard' mentioned in the *Tecmed* award to the facts of this case.[163]
- The *Oxus* Tribunal indicated that it was not necessary to take a position on this issue, but acknowledged the importance of the wording of an FET clause when being interpreted by tribunals.[164] The Tribunal took a rather broad approach regarding the content of the FET standard.[165]

What these awards have in common is that, while not taking a position on the controversial debate about the status of the clause and its relationship with the MST, they have in fact used broad interpretations just like other tribunals that considered the standard had an autonomous character. I have also found awards where tribunals took a narrow approach to the concept of legitimate expectations.[166]

160. *Ibid.*, paras 443-445.
161. *Ibid.*, para. 446, indicating that the FET 'also requires that the host state maintain a legal order that is stable and predictable, so as to afford the investor the opportunity to plan and operate its investments in accordance with the state's legal and business framework. The elements of stability and predictability of the state's legal order go hand in hand with the need that the state act with reasonable consistency and transparency, as part of an overall aim of enhancing legal certainty'.
162. *MTD Equity Sdn. Bhd. & MTD Chile S.A. v. Chile*, ICSID Case No. ARB/01/7, Award, 25 May 2004, paras 110-112.
163. *Ibid.*, para. 115.
164. *Oxus Gold plc v. Uzbekistan, the State Committee of Uzbekistan for Geology & Mineral Resources, and Navoi Mining & Metallurgical Kombinat*; UNCITRAL, Final Award, 17 Dec. 2015, para. 313. The Tribunal 'acknowledge[d] that there is a great variation in the way this standard is applied by international tribunals, partly because of the different approaches towards the origins and nature of the FET standard (e.g. whether conceived as an international minimum standard or as an autonomous standard) (for a summary of the situation, see El Paso v. Argentina, paras. 330ff), partly because the relevant provisions contemplating the FET standards in BITs differ in their structure and wording, thereby requiring a case by case analysis and application'.
165. *Ibid.*, para. 313 ('the concept of "legitimate expectations" is an objective concept, that is the result of interests and rights of both the investor and the State, and that the result of such balancing may thus vary according to the specific context'), para. 786 (indicating that the FET standard 'must be understood as a means to guarantee justice to foreign investors, and when doing so, for the States' actions to give due regard to an investor's legitimate expectations by refraining from taking measures which are not justified under the circumstances, i.e., which are unreasonable, disproportionate or discriminatory').
166. *Houben, supra* n. 156, paras 185-187, indicating that legitimate expectations must take into account the 'caractéristiques de l'Etat d'accueil et de l'investisseur, notamment de l'expérience professionnelle de ce dernier dans le pays concerné', that 'il convenait de prendre en compte le niveau de développement de l'Etat d'accueil', as well as the fact that 'l'investisseur connaissait ou aurait dû connaître les risques inhérents à chaque Etat'.

1.3.3 *Award Not Addressing the Issue at All*

Finally, I have found several awards (74) where the tribunals do not mention at all the debate about the status of the clause and its relationship with the MST. This group represents the largest bulk of awards (more than 60% of awards examining stand-alone clauses).

In about half of these awards, the tribunal did not say much about the meaning, scope and content of the FET clause. This is the case for about 30 awards.[167] Other

---

167. *See*, for instance (the list is not meant to be exhaustive): *Emilio Agustín Maffezini v. Spain*, ICSID Case No. ARB/97/7, Award, 13 Nov. 2000, para. 83; *Wena Hotels Ltd. v. Egypt*, ICSID Case No. ARB/98/4, Award, 8 Dec. 2000, para. 84; *CME Czech Republic B.V. v. Czech Republic*, UNCITRAL, Award, 14 Mar. 2003, para. 611; *Eureko B.V. v. Poland*, ad hoc arbitration, Partial Award, 19 Aug. 2005, para. 234 (indicating that it had 'no hesitation' in finding that the clause had been 'clearly' violated and referring to 'outrageous' and 'shocking' conduct, and adding that 'even though, to constitute breach of treaty, actions and inactions need not be of that degree of extremity'); *Iurii Bogdanov, Agurdino-Invest Ltd. and Agurdino-Chimia JSC v. Moldova*, SCC, Award, 22 Sep. 2005, paras 16ff.; *ADC Affiliate Limited and ADC & ADMC Management Limited v. Hungary*, ICSID Case No. ARB/03/16, Award, 2 Oct. 2006, para. 445; *Eastern Sugar B.V. (Netherlands) v. Czech Republic*, SCC Case No. 088/2004, Partial Award, 27 Mar. 2007, para. 198; *Desert Line Projects LLC v. Yemen*, ICSID Case No. ARB/05/17, Award, 6 Feb. 2008, paras 191ff.; *Gemplus S.A., SLP S.A., Gemplus Industrial S.A. de C.V. v. Mexico*, ICSID Case No. ARB(AF)/04/3, Award, 16 Jun. 2010, para. 7-76 (dealing with two BITs, one stand-alone FET clause and one 'in accordance with international law' clause, and concluding that the Respondent's conduct 'was manifestly irrational, arbitrary and perverse, being also conducted in bad faith towards the Claimants and their rights as investors under the two BITs'); *Yury Bogdanov v. Moldova*, SCC Arbitration No. V 114/2009, Award, 30 Mar. 2010, paras 86ff.; *Peter Franz Vocklinghaus v. Czech Republic*, Ad Hoc, Final Award, 19 Sep. 2011, paras 209ff.; *GEA Group Aktiengesellschaft v. Ukraine*, ICSID Case No. ARB/08/16, Award, 31 Mar. 2011, paras 268ff.; *British Caribbean Bank Limited v. Belize*, PCA Case No. 2010-18, Award, 19 Dec. 2014, paras 279ff.; *Hesham T. M. Al Warraq v. Indonesia*, UNCITRAL Ad hoc, Final Award, 15 Dec. 2014, paras 540ff. (dealing with allegations of denial of justice); *Tulip Real Estate and Development Netherlands B.V. v. Turkey*, ICSID Case No. ARB/11/28, 10 Mar. 2014, para. 401; *Bernhard von Pezold and Others v. Zimbabwe*, ICSID Case No. ARB/10/15, Award, 28 Jul. 2015, para. 546; *OOO Manolium Processing v. Belarus*, PCA Case No. 2018-06, Final Award, 22 Jun. 2021, paras 511ff.; *IC Power Asia Development Ltd. v. Guatemala*, PCA Case No. 2019-43, Award, 7 Oct. 2020, paras 465ff.; *Lidercón S.L. v. Peru*, ICSID Case No. ARB/17/9, Award, 6 Mar. 2020; *B3 Croatian Courier Coöperatief U.A. v. Croatia*, ICSID Case No. ARB/15/5, Award, 5 Apr. 2019, para. 835 (simply indicating that FET is breached by 'conduct that is arbitrary, in bad faith, that fails to afford due process or to ensure appropriate levels of transparency', but only focusing on arbitrariness); *Fouad Alghanim & Sons Co. for General Trading & Contracting, W.L.L. and Mr. Fouad Mohammed Thunyan Alghanim v. Jordan*, ICSID Case No. ARB/13/38, Award, 14 Dec. 2017; *Garanti Koza LLP v. Turkmenistan*, ICSID Case No. ARB/11/20, Award, 19 Dec. 2016, para. 38 (referring to awards using a rather high threshold, including the *Mondev* and *ELSI* decisions, and also using this terminology: 'fundamentally unfair' 'fundamental departure from international norms', at paras 383, 387); *Zhongshan Fucheng v. Nigeria*, Award, 26 Mar. 2021, para. 130; *CMC Muratori Cementisti CMC Di Ravenna SOC. Coop., et al., v. Mozambique*, ICSID Case No. ARB/17/23, 24 Oct. 2019, para. 424 (not 'denying' that the FET duty 'may include an obligation of transparency', but finding no breach); *Swisslion DOO Skopje v. Macedonia*, ICSID Case No. ARB/09/16, Award, 6 Jul. 2012, paras 272ff. (indicating that the standard 'basically ensures that the foreign investor is not unjustly treated, with due regard to all surrounding circumstances, and that it is a means to guarantee justice to foreign investors' and finding that 'a series of measures that collectively amount to a composite act' is in breach of FET); *A.M.F. Aircraftleasing Meier & Fischer GmbH & Co. KG v. Czech Republic*, PCA Case No. 2017-15, Award, 11 May 2020, para. 699 (referring to investors' legitimate expectations 'defined somewhat differently by different tribunals' without any further analysis); *Hochtief*

awards in this group contain more analysis on the issue. Their reasoning is not uniform.

Some of the awards have adopted a rather broad interpretation of the FET standard in relation to the concepts of legitimate expectations and transparency,[168] and

Aktiengesellschaft v. Argentina, ICSID Case No. ARB/07/31, Decision on Liability, 29 Dec. 2014, para. 219 (simply indicating that it agrees that the proper approach to the interpretation of the FET obligation is 'the threshold for a treaty breach set by *Waste Management II*', which is 'representative of the approach taken by investment tribunals to this question').

168. *Walter Bau Ag (In Liquidation) v. Thailand*, UNCITRAL, Award, 1 Jul. 2009, para. 12.3 ('In spite of the fact that there was no guarantee by the Respondent of an explicit rate of return, the Tribunal considers that a reasonable rate of return (...) was part of the Claimant's legitimate expectations and the failure to fulfil such a reasonable expectation was a breach of the Respondent's FET obligations'). *See also, L.E.S.I. S.p.A. and ASTALDI S.p.A. v. Algeria*, ICSID Case No. ARB/05/3, Award, 12 Nov. 2008 (given that the Italy-Algeria BIT did not include an FET clause, the Tribunal imported a stand-alone FET clause via the MFN clause. Citing the *Tecmed* award (*supra* n. 28), the Tribunal gave a rather broad definition of the standard: 'Le présent Tribunal arbitral considère que cette obligation signifie que l'Etat doit agir de manière cohérente, dénuée d'ambiguïté, transparente, qu'il doit maintenir un environnement suffisamment stable pour permettre à un investisseur raisonnablement diligent d'adopter une stratégie commerciale et la mettre en œuvre dans la durée, et qu'il doit agir de façon non arbitraire ou discriminatoire et sans détournement de pouvoir et dans le respect de ses engagements'). *See also, Maffezini, supra* n. 167, para. 83 (providing no analysis of the FET clause and only stating that 'the lack of transparency with which this loan transaction was conducted is incompatible with Spain's commitment to ensure the investor a fair and equitable treatment in accordance with Article 4(1) of the same treaty'); *Waguih Elie George Siag and Clorinda Vecchi v. Egypt*, ICSID Case No. ARB/05/15, Award, 1 Jun. 2009, para. 450 (indicating that it is 'widely recognised that the principle of good faith underlies fair and equitable treatment' and that 'numerous arbitral tribunals have held that, in international investment arbitration, the host State's duty to respect the investor's legitimate expectations arises from its more general duty to act in good faith towards foreigners' and that one of the 'categories of frequent application' includes 'transparency, protection of legitimate expectations'); *Toto Costruzioni Generali S.p.A v. Lebanon*, ICSID Case No. ARB/07/12, Award, 7 Jun. 2012, paras 152ff., 159 ('legitimate expectations may follow from explicit or implicit representations made by the host state, or from its contractual commitments. The investor may even sometimes be entitled to presume that the overall legal framework of the investment will remain stable. Much depends, however, on the circumstances of the case'); *Alpha Projektholding GmbH v. Ukraine*, ICSID Case No. ARB/07/16, Award, 8 Nov. 2010, para. 420 (indicating that FET 'includes the obligation not to upset an investor's legitimate expectations', citing the *Tecmed* award (*supra* n. 28) and defining at para. 422 the concept broadly: 'Claimant did possess a legitimate expectation that the government would not interfere with the contractual relationship between Claimant and the Hotel, and that the agreements would be honored, albeit with the reformation to the payment terms necessitated by the Ukrainian law on joint activities as discussed below. Those expectations arose not only by the terms of the original agreements, but, for example, also by the terms of the amendments to those agreements negotiated during or after the corporatization, and by the assurances given by the new management of the Hotel in June 2004 that the relationship would continue'). *See also, Ioannis Kardassopoulos v. Georgia*, ICSID Case No. ARB/05/18, Award, 3 Mar. 2010, para. 428, noting the parties' position on the debate, but not taking a position. Yet, later at para. 439, the Tribunal mentioned that it considered that the 'Respondent's interpretation of the legitimate expectations element of the FET standard' (i.e., that the specific assurances of compensation alleged to have been given to the investor were made many years after his initial investment) would 'presuppose limitations upon the notion of fair and equitable treatment that are not established as a matter of law and that are inconsistent with the terms of the BIT read in their proper context'. The Tribunal then referred to the *Tecmed* (*supra* n. 28) and *Sempra* (*supra* n. 345) awards and referred at para. 441 to the following broad definition of the concept: the investor had 'throughout the term of his

proportionality.[169] Other tribunals have simply mentioned that stand-alone FET clauses had been interpreted broadly by tribunals,[170] but they did *not* apply broad definitions of legitimate expectations and stability/predictability.[171]

I have also found several other awards where the tribunals were silent on the debate, but have adopted a rather balanced approach regarding the scope of the concept of legitimate expectations (and transparency). This is the case for a number of 'older' awards.[172] This is also the case for about 20 more recent awards rendered in the

investment the legitimate expectation that Georgia would conduct itself vis-à-vis his investment in a manner that was reasonably justifiable and did not manifestly violate basic requirements of consistency, transparency, even-handedness and non-discrimination'. *See also, Sergei Paushok, CJSC Golden East Company and CJSC Vostokneftegaz Company v. Mongolia*, UNCITRAL, Award on Jurisdiction and Liability, 28 Apr. 2011, paras 250-255, 301, 304 (referring to the *Rumeli* award, *supra* n. 147, indicating that, *inter alia*, transparency, good faith and were 'principles to be applied' under the standard); *Spyridon Roussalis v. Romania*, ICSID Case No. ARB/06/1, Award, 7 Dec. 2011, paras 313ff. (referring to the *Rumeli* award (*supra* n. 147) and to *Tecmed's* (*supra* n. 28) wide definition of legitimate expectations, but also to the narrower approach followed in *Saluka, supra* n. 51); *Krederi Ltd. v. Ukraine*, ICSID Case No. ARB/14/17, Award, 2 Jul. 2018, paras 437-438 (focusing on denial of justice, but noting, quoting the *Lemire* dictum, that FET includes transparency, stable and predictable legal framework and legitimate expectations in the general sense); *Olin Holdings Limited v. Libya*, ICC Case No. 20355/MCP, Final Award, 25 May 2018, paras 304ff. (narrowly defining legitimate expectations, but speaking more generally at para. 311 of the obligation to respect 'the investor's ability to operate its investment with a minimum level of certainty as to its fate and as to the ability to implement basic business decisions in an unfettered manner' and also defining transparency broadly at para. 320); *Mytilineos Holdings v. Serbia (II)*, PCA Case No. 2014-30, Award, August 2017, reported in IAReporter, 30 Sep. 2019 (endorsing the view that the investor had a legitimate expectation that Serbia would 'act lawfully and reasonably in determining how to deal with RTB Bor' and that this expectation was 'reasonable' and that 'the investor would be able to enforce its claims against RTB Bor in a reasonable time').

169. *Marfin Investment Group Holdings S.A., Alexandros Bakatselos and others v. Cyprus*, ICSID Case No. ARB/13/27, Award, 26 Jul. 2018, paras 1211ff.

170. *Parkerings-Compagniet, supra* n. 1, examining a clause providing for 'equitable and reasonable' and finding that it has the same meaning as 'fair and equitable' (paras 271-278) and simply indicating that the clause 'has been interpreted broadly by Tribunals' (para. 277).

171. *Ibid.* The Tribunal noted that 'a State has the right to enact, modify or cancel a law at its own discretion', but also that the investor has a 'right to a certain stability and predictability of the legal environment of the investment' and that 'The investor will have a right of protection of its legitimate expectations provided it exercised due diligence and that its legitimate expectations were reasonable in light of the circumstances' (paras 332-333). *See also*: *Horthel Systems BV, Poland Gaming Holding BV and Tesa Beheer BV v. Poland*, PCA Case No. 2014-31, Award, 2 Feb. 2017, paras 236ff., 238-240, referring to a narrow definition of legitimate expectations: 'general statutory norms (...) do not give rise to legitimate expectations unless they contain a specific commitment of stability', and also speaking of 'specific, individualized undertakings of a state'.

172. *Metalpar S.A. and Buen Aire S.A. v. Argentina*, ICSID Case No. ARB/03/5, Award on the Merits, 6 Jun. 2008, paras 180ff.; *EDF (Services) Limited v. Romania*, ICSID Case No. ARB/05/13, Award, 8 Oct. 2009, paras 215ff.; *Nordzucker v. Poland*, UNCITRAL, Second Partial Award on Merits, 23 Nov. 2009 (referring to an obligation of transparency, paras 12ff., but also using a narrow definition of legitimate expectations, at paras 86ff.); *Invesmart v. Czech Republic*, UNCITRAL, Ad hoc, Award, 26 Jun. 2009, paras 199, 202, 250ff.; *White Industries Australia Limited v. India*, UNCITRAL, Award, 30 Nov. 2011, para. 10.3.1; *Jan Oostergetel and Theodora Laurentius v. Slovak Republic*, UNCITRAL, Ad Hoc, Award, 25 Oct. 2012, paras 220ff.; *Flemingo Duty Free Shop Private Limited v. Poland*, PCA Case No. 2014-11, Award, 12 Aug. 2016, paras 529ff. (referring to 'predictability' as part of FET and other elements, including legitimate expectations, citing *Saluka, supra* n. 51); *Impregilo S.p.A. v. Argentina I*,

last five years.[173] It seems that these tribunals no longer find it necessary to examine the question of whether a stand-alone clause should be characterised as an autonomous

ICSID Case No. ARB/07/17, Award, 21 Jun. 2011, paras 285-291; *Marion Unglaube v. Costa Rica*, ICSID Case No. ARB/08/1, Award, 16 May 2012, para. 249; *Renée Rose Levy de Levi v. Peru*, ICSID Case No. ARB/10/17, Award, 26 Feb. 2014, para. 319 (agreeing that 'for an investor to make a decision on an investment, an important element usually considered is the stability of the country's legal system', but adding that 'stability does not mean a freezing of the legal system or making it impossible for the State to reform laws and other regulations in force at the time the investor made the investment'); *Yuri Bogdanov and Yulia Bogdanova v. Moldova*, SCC Case No. V091/2012, Award, 16 Apr. 2013, paras 183ff.; *Bosca, supra* n. 1, para. 235; *Convial Callao S.A. and CCI, Compañía de Concesiones de Infraestructura S.A. v. Peru*, ICSID Case No. ARB/10/2, Award, 21 May 2013, paras 561ff.

173. *South American Silver Limited v. Bolivia*, PCA Case No. 2013-15, Award, 30 Aug. 2018, paras 645ff. *See also*, *Pawlowski AG and Project Sever s.r.o. v. Czech Republic*, ICSID Case No. ARB/17/11, Award, 1 Nov. 2021, paras 288-289, noting that the clause 'is a rule of laconic brevity and delphic obscurity', but that its 'scope of protection is intimately related: to the legitimate and reasonable expectations on which the investor relied, including the stability of the host State's legal framework; and to the specific undertakings and representations proffered by the host State at the time when the investment was made'. Importantly, the Tribunal also mentioned that 'the legitimacy or reasonableness of the investor's expectations must be assessed in conjunction with the political, socioeconomic, cultural and historical conditions in the host State, and in particular, balancing the right of the State under international law to regulate within its borders' (para. 290). The Tribunal applied a narrow view of the concept, requiring specific representations, assurances, or commitments, but also noted that 'legal expectations can also be created in some cases by the State's general legislative and regulatory framework' (para. 613). *See also*, *Naturgy Energy Group, S.A. and Naturgy Electricidad Colombia, S.L. (formerly Gas Natural SDG, S.A. and Gas Natural Fenosa Electricidad Colombia, S.L.) v. Colombia*, ICSID Case No. UNCT/18/1, Award, 12 Mar. 2021, adopting a rather narrow approach and speaking of 'objectively reasonable' legitimate expectations that must be assessed when the investment is made (paras 322ff.) and referring to the high level of arbitrariness set in the ICJ *ELSI* case to find a breach (paras 343ff.). *See also*, *Glencore International A.G. y C.I. Prodeco S.A. v. Colombia*, ICSID Case No. ARB/16/6, Award, 27 Aug. 2019, para. 1308, where the Tribunal explained that the content of the FET can be 'established by the rules of interpretation of the VCLT, aided by the jurisprudence of international tribunals' and that 'a host State breaches such minimum standard and incurs international responsibility if its actions (or in certain circumstances omissions) violate certain thresholds of propriety or contravene basic requirements of the rule of law, causing harm to the investor'. It is not entirely clear whether this is a reference to the MST. It is probably not. The Tribunal also noted that 'the threshold of propriety required by FET must be determined by the tribunal in light of all the relevant circumstances of the case', including some factors, such as, *inter alia*, specific representations made by the State, whether the State has respected the principles of 'due process, consistency, and transparency when adopting the measures at issue' or 'failed to offer a stable and predictable legal framework, in breach of the investor's legitimate expectations' (para. 1310). But the Tribunal also noted that such rights must be balanced taking into account States' 'sovereign right to amend their laws and regulations and to adopt new ones in furtherance of public interest, the conception of which can change over time' (para. 1311). It later adopted a rather balanced definition of legitimate expectations (paras 1366ff.) but also noted that 'legal expectations can also be created in some cases by the State's general legislative and regulatory framework: an investor may make an investment in reasonable reliance upon the stability of that framework, so that in certain circumstances a reform of the framework may breach the investor's legitimate expectations'. *See also*: *Ortiz Construcciones y Proyectos S.A. v. Algeria*, ICSID Case No. ARB/17/1, Award, 29 Apr. 2020, paras 275ff., 283ff.; *Viorel Micula and others v. Romania [II]*, ICSID Case No. ARB/14/29, Award, 5 Mar. 2020, paras 357ff.; *Staur Eiendom AS, EBO Invest AS and Rox Holding AS v. Latvia*, ICSID Case No. ARB/16/38, Award, 28 Feb. 2020, para. 420 (referring to 'specific undertakings of the State upon which the Claimants could reasonably have been expected to rely', but also referring to an obligation to provide a 'transparent, consistent and stable business framework', para. 470); *Cengiz İnşaat*

clause or whether it is linked to international law or the MST. Instead, they are focusing on assessing whether the FET standard's elements have been breached. They are increasingly applying the NAFTA-style narrow definition of the concept of legitimate expectations. It is also noteworthy that in only six of these recent cases (about 30%), tribunals found a breach of the FET clause.

1.3.4 Conclusion

What has been the outcome of these cases in terms of liability for these three categories of awards (examined in sections 1.3.1, 1.3.2 and 1.3.3) where tribunals did not formally take a position on the question of the status of a stand-alone FET clause and its relationship with the MST? These awards can be divided into two groups.

On the one hand, in about half of the cases (47 awards out of 91) the FET claims were rejected.[174] As mentioned above, many of these awards have been rendered in the

---

Sanayi ve Ticaret A.S v. Libya, ICC Case No. 21537/ZF/AYZ, Award, 7 Nov. 2018, para. 547 (speaking of 'specific representations or commitments' leading an investor to invest); *Agility Public Warehousing Company K.S.C. v. Iraq*, ICSID Case No. ARB/17/7, Award, 22 Feb. 2021, para. 160 (indicating that 'the standard is a broad and flexible protection, requiring a fact-specific assessment to determine whether conduct is "fair" and "equitable" in the context and the particular circumstances of the dispute', but also applying a narrow definition of legitimate expectations, at para. 162); *Consutel Group S.p.A. in liquidazione v. Algeria*, PCA No. 2017-33, Award, 3 Feb. 2020, para. 416 (the BIT contained no FET clause, but the FET clause found in the Belgian-Lux.-Algeria BIT was imported through the MFN clause. The Tribunal used a rather narrow definition of legitimate expectations, at paras 421, 459, 470, 473); *Etrak İnşaat Taahut ve Ticaret Anonim Sirketi v. Libya*, ICC Case No. 22236/ZF/AYZ, Final Award, 22 Jul. 2019, paras 313ff.; *United Utilities (Tallinn) B.V. and Aktsiaselts Tallinna Vesi v. Estonia*, ICSID Case No. ARB/14/24, Award, 21 Jun. 2019, paras 574ff.; *Cyprus Popular Bank Public Co. Ltd. v. Greece*, ICSID Case No. ARB/14/16, Award, 15 Apr. 2021, paras 1128-1129; *Georg Gavrilovic and Gavrilovic d.o.o. v. Croatia*, ICSID Case No. ARB/12/39, Award, 26 Jul. 2018, paras 954ff., 984ff.; *Mohammad Reza Dayyani and others v. Korea*, PCA Case No. 2015-38, Award, June 2018, reported in: IAReporter, 22 Jan. 2019 (apparently referring to 'reasonable expectations derived from specific representations made at the time of the investments', and that 'expectations were to be assessed 'objectively and reasonably in light of the circumstances'); *UAB E Energija v. Latvia*, ICSID Case No. ARB/12/33, Award, 22 Dec. 2017 (mentioning the 'considerable debate as to the content of this standard, including as to whether it confers protection going beyond the minimum standard of treatment required as a matter of customary international law', para. 833, but not taking any position, and adopting a narrow definition of legitimate expectations and stability and predictability of the legal environment, paras 835-838); *G.I.H.G. Limited, Natland Group Limited, Natland Investment Group NV, and Radiance Energy Holding S.A.R.L. v. Czech Republic*, PCA Case No. 2013-35, Partial Award, 20 Dec. 2017, reported in IAReporter, 26 Jul. 2018 (apparently adopting a balanced position); *JSW Solar (zwei) GmbH & Co.KG, Gisela Wirtgen, Jürgen Wirtgen, and Stefan Wirtgen v. Czech Republic*, PCA Case No. 2014-03, Final Award, 11 Oct. 2017, paras 407ff.; *JKX Oil & Gas plc, Poltava Gas B.V. and Poltava Petroleum Company v. Ukraine*, PCA Case No. 2015-11, Award, 6 Feb. 2017, reported in IAReporter, 29 Jun. 2020; *WCV World Capital Ventures Cyprus Ltd. & Channel Crossings Ltd. v. Czech Republic*, PCA Case No. 2016-1, Award, 26 Jul. 2023, paras 266, 278, 280, 293.

174. *South American Silver*, *supra* n. 173, para. 674; *Consortium RFCC*, *supra* n. 156; *L.E.S.I.*, *supra* n. 168, para. 164; *Metalpar*, *supra* n. 172, para. 235; *EDF*, *supra* n. 172, para. 330; *Invesmart*, *supra* n. 172, paras 199, 202, 250ff.; *Vocklinghaus*, *supra* n. 167, para. 214; *Roussalis*, *supra* n. 168, paras 313ff.; *GEA Group*, *supra* n. 167, para. 367; *White Industries*, *supra* n. 172, para. 10.3.1; *Jan Oostergetel*, *supra* n. 172, para. 341; *Convial*, *supra* n. 172, para. 619; *Bogdanov*

last five years and involve tribunals not addressing the question of the status of the FET clause at all.

On the other hand, in the other half of the awards (44 cases out of 91) tribunals have found a breach of the FET clause. A few tribunals (seven) have found that the clause had been breached but held that no damage had been proven.[175] In most cases, the tribunals awarded compensation. Some tribunals concluded that the clause had been breached along with other provisions.[176] Other tribunals only found a breach of the FET clause.[177]

(2013 award), *supra* n. 172, para. 211; *Levy, supra* n. 172, para. 391; *Enkev Beheer, supra* n. 155, para. 376; *Tulip, supra* n. 167, para. 414; *ECE, supra* n. 157, paras 4.754-4.757; *MNSS, supra* n. 152, para. 346; *CMC Muratori, supra* n. 167; *Alghanim, supra* n. 167; *Lidercón, supra* n. 167; *IC Power Asia, supra* n. 167; *Tokios Tokelés, supra* n. 156; *Binder, supra* n. 159; *WCV, supra* n. 173; *Unglaube, supra* n. 172; *Toto, supra* n. 168; *Naturgy Energy, supra* n. 173; *Ortiz, supra* n. 173; *Micula, supra* n. 173; *Bayindir, supra* n. 76; *Staur, supra* n. 173; *Gosling, supra* n. 154; *Cengiz, supra* n. 173; *Agility, supra* n. 173, para. 279; *Consutel, supra* n. 173; *United Utilities, supra* n. 173, para. 939; *Marfin, supra* n. 169, paras 1211ff.; *Gavrilovic, supra* n. 173, paras 954ff., 984ff.; *Krederi, supra* n. 168; *JSW Solar, supra* n. 173; *JKX Oil & Gas, supra* n. 173; *Houben, supra* n. 156; *G.I.H.G., supra* n. 173; *A.M.F. Aircraftleasing Meier, supra* n. 167; *Paushok, supra* n. 168.

175. *Rompetrol, supra* n. 134; *Pawlowski, supra* n. 173; *B3 Croatian Courier, supra* n. 167; *Al Warraq, supra* n. 167, para. 683; *Bosca, supra* n. 1, para. 329 (indicating that the claimant had already been reimbursed for its direct losses by virtue of a 2006 Supreme Court of Lithuania decision); *Nordzucker, supra* n. 172 (awarding no damages in subsequent Award, 28 Nov. 2009); *Eureko, supra* n. 167, para. 234 (finding a breach of FET and other clauses, the case was later settled).
176. *CC/Devas, supra* n. 137, para. 470 (USD 100 million); *Quiborax, supra* n. 131 (USD 48.6 million); *Belokon, supra* n. 143 (USD 15 million, the award was later set aside); *PAO Tatneft, supra* n. 145 (USD 120 million); *Rumeli, supra* n. 147 (USD 125 million); *Cyprus Popular Bank, supra* n. 173 (reported in IAReporter, 8 Jun. 2023, EUR 34.5 million); *Alpha, supra* n. 168, para. 420 (USD 2.9 million); *Kardassopoulos, supra* n. 168 (USD 45 million); *Glencore, supra* n. 173 (USD 19 million); *Olin Holdings, supra* n. 168, para. 551 (EUR 18.2 million); *Mytilineos, supra* n. 168 (USD 40 million awarded for breach of FET and expropriation); *Garanti Koza, supra* n. 167 (finding a breach of FET and the umbrella clause, and awarding USD 2.5 million in a subsequent award, 19 Dec. 2016); *Flemingo, supra* n. 172, para. 976 (also finding a breach of expropriation and awarding EUR 17.9 million); *von Pezold, supra* n. 167 (USD 100 million); *Manolium, supra* n. 167 (USD 20 million); *Venezuela Holdings, B.V., et al (case formerly known as Mobil Corporation, Venezuela Holdings, B.V., et al.) v. Bolivarian Republic of Venezuela*, ICSID Case No. ARB/07/27, Award, 9 Oct. 2014, paras 256ff., 270 (USD 9 million for breach of legitimate expectations only, the sum awarded for expropriation is USD 1.4 billion. The award was later annulled: Decision on Annulment, 9 Mar. 2017); *Bogdanov, supra* n. 167, paras 86ff. (475 386.41 lei); *Gemplus, supra* n. 167 (USD 16 million); *Siag, supra* n. 168, para. 450 (USD 74.5 million); *ADC, supra* n. 167, paras 445, 543 (USD 76.2 million); *CME, supra* n. 167, para. 611, Final Award, 14 Mar. 2003 (USD 269.8 million); *Wena Hotels, supra* n. 167, paras 133ff. (USD 20.6 million); *Maffezini, supra* n. 167, para. 83 (ESP 57.6 million).
177. *MTD Equity, supra* n. 162 (USD 5.8 million); *BG Group, supra* n. 133 (USD 185 million); *Impregilo, supra* n. 172, para. 331 (USD 21 million); *Etrak, supra* n. 173, para. 450 (USD 21.8 million); *Dayyani, supra* n. 173 (USD 50 million); *UAB, supra* n. 173 (EUR 1.5 million); *Hochtief, supra* n. 167 (finding a breach of FET and deciding not to examine other provisions, awarding damages of USD 13.4 million in a subsequent award, 21 Dec. 2016); *Oxus Gold, supra* n. 164, para. 313 (USD 10.2 million); *British Caribbean Bank, supra* n. 167, paras 287ff. (USD 40 million); *Swisslion, supra* n. 167, para. 360 (EUR 350,000); *Bau, supra* n. 168, para. 17.1 (EUR 29.2 million); *Desert Line, supra* n. 167, paras 191ff. (YR 3.5 billion); *Eastern Sugar, supra* n. 167, para. 198 (EUR 25.4 million); *Bogdanov* (2005 award), *supra* n. 167, paras 16ff. (Lie

1.4 Award Interpreting the ECT

I have examined 54 awards which have dealt with an FET claim under the ECT. This Treaty contains the following FET clause (Article 10):

> Each Contracting Party shall, in accordance with the provisions of this Treaty, encourage and *create stable, equitable, favourable and transparent conditions* for Investors of other Contracting Parties to make Investments in its Area. Such conditions shall include a commitment to accord at all times to Investments of Investors of other Contracting Parties *fair and equitable treatment*. Such Investments shall also enjoy the most constant protection and security and no Contracting Party shall in any way impair by unreasonable or discriminatory measures their management, maintenance, use, enjoyment or disposal. In no case shall such Investments be accorded treatment *less favourable than that required by international law*, including treaty obligations. (emphasis added).

A few observations can be made about the scope of this provision. The clause is broader than a typical bare or stand-alone FET clause. It explicitly refers to the 'stable, equitable, favourable and transparent conditions', adding that one such condition is to provide the FET.[178] As noted by some tribunals, 'legal stability is part of the FET standard under the ECT'.[179] The last sentence of Article 10 importantly adds that investments must always be accorded a treatment no less favourable than that required by 'international law'. Yet, the treatment referred to includes many elements of protection, not just the FET. In other words, the reference to 'international law' is *not directly* linked to the FET standard.[180] The *SunReserve* award speaks of a 'demarcation' between the two elements.[181] In *Hydro Energy*, the Tribunal referred to this last

694,896); *Parkerings-Compagniet, supra* n. 1 (finding an FET breach, but the amount of damages is not known); *Horthel, supra* n. 171 (finding a breach, but the amount of compensation is redacted).

178. *LSG Building Solutions GmbH and others v. Romania*, ICSID Case No. ARB/18/19, Decision on Jurisdiction, Liability and Principles of Reparation, 11 Jul. 2022, para. 1007 ('the requirement that the host State afford "stable" or "transparent" conditions is seldom found. The ECT differs from other traditional FET provisions because it makes an explicit reference to the concept of stability').
179. *Luxembourg Solar 1 S.Á.R.L. et al. v. Spain*, SCC Case No. 2015/150, Award, 14 Nov. 2018, para. 351. *See also, Plama Consortium Limited v. Bulgaria*, ICSID Case No. ARB/03/24, Award, 27 Aug. 2008, para. 173; *Eiser Infrastructure Limited and Energía Solar Luxembourg S.à r.l. v. Spain*, ICSID Case No. ARB/13/36, Award, 4 May 2017, para. 381.
180. OECD, *supra* n. 9, 11: 'Some treaties contain an unspecified "fair" and "equitable" treatment clause and, *separately*, state that parties are obliged to afford at least treatment according to international law. The Energy Charter Treaty is a prominent but not the only example of this approach' (emphasis in the original).
181. *SunReserve Luxco Holdings S.à.r.l. (Luxembourg) et al. v. Italy*, SCC Case No. 2016/32, Final Award, 25 Mar. 2020, para. 672: 'the Tribunal considers that the text of Article 10(1) ECT itself creates a distinction between the FET obligation therein, and the international minimum standard for FET obligations. This independent reference to the treatment required by international law creates a demarcation between the legal standard for the FET obligation contained in the second sentence and the treatment required by international law. This demarcation becomes apparent when Article 10(1) ECT is juxtaposed against Article 1105 NAFTA, which is titled "Minimum Standard of Treatment", and requires the host State to "accord to investments of investors of another Party treatment in accordance with international law, including fair and equitable treatment…". Thus, as Claimants rightly submit, NAFTA

reference as one of the 'other obligations in Article 10(1)', which has 'not played any significant role in this arbitration'.[182] Importantly, awards assessing Article 10(1) have *not* considered this reference to 'international law' as a 'no less' type of clause (a type of clause is further discussed in the next chapter).

One of the issues debated by tribunals is whether the reference in Article 10 to 'stable, equitable, favourable and transparent conditions' offers foreign investors a standard of protection that is *distinct* from the FET standard. The *Plama* award was one of the first to examine the issue. The Tribunal stated that the standards of protection in Article 10(1) of the ECT were 'closely interrelated', but added that this 'does not mean, however, that each standard could not be defined autonomously'.[183] Yet, the Tribunal also noted that 'stable and equitable conditions are clearly part of the fair and equitable treatment standard under the ECT'.[184] Similarly, the question was mentioned in *Cavalum*, but the Tribunal noted that 'nothing turns on the point in this arbitration because it is clear that stability and transparency are also part of the FET standard itself'.[185] Since then, all awards dealing with this issue (with very few exceptions)[186] have considered that both 'stability' and FET offer the same protection and therefore have been examined together.[187] A few awards have mentioned the issue but decided not to take a position on the question.[188]

explicitly equates the standard of treatment to the international law minimum standard, within which the FET obligations are subsumed. Article 10(1) ECT does not create any such link between the FET obligation therein and the customary international law minimum standard'.

182. *Hydro Energy 1 S.à.r.l and Hydroxana Sweden AB v. Spain*, ICSID Case No. ARB /15/42, Decision on Jurisdiction, Liability and Directions on Quantum, 9 Mar. 2020, para. 544.

183. *Plama, supra* n. 179, para. 163, quoting (at paras 25-26). C.H. Schreuer, *Fair and Equitable Treatment (FET): Interaction with other Standards*, 4(5) TDM (2007), stating that 'The better view is that these standards, though related, are separate and autonomous.'

184. *Plama, supra* n. 179, para. 173.

185. *Cavalum SGPS, S.A. v. Spain*, ICSID Case No. ARB/15/34, Decision on Jurisdiction, Liability and Directions on Quantum, 31 Aug. 2020, para. 403.

186. *See*, for instance, *Enrus Energy Holdings Corporation v. Spain*, ICSID Case No. ARB/16/4, Decision on Jurisdiction and Liability, 17 Mar. 2021, Partial Dissent of Garibaldi, paras 19 ('there is no reason why the two sentences cannot be applied separately, each in accordance with its own prescriptive content') 45 ('in the context of the second sentence of Article 10(1), stability, transparency, and consistency are factors to be taken into account in a fair-and equitable-treatment analysis; they are not requirements to be used as a substitute for the 'fair and equitable treatment' standard'). *See also, WA Investments Europa Nova Ltd v. Czech Republic*, PCA Case No. 2014-19, Award, 15 May 2019, paras 569-570, dealing with the 'question whether an obligation to provide a stable and predictable legal framework for foreign investment is, in any event, a separate and distinguishable part of the treaty obligation to accord FET' and concluding that 'the Tribunal agrees with the Claimant that such a separate obligation exists as part of the FET standard'.

187. *ESPF Beteiligungs GmbH et al. v. Italy*, ICSID Case No. ARB/16/5, Award, 14 Sep. 2020, paras 443-444; *Silver Ridge Power BV v. Italy*, ICSID Case No. ARB /15/37, Award, 26 Feb. 2021, para. 393; *Enrus, supra* n. 186, para. 314 (majority of the Tribunal, Garibaldi dissenting); *Hydro Energy, supra* n. 182, paras 544, 547-548 (noting that 'on the face of Article 10(1) there is a separate obligation', but adding that it is 'clear that even without an express obligation to create stable, equitable and transparent conditions, that such an obligation would be included in the fair and equitable treatment standard') 546 ('these obligations overlap to a very great degree'); *I.C.W. Europe Investments Limited v. Czech Republic*, PCA Case No. 2014-22, Award, 15 May 2019, para. 529 ('Investment tribunals have consistently decided, and this Tribunal agrees, that the obligation to guarantee a stable and predictable investment framework forms part of the FET standard'); *Voltaic Network GmbH v. Czech Republic*, PCA Case No. 2014-20, Award, 15

The majority of awards (37 out of 54) have not mentioned or dealt with the question of the status of the FET clause and whether it should be considered an autonomous FET clause or if it is linked to international law or to the MST under custom.[189]

May 2019, para. 487; *Sevilla Beheer B.V. and others v. Spain,* ICSID Case No. ARB/16/27, Decision on Jurisdiction, Liability, and Principles of Quantum, 11 Feb. 2022, paras 714-715 (Cameron dissenting on this point); *Photovoltaic Knopf Betriebs GMBH v. Czech Republic,* PCA Case No. 2014-21, Award, 15 May 2019, para. 483; *LSG, supra* n. 178, para. 1020 ('FET is inseparable from stability and predictability'); *Renergy S.à r.l. v. Spain,* ICSID Case No. ARB/14/18, Award, 6 May 2022, para. 610 (Sands dissenting and taking a different position); *Isolux Infrastructure Netherlands, B.V. v. Spain,* SCC V2013/153, Award, 12 Jul. 2016, paras 764-766; *Novenergia II – Energy & Environment (SCA) (Grand Duchy of Luxembourg) v. Spain,* SCC Case No. 2015/063, Final Award, 15 Feb. 2018, para. 646; *Charanne B.V. and Construction Investments S.a.r.l. v. Spain,* SCC Case No. 062/2012, Final Award, 21 Jan. 2016, paras 476-477; *Foresight Luxembourg Solar 1 S. Á.R1., et al. v. Spain,* SCC Case No. 2015/150, Final Award, 14 Nov. 2018, para. 351; *Eurus Energy Holdings Corporation v. Spain,* ICSID Case No. ARB/16/4, Decision on Jurisdiction and Liability, 17 Mar. 2021, para. 314; *BayWa r.e. Renewable Energy GmbH and BayWa r.e. Asset Holding GmbH v. Spain,* ICSID Case No. ARB/15/16, Decision on Jurisdiction, Liability and Directions on Quantum, 2 Dec. 2019, para. 458; *Luxembourg Solar, supra* n. 179, paras 360ff.; *RWE Innogy GmbH and RWE Innogy Aersa S.A.U. v. Spain,* ICSID Case No. ARB/14/34, Decision on Jurisdiction, Liability and Certain Issues of Quantum, 30 Dec. 2019, para. 429; *PV Investors v. Spain,* PCA Case No. 2012-14, Final Award, 28 Feb. 2020, para. 567; *AES Corporation and Tau Power B.V. v. Kazakhstan,* ICSID Case No. ARB/10/16, Award, 1 Nov. 2013, paras 380, 383.

188. *Mercuria Energy Group Limited v. Poland,* SCC Case No. 096/2008, Award, 29 Dec. 2022, para. 833 ('Whether or not it is an independent obligation, the Tribunal notes that it is intrinsically connected in the ECT to the FET and can inform the interpretation of the latter'); *ESPF, supra* n. 187, paras 442-443; *9REN Holding S.a.r.l v. Spain,* ICSID Case No. ARB/15/15, Award, 31 May 2019.

189. *RWE, supra* n. 187; *Renergy, supra* n. 187, para. 610; *Petrobart Ltd. v. Kyrgyz Republic,* SCC Case No. 126/2003, Award, 29 Mar. 2005, para. 26; *Nykomb Synergetics Technology Holding AB v. Latvia,* SCC, Award, 16 Dec. 2003, paras 33ff.; *Isolux, supra* n. 187, paras 764-766; *Enrus, supra* n. 186 (majority of the Tribunal) paras 312ff.; *Hydro Energy, supra* n. 182, para. 544; *I.C.W., supra* n. 187, paras 525ff.; *Photovoltaic, supra* n. 187, paras 476ff.; *Voltaic, supra* n. 187, paras 484ff.; *WA Investments, supra* n. 186, paras 564ff.; *STEAG GmbH v. Spain,* ICSID Case No. ARB/15/4, Decision on Jurisdiction, Liability and Principles of Quantum, 8 Sep. 2020; *MOL Hungarian Oil and Gas Company Plc v. Croatia,* ICSID Case No. ARB/13/32, Award, 5 Jul. 2022; *Mathias Kruck and others v. Spain,* ICSID Case No. ARB/15/23, Decision on Jurisdiction, Liability and Principles of Quantum, 14 Sep. 2022, paras 158ff.; *FREIF Eurowind Holdings Ltd. v. Spain,* SCC Case No. 2017/060, Final Award, 8 Mar. 2021; *Festorino Invest Limited and others v. Poland,* SCC Case No. V2018/098, Award, 30 Jun. 2021, paras 707ff.; *Mercuria, supra* n. 188; *Sevilla Beheer, supra* n. 187; *Infracapital F1 S.à r.l. and Infracapital Solar B.V. v. Spain,* ICSID Case No. ARB/16/18, Decision on Jurisdiction, Liability, and Directions on Quantum, 13 Sep. 2021; *Antaris GmbH and Göde v. Czech Republic,* PCA Case No. 2014-01, UNCITRAL, Award, 2 May 2018, para. 360; *Novenergia, supra* n. 187; *ESPF, supra* n. 187; *Eurus, supra* n. 187, paras 314ff.; *9REN, supra* n. 188; *BayWa r.e., supra* n. 187, paras 458ff.; *Luxembourg Solar, supra* n. 179; *Cavalum, supra* n. 185; *Stadtwerke München GmbH and others v. Spain,* ICSID Case No. ARB/15/1, Award, 2 Dec. 2019; *Masdar Solar & Wind Cooperatief v. Spain,* ICSID Case No. ARB/14/1, Award, 16 May 2008, paras 482ff.; *Mamidoil Jetoil v. Albania,* ICSID Case No. ARB/11/24, Award, 30 Mar. 2015, paras 598ff.; *NextEra Energy Global Holdings B.V. and NextEra Energy Spain Holdings B.V. v. Spain,* ICSID Case No. ARB/14/11, Decision on Jurisdiction, Liability and Quantum Principles, 12 Mar. 2019, paras 580ff.; *Eiser, supra* n. 179, paras 362ff.; *RREEF Infrastructure Services Luxembourg S.à.r.l. and Energia Termosolar B.V. (formerly Antin Infrastructure Services Luxembourg S.à.r.l. and Antin Energia Termosolar B.V.) v. Spain,* ICSID Case No. ARB/13/31, Award, 15 Jun. 2018; *Charanne, supra* n. 187, para. 476; *PV Investors, supra* n. 187, paras 557ff.; *AES, supra* n. 187, paras 376ff.; *Ascom Group S.A.,*

Of the awards that did say something on the issue, the vast majority of them (9 out of 14 awards) explicitly considered that the provision was an autonomous FET clause. The first one to take that position was the *Liman Caspian* Tribunal:

> [T]he purpose of ECT Article 10(1), second sentence, is to provide a protection which goes beyond the minimum standard to treatment under international law. The ECT was intended to go further than simply reiterating the protection offered by the latter. In this respect, ECT Article 10(1), second sentence, differs from NAFTA Article 1105 (in its interpretation given by the Free Trade Commission on 31 July 2001) which contains an express reference to international law. Therefore, when assessing Respondent's actions, a specific standard of fairness and equitableness above the minimum standard must be identified and applied for the application of the ECT.[190]

As explained by the *Silver Ridge Power* Tribunal, 'the special features' of the ECT 'make it evident' that the FET standard 'differs from, and goes beyond, the minimum standard of protection under customary international law and must therefore be determined autonomously'.[191] In the words of the *Belenergia* Tribunal, Article 10(1) ECT 'provides an autonomous, self-contained definition of FET, with no reference' to the MST.[192] According to another tribunal, in this context, the phrase 'less favourable than ... required by international law' indicates that the MST 'does get incorporated into the ECT, but only as the bare minimum threshold that the host State's treatment of investments must meet'.[193] In other words, as stated by the Tribunal in *Azurix v. Argentina* (dealing with a different type of FET clause) the MST sets a 'floor, [but] not a ceiling'[194] of the standard of treatment required from host States under the treaty.[195] In the words of another tribunal, the MST 'operates as a floor, while the FET standard affords additional protection'.[196] Since the standard 'is not strictly equivalent to international law', this means that 'this non-restrictive standard confers on the Tribunal some interpretation leeway'.[197] Other awards adopted the same position.[198]

Anatolie Stati, Gabriel Stati and Terra Raf Trans Trading Ltd. v. Kazakhstan, SCC Case No. 116/2010, Award, 19 Dec. 2013, paras 941ff.; *AES Summit Generation Limited and AES-Tisza Erömü Kft. v. Hungary (II)*, ICSID Case No. ARB/07/22, Award, 23 Sep. 2010.

190. *Liman Caspian Oil B.V. & NCL Dutch Investment B.V. v. Kazakhstan*, ICSID Case No. ARB/07/14, Award, 22 Jun. 2010, para. 263.
191. *Silver Ridge, supra* n. 187, para. 401.
192. *Belenergia S.A. v. Italy*, ICSID Case No. ARB/15/40, Award, 6 Aug. 2019, para. 568.
193. *SunReserve, supra* n. 181, para. 673. The Tribunal also made this other comment: 'Tribunal is neither persuaded by Respondent's suggestion that there exists a hermeneutical principle of interpretation that requires international treaties to be interpreted consistent with customary international law, nor does it consider that interpretation of Article 10(1) ECT in accordance with the principles of interpretation in international law results in the application of the customary international law minimum standard.'
194. *Azurix Corp. v. Argentina*, ICSID Case No. ARB/01/12, Award, 14 Jul. 2006, para. 361.
195. *SunReserve, supra* n. 181, para. 673.
196. *LSG, supra* n. 178, para. 1019 (also noting that 'nothing in the ECT suggests that its drafters had the intention to equate the modern FET standard and the old, customary minimum standard of treatment of aliens'). *See also*: *SolEs Badajoz GmbH v. Spain*, ICSID Case No. ARB/15/38, Award, 31 Jul. 2019, para. 332.
197. *Belenergia, supra* n. 192, para. 569.
198. *OperaFund Eco-Invest SICAV PLC and Schwab Holding AG v. Spain*, ICSID Case No. ARB/15/36, Award, 6 Sep. 2019, para. 425 ('The express inclusion of this commitment in Article 10 also

Only a handful of awards have supported the opposite view that the FET clause is a reference to the MST or custom.[199] I have also found a few awards which contain rather ambiguous passages that may suggest that the Tribunal was also leaning towards this approach.[200]

How have ECT tribunals assessed the question of the content of the FET obligation? In *Plama*, the Tribunal mentioned that 'the Parties agree that the standard includes to a certain extent the protection of the investor's legitimate expectations and the provision of a stable legal framework', but it also added that it was 'nonetheless conscious that this may now be a controversial area, particularly with different interpretations being given to the decision of the ad hoc Committee in *MTD v. Chile*'.[201] Since then, the reasoning of tribunals have been much more straightforward on the

---

clarifies that its standard is autonomous, and beyond the MST. As clarified in Liman v. Kazakhstan, had the Contracting Parties to the ECT intended to limit their FET obligations to the MST, they could and would have made that intention clear'); *Watkins Holdings S.à r.l. and others v. Spain*, ICSID Case No. ARB/15/44, Award, 21 Jan. 2020, paras 511-513; *InfraRed Environmental Infrastructure GP Limited and others v. Spain*, ICSID Case No. ARB/14/12, Award, 2 Aug. 2019, paras 347, 350.

199. *Blusun S.A., Jean-Pierre Lecorcier and Michael Stein v. Italy*, ICSID Case No. ARB/14/3, Award, 27 Dec. 2016, para. 319(3), indicating that 'the core commitment' under Art. 10 of the ECT is to accord FET, adding that 'this incorporates the fair and equitable treatment standard under customary international law and as applied by tribunals'. The passage could be interpreted as suggesting that for the Tribunal the FET clause is a reference to the MST. This is indeed what the Tribunal said in *RWE, supra* n. 187, para. 443 ("The conclusion of the Blusun tribunal is that the second sentence of Article 10(1) incorporates the fair and equitable treatment standard under customary international law")', and concluding at para. 447: 'The formula "fair and equitable treatment" was not agreed to by the ECT Contracting Parties in a legal vacuum, but against a backdrop where the formula had been used for many decades as a standard of investment protection closely tied to customary international law (...).'

200. *Electrabel v. Hungary*, ICSID Case No. ARB/07/19, Decision on Jurisdiction, Applicable Law and Liability, 30 Nov. 2012, para. 7.155, examining the claimant's allegation that Hungary violated the obligation under Art. 10(1) ECT not to accord to its investment treatment less favourable than that required by international law. The Tribunal agreed with the claimant that 'the content of this standard is, at the present time, similar to the other standards expressly mentioned in Article 10(1) ECT, which also exist as standards of protection in customary international law' (para. 7.158). This passage may be understood as suggesting that the standard under international and the FET treaty standard under the ECT are the same. *See also*, *RREEF, supra* n. 189, para. 258, indicating that 'this discussion remains rather academic'. The *RREEF* Tribunal also added this comment: 'this provision guarantees FET to foreign investors, with the precision that this treatment will not be "less favourable than that required by international law" (an expression which can be assimilated to imposing the minimum standard of protection) (paragraph 1) together with national treatment (paragraph 3). In other words, the minimum standard as applied traditionally in international law is included in the FET which adds to it in favour of the investor'. This passage could be suggesting that for the Tribunal the words 'international law' in the provision is a reference to the MST. But later, the *RREEF* Tribunal added that 'the FET principle includes, but goes beyond, the traditional "minimum standard" as conceived in the Neer Case' (para. 263). *See also*, *Limited Liability Company Amto v. Ukraine*, SCC Case No. 080/2005, Final Award, 26 Mar. 2008, para. 74: 'There is clearly overlapping within Article 10(1). It refers to both fair and equitable treatment and the minimum standard required by international law, when these two standards may be identical in many contexts.' This passage is ambiguous. On the one hand, it suggests that these are two different concepts. But, on the other hand, it also seems to indicate that they may be identical.

201. *Plama, supra* n. 179, para. 175. It adopted a narrow definition of legitimate expectations, at para. 176.

issue. All tribunals which have explicitly commented on Article 10 have considered that legitimate expectations are part of the FET. Thus, as mentioned by one tribunal, 'stability is also part of the legitimate expectation of the investor'.[202]

I have found only one award where the tribunal seems *not* to have considered legitimate expectations as a stand-alone element of the FET standard.[203] A similar position was adopted by Douglas in his dissenting opinion in the *Kruck* case.[204] In any event, to the best of my knowledge, all other tribunals have adopted a narrow definition of the concept of legitimate expectations and a balanced position on the scope of the obligation to provide a stable and transparent legal framework.[205] Some tribunals have also adopted a high threshold of gravity to find a breach of that element of protection.[206]

Several questions regarding the scope of legitimate expectations have arisen. I will briefly mention just a few of them. As mentioned by the *Masdar v. Spain* Tribunal, 'in essence, one school of thought considers that such commitments can result from general statements in general laws or regulations. The other considers that any such

202. *Cavalum, supra* n. 185, para. 405.
203. *Enrus, supra* n. 186, majority of the Tribunal, para. 317: 'On this view, legitimate expectations are essentially consideranda. The term itself does not appear in the ECT, or for that matter in BITs, and there is no rule that legitimate expectations are to be observed, analogous to the pacta sunt servanda rule in the law of treaties. Rather, they are relevant factors to be taken into account in the interpretation and application of treaty standards such as Article 10(1) of the ECT, first and second sentences.' *See also,* Partial Dissent of Garibaldi, para. 46, agreeing.
204. *Kruck, supra* n. 189, Dissenting opinion, Douglas, para. 5, stating that 'the concept of legitimate expectations has no textual embodiment in the ECT and in investment treaties more generally' and that 'the only path to a doctrine of legitimate expectations through the FET standard is by interpretation'. For him, 'the only bridge that seems plausible, and it is far from uncontroversial, is to say that the doctrine of legitimate expectations is a "general principle of law recognised by civilised nations" in the sense of Article 38 ICJ Statute that can then qualify as a "relevant rule of international law applicable in the relations between the parties" for the purposes of Article 31(3)(c) VCLT' (para. 18).
205. *Silver Ridge, supra* n. 187, paras 403ff.; *Eskosol S.p.A. in liquidazione v. Italy*, ICSID Case No. ARB/15/50, Award, 4 Sep. 2020, para. 416; *Hydro Energy, supra* n. 182, paras 544ff.; *I.C.W., supra* n. 187, paras 525ff.; *Photovoltaic, supra* n. 187, paras 476ff.; *Voltaic, supra* n. 187, paras 484ff.; *WA Investments, supra* n. 186, paras 664ff.; *Enrus, supra* n. 186, majority of the Tribunal; *Blusun, supra* n. 199, paras 365ff.; *STEAG, supra* n. 189, paras 503-504; *LSG, supra* n. 178, paras 1015, 1027ff.; *Kruck, supra* n. 189, paras 188ff.; *FREIF, supra* n. 189, para. 449; *Renergy, supra* n. 187, paras 611ff.; *Festorino, supra* n. 189, paras 707ff.; *Mercuria, supra* n. 188, paras 834-835; *Sevilla Beheer, supra* n. 187, paras 793ff.; *Infracapital, supra* n. 189, paras 569ff.; *SunReserve, supra* n. 181, paras 694ff., 729ff.; *Antaris, supra* n. 189, paras 360ff.; *Novenergia, supra* n. 187, paras 647ff.; *ESPF, supra* n. 187, paras 508ff.; *9REN, supra* n. 188, paras 292ff.; *BayWa r.e., supra* n. 187, paras 463ff.; *Eskosol, supra* n. 205, paras 424ff.; *Greentech Energy Systems A/S, NovEnergia II Energy & Environment (SCA) SICAR, and NovEnergia II Italian Portfolio SA v. Italy*, SCC Case No. 2015/095, Final Award, 23 Dec. 2018, paras 445ff.; *Luxembourg Solar, supra* n. 179, paras 365ff.; *Belenergia, supra* n. 192, paras 571ff.; *Cavalum, supra* n. 185, paras 418ff.; *Cube Infrastructure Fund SICAV and others v. Spain*, ICSID Case No. ARB/15/20, Decision on Jurisdiction, Liability and Partial Decision on Quantum, 19 Feb. 2019, paras 383ff.; *OperaFund, supra* n. 198, paras 426, 480ff.; *SolEs Badajoz, supra* n. 196, para. 310; *Stadtwerke, supra* n. 189, paras 263ff.; *Watkins, supra* n. 198, paras 515ff.; *InfraRed Environmental, supra* n. 198, paras 366ff.; *Masdar, supra* n. 189, paras 482ff.; *Mamidoil Jetoil, supra* n. 189, paras 598ff.; *NextEra, supra* n. 189, paras 582ff.; *RWE, supra* n. 187, paras 452ff.
206. *SunReserve, supra* n. 181, para. 688.

commitments have to be specific'.[207] While some tribunals support the second approach,[208] others have followed the first approach.[209] Many tribunals have mentioned that the ECT requires that a 'balance be struck between two principles which are both recognized by this treaty'. On the one hand, 'the interest of investors in a stable and transparent legal framework as well as in respect for their legitimate expectations', and, on the other hand, the 'host State's sovereignty, notably including the ability to adapt its legislative and regulatory framework to new developments, which are unavoidable in a long-term cooperation'.[210] A detailed analysis of these questions is beyond the scope of this book.

In terms of liability and compensation, I have found 32 awards (out of 54) which held that the FET clause (sometimes alongside other clauses) had been breached.[211] The success rate for claimants is therefore 60%. That rate is higher than that of tribunals which have assessed stand-alone FET clauses (examined in Chapter section I). In one case the tribunal awarded no compensation.[212] In some of these cases, the quantum phase was still pending at the time of writing.[213] In two cases, the awards were later annulled.[214] I also have found 22 cases where the FET claim was rejected.[215]

207. *Masdar, supra* n. 189, paras 490ff. examining the question in detail.
208. *See*, for instance, *Hydro Energy, supra* n. 182, paras 584 ('in the absence of specific promises or representations by the State to the investor, the investor may not rely on an investment treaty as a kind of insurance policy against the risk of any changes in the host State's legal and economic framework'), 586 ('general laws are not promises, and the risk of change is for entrepreneurs to assess and assume').
209. *Silver Ridge, supra* n. 187, paras 406ff.; *STEAG, supra* n. 189, paras 506-508.
210. *Silver Ridge, supra* n. 187, para. 401. The question has been raised and debated in, *inter alia* (the list is not exhaustive): *Novenergia, supra* n. 187, para. 694 ('a balancing exercise, where the state's regulatory interests are weighed against the investors' legitimate expectations and reliance'); *Antaris, supra* n. 189, para. 360(8) and (9); *Infracapital, supra* n. 189, para. 566; *LSG, supra* n. 178, para. 1015; *Luxembourg Solar, supra* n. 179, para. 359. *See also, Eiser, supra* n. 179, para. 382.
211. *PV Investors, supra* n. 187, paras 557ff.; *AES, supra* n. 187, paras 376ff.; *9REN, supra* n. 188; *Cube Infrastructure, supra* n. 205 (EUR 33.7 million); *SolEs Badajoz, supra* n. 196 (EUR 40.98 million); *RREEF, supra* n. 189, Award, 11 Dec. 2019 (EUR 59.6 million); *OperaFund, supra* n. 198 (USD 29.3 million); *Watkins, supra* n. 198 (EUR 77 million); *InfraRed Environmental, supra* n. 198 (EUR 28.2 million); *Ascom, supra* n. 189 (USD 497 million); *Luxembourg Solar, supra* n. 179; *RREEF, supra* n. 189 (EUR 112 million); *Masdar, supra* n. 189 (EUR 64.5 million); *NextEra, supra* n. 189 (EUR 290.6 million); *Infracapital, supra* n. 189 (EUR 24.9 million); *MOL, supra* n. 189 (USD 167.8 million); *Kruck, supra* n. 189 (EUR 15 million); *STEAG, supra* n. 189 (EUR 27.6 million); *Petrobart, supra* n. 189 (USD 1.1 million); *Nykomb, supra* n. 189 (LVL 1.6 million); *Cavalum, supra* n. 185, Award, 29 Sep. 2022 (EUR 7.4 million); *Eurus, supra* n. 187 (EUR 106.2 million); *ESPF, supra* n. 187 (USD 16 million); *BayWa r.e., supra* n. 187, Award, 25 Jan. 2021 (EUR 22 million).
212. *AES, supra* n. 187.
213. *LSG, supra* n. 178; *Hydro Energy, supra* n. 182; *Sevilla Beheer, supra* n. 187.
214. *Novenergia, supra* n. 187 (EUR 53.3 million, the award was later set aside by a Swedish appellate court: Svea Court of Appeal Case No. T 4658-18, December 2022); *Eiser, supra* n. 179 (EUR 128 million, the award was annulled by a decision of the Annulment Committee, 11 Jun. 2020).
215. *Amto, supra* n. 200; *Eskosol, supra* n. 205; *Blusun, supra* n. 199; *Electrabel, supra* n. 200; *Belenergia, supra* n. 192; *Mamidoil Jetoil, supra* n. 189; *FREIF, supra* n. 189; *Photovoltaic, supra* n. 187; *Voltaic, supra* n. 187; *Mercuria, supra* n. 188; *Charanne, supra* n. 187; *Isolux, supra* n. 187; *Plama, supra* n. 179; *SunReserve, supra* n. 181; *WA Investments, supra* n. 186; *Silver Ridge,*

1.5 Conclusion on Stand-Alone FET Clauses

From my analysis of all awards (120 + 54 ECT awards) which have examined stand-alone FET clauses, the following points should be highlighted.

First, the vast majority of awards which took a position on the issue of the status of the clause and its relationship with the MST concluded that the clause should be interpreted to have an autonomous character (23 out of 29 awards, i.e., some 80% awards).[216] All these awards have concluded that the FET standard encompasses the protection of investors' legitimate expectations. Yet, most tribunals have narrowly defined the concept of legitimate expectations.

Second, the vast majority of tribunals (about 75%) did not formally take a position on the status of the FET clause. In fact, a larger number of awards (74 out of 120) did not mention the issue at all. Yet, the approach they adopted is very similar to that of other tribunals which did take a position on the status of the clause. They have all adopted broad interpretations when defining the content of FET.

Third, the success rate of FET claims is higher for tribunals which have expressly stated that a stand-alone FET clause has an 'autonomous' character compared to others which did not take a position on this question (2\3 versus 50%). The difference is much greater if one considers the awards rendered in the last five years, which are characterised by tribunals not taking a position at all on the issue and most of them (70%) not finding any breach. These findings suggest that when a tribunal discusses the status of the FET clause and takes a position on the matter, it is more likely that it will conclude that a breach has been committed.

Fourth, the most important finding is that the overall success rate for all 120 awards where tribunals have examined stand-alone FET clauses is high (63 awards out of 120). Claimants have a 50% chance of being successful. The success rate is even higher if one takes into account the 54 awards rendered under the ECT where claimants have been successful in 60% of cases. In any event, this success rate is much higher compared to that of awards examining FET clauses where the standard is expressly linked to the MST. Thus, NAFTA tribunals have found a breach in only 25% of claims (6 out of 27 awards).[217]

These findings are important given that new trends are emerging regarding how States are drafting FET clauses in their new investment treaties. As mentioned in the Introduction, States are increasingly expressing their willingness to adopt new FET clauses (or to modify existing ones) to better protect their needs and interests.[218] In this context, there is one important finding contained in this study that they may want to keep in mind. The possibility that a tribunal will interpret a stand-alone FET clause as

---

supra n. 187; *I.C.W.*, *supra* n. 187; *Festorino, supra* n. 189, paras 707ff.; *Antaris, supra* n. 189; *AES Summit, supra* n. 189; *Liman, supra* n. 190; *Stadtwerke, supra* n. 189.

216. The same is true for awards examining the ECT: almost all tribunals which have taken a position on the issue have adopted the same approach.

217. As further examined below in Chapter III, the success rate is higher for other (non-NAFTA) FET clauses also linked to the MST.

218. *See*, OECD 'Track 2' program: https://www.oecd.org/investment/investment-policy/investment-treaties.htm.

an implicit reference to the MST or 'international law' is very low (about 5% of awards). Faced with a stand-alone FET clause, a tribunal is very likely to adopt a broad interpretation of the standard. It is also more likely to conclude that a breach has been committed compared to tribunals assessing FET clauses linked to the MST.

II FET CLAUSES REFERRING TO 'INTERNATIONAL LAW'

Introduction

The above-mentioned 2023 OECD paper refers to a second category of FET clauses where the treatment is associated with 'international law' or 'principles of international law'.[219] The OECD paper indicates that an association with 'principles of international law' is found in 140 treaties and with 'international law' in 115 treaties.[220] Together these 255 treaties represent about 10% of all treaties containing an FET clause. According to two authors, tribunals have considered that such clauses should be equated with 'MST, given autonomous interpretation', or they have simply 'not taken any position for that relationship'.[221] As further explained below, the case law is not uniform, and tribunals have indeed adopted different views. I will show there are nevertheless clear patterns emerging from the analysis of these awards that particularly stand out when two different variants of this type of clause are examined separately.

FET clauses containing a reference to either 'international law' or 'principles of international law' can be divided into two groups. I will first examine how tribunals have interpreted clauses where the FET must be 'in accordance with international law' (section 2.1). A typical example of such clauses is found in these two treaties:

> Each Contracting Party shall accord investments or returns of investors of the other Contracting Party
>
> a. fair and equitable treatment in accordance with principles of international law, and
> b. full protection and security. (Canada-Egypt BIT, 1996, Art. II)
>
> Each Contracting Party shall in its Area accord to investments of investors of the other Contracting Party treatment in accordance with international law, including fair and equitable treatment and full protection and security. (Japan-Myanmar BIT, 2013, Art. 4).

Other treaties use a different formulation. They refer to the obligation to offer investors an FET, with this additional clarification: '[i]n no case shall such Investments be accorded treatment less favourable than that required by international law'. These clauses will be referred to as 'no less' FET clauses (section 2.2). This clause is an example:

219. OECD, *supra* n. 9, 11.
220. *Ibid.*
221. Emami & Rehna, *supra* n. 14, 90.

> Investment shall at all times be accorded fair and equitable treatment, shall enjoy full protection and security and shall in no case be accorded treatment less than that required by international law (Argentina-United States BIT, Art. 2)

It should be recalled that under Article 38(1) of the Statute,[222] custom is one of the three sources of 'international law' applied by the ICJ. It would therefore be entirely legitimate to expect that tribunals interpreting the words 'international law' in FET clauses would consider it as a reference to the MST, a rule of custom applicable in the context of international investment law. In fact, in its 2012 Report, UNCTAD said (in reference to 'in accordance with international law' FET clauses) that this 'formulation prevents the use of a purely semantic approach to the interpretation of the FET standard and is meant to ensure that the interpreter uses principles of international law, including, but not limited to, customary international law'.[223] In this context, the expression 'purely semantic approach' is undeniably a reference to the tendency of many tribunals to give a very broad interpretation to an FET clause whenever it contains no reference to 'international law' or the MST.[224] The UNCTAD Report suggests that the inclusion of the words 'international law' in an FET was meant to *prevent* tribunals from adopting such a broad approach. In fact, the Report also added that 'a tribunal faced with such language may not go beyond what the sources of international law dictate the scope and meaning of FET to be'.[225]

One surprising finding of my empirical study of all awards dealing with that type of clause is that the inclusion of the words 'international law' has *not at all prevented* tribunals from adopting whatever interpretation they wanted regarding the meaning and the scope of the clause. If the aim of adding these two words in an FET clause was to 'ensure' that the interpreter would not go beyond the traditional sources of international law, it has *not* been successful. Overall, tribunals have interpreted these clauses in very much the same way as stand-alone autonomous FET clauses containing *no* reference to 'international law'. Only a minority of tribunals have held that the term should be considered a reference to the MST or to custom. Another even more remarkable finding is that there is a clear correlation between the way a tribunal answers this question, the way it interprets the content of the standard, and how it deals with matters of liability and compensation. In other words, how a tribunal assesses the meaning of the inclusion of the words 'international law' in an FET clause has a direct impact on the way it determines whether a breach has been committed. I will show that when a tribunal considers that these words are *not* a reference to the MST, it is more likely to give it a broad interpretation and, in turn, to find that a violation has been committed. In contrast, tribunals that have considered that the term 'international law' in an FET clause is a reference to the MST have been much more reluctant to find a breach of the standard. The emergence of these two patterns of case law was something that UNCTAD did not envisage in its 2012 Report.

222. *Statute of the ICJ*, reprinted in International Court of Justice, Charter of the United Nations, Statute and Rules of Court and other Documents 61 (No. 4, 1978).
223. UNCTAD, *supra* n. 2, 22.
224. *See*, awards examined in Chapter I, Section 1.1.
225. UNCTAD, *supra* n. 2, 22.

2.1 FET Clauses Where Treatment Must Be 'in Accordance with International Law'

I have found 30 awards examining this type of clause. In several awards (11), the tribunals did not take a position on the issue.[226] In some of them, the tribunals did mention the debate, and the parties' arguments, but they decided to leave the question open.[227]

In the following sections, I will explain this:

- The vast majority of awards where tribunals took a position on the question of the status of this clause concluded that 'in accordance with international law' is *not* a reference to the MST under custom. I have found only a few awards adopting a different position (section 2.1.1).
- Yet, very few awards have actually examined what the sources of international law are (section 2.1.2).
- Most tribunals have interpreted this provision in very much the same way as other tribunals[228] which have considered that a stand-alone FET clause has an autonomous character (section 2.1.3).
- The findings of these tribunals on the question of the status of the clause and its relationship with the MST have had a direct impact in terms of how they have assessed matters of liability and compensation (section 2.1.4).

---

226. *See*, *Frontier Petroleum Services Ltd. v. Czech Republic*, UNCITRAL, Ad Hoc, Award, 12 Nov. 2010, paras 285ff.; *Eutelsat S.A. v. Mexico*, ICSID Case No. ARB(AF)/17/2, Award, 15 Sep. 2021, paras 384-385 (concluding that legitimate expectations is part of the FET, but had not been breached, at paras 405-409); *PSEG Global Inc. and Konya Ilgin Elektrik Üretim ve Ticaret Limited Şirketi v. Turkey*, ICSID Case No. ARB/02/5, Award, 19 Jan. 2007, paras 238ff. (the Tribunal found a breach of the FET, at para. 256); *Copper Mesa Mining Corporation v. Ecuador*, PCA No. 2012-2, Award, 15 Mar. 2016, para. 6.51; *Dan Cake S.A. v. Hungary*, ICSID Case No. ARB/12/9, Decision on Jurisdiction and Liability, 24 Aug. 2015, paras 145ff.; *Serafín García Armas and Karina García Gruber v. Venezuela*, PCA Case No. 2013-3, Award, 26 Apr. 2019, para. 342; *Gold Reserve Inc. v. Venezuela*, ICSID Case No. ARB(AF)/09/1, Award, 22 Sep. 2014, para. 567.
227. *Peter A. Allard v. Barbados*, PCA Case No. 2012-06, Award, 27 Jun. 2017, paras 192-193 (indicating that the debate was 'not material for the outcome of the case'); *Saint-Gobain Performance Plastics Europe v. Venezuela*, ICSID Case No. ARB/12/13, Decision on Liability and the Principles of Quantum, 30 Dec. 2016, para. 488 (indicating that the reference to the 'rules and principles of international law' 'might, in principle, raise doubts as to the correct interpretation of the FET clause', but that it 'does not have to make a finding in this regard' because the measures adopted would, if proven, 'also be in breach of the more restrictive FET concept as described by Respondent in this case'); *Tenaris S.A. and Talta - Trading e Marketing Sociedade Unipessoal Lda. v. Venezuela*, ICSID Case No. ARB/11/26, Award, 29 Jan. 2016 (referring to the position of the parties on whether the wording was a reference to an autonomous FET clause, but deciding not to take position, at paras 385ff.; the Tribunal found no FET breach, paras 423-424). *See also*, *Louis Dreyfus Armateurs SAS v. India*, PCA Case No. 2014-26, Award, 11 Sep. 2018, examining the India-France BIT which contains a unique FET clause whereby each party 'extend fair and equitable treatment in accordance with internationally established principles (...)'. The Tribunal found no breach of the clause and said that it was 'not necessary to resolve the Parties' considerable debate about the scope' of the clause (para. 369).
228. *See*, awards examined in Chapter I, Section 1.1.

2.1.1 *Is the Term 'International Law' in an FET Clause a Reference to the MST?*

Out of the 19 awards which examined the meaning of the term 'international law' in an FET clause, the vast majority (15 awards) have concluded that this is *not* a reference to the MST under custom. Other awards have come to different conclusions. In the next sections, I will examine the following points:

- Awards finding that 'international law' is not a reference to the MST (section 2.1.1.1).
- Awards downplaying the importance of the distinction (section 2.1.1.2).
- The *Infinito Gold* award: clash of ideas (section 2.1.1.3).
- Awards finding that 'international law' is a reference to the MST (section 2.1.1.4).

2.1.1.1 *Awards Finding That 'International Law' Is Not a Reference to the MST*

In *Tecmed*, the Tribunal said that the clause should be given an 'autonomous interpretation'.[229] Other tribunals have come to the same conclusion. In *Crystallex*, the Tribunal noted that in the absence of any reference to a minimum standard, the FET standard embodied in the Treaty 'cannot – by virtue of that formulation or otherwise – be equated to' the MST under custom.[230] For the Tribunal, it 'rather constitutes an *autonomous* treaty standard'.[231] The *Air Canada* Tribunal adopted the same position.[232] Other tribunals have simply indicated that the clause's language referenced 'international law', not the MST. One of the most comprehensive analyses was made by the *Vivendi* Tribunal indicating that the clause refers to FET 'in conformity with the principles of international law, and not to the minimum standard of treatment'.[233] The

229. *Tecmed, supra* n. 28, para. 155: 'The Arbitral Tribunal understands that the scope of the undertaking of fair and equitable treatment under Article 4(1) of the Agreement described above is that resulting from an autonomous interpretation (...).'
230. *Crystallex International Corporation v. Venezuela*, ICSID Case No. ARB(AF)/11/2, Award, 4 Apr. 2016, para. 530, adding that 'Unlike treaties such as NAFTA, which expressly incorporate the minimum standard of treatment, the Canada-Venezuela BIT nowhere refers to such minimum standard.'
231. *Ibid.*, emphasis added. *See also*: *Franck Charles Arif v. Moldova*, ICSID Case No. ARB/11/23, Award, 8 Apr. 2013, para. 529: 'the Tribunal is satisfied that the fair and equitable treatment standard in Article 3 of the France-Moldova BIT *is an autonomous standard* given: the title of Article 3; the use of the expression "fair and equitable treatment" three times in Article 3; the elaboration of a series of non-exclusive obstacles to fair and equitable treatment in Article 3, as well as the object and purpose of the BIT already referred to', emphasis added.
232. *Air Canada v. Venezuela*, ICSID Case No. ARB(AF)/17/1, Award, 13 Sep. 2021, para. 447: 'The Tribunal reads this provision *as a stand-alone norm*. It is clearly not synonymous with the standard of protection in the NAFTA context. The fact that Article II(2) refers to "principles of international law" does not imply that these "principles" are synonymous with customary international law or to the "international minimum standard",' emphasis added.
233. *Compañía de Aguas del Aconquija SA and Vivendi Universal SA v. Argentina*, ICSID Case No. ARB/97/3, Second Presentation of the Case, Award, 20 Aug. 2007, para. 7.4.6.

Tribunal saw no 'basis for equating principles of international law with the minimum standard of treatment' for the following three reasons:

> First, the reference to principles of international law supports a broader reading that invites consideration of a wider range of international law principles than the minimum standard alone. Second, the wording of Article 3 requires that the fair and equitable treatment conform to the principles of international law, but the requirement for conformity can just as readily set a floor as a ceiling on the Treaty's fair and equitable treatment standard. Third, the language of the provision suggests that one should also look to contemporary principles of international law, not only to principles from almost a century ago.[234]

The *Vivendi* Tribunal also referred, *inter alia*, to the above-mentioned article by Mann which stated that the FET clause 'envisage[s] conduct which goes far beyond' the MST and 'afford[s] protection to a greater extent' than under that standard; the terms 'are to be understood and implied independently and autonomously' from the MST.[235]

The same approach has been subsequently adopted by other tribunals.[236] They have held that 'in accordance with international law' is *not* synonymous with the MST under international law.[237] The *Global Telecom* award illustrates this reasoning:

> Dealing first with Canada's argument that the fair and equitable treatment standard set out in the BIT is limited to the minimum standard of treatment under customary international law, the Tribunal concludes that there is no basis for such an interpretation. Any such limitation runs counter to the explicit terms used in Article II(2)(a) and to the ordinary meaning to be given to those terms in their context and in the light of the BIT's object and purpose.

234. *Ibid.*, para. 7.4.7.
235. *Ibid.*, para. 7.4.8, quoting Mann, *supra* n. 41.
236. *Total S.A. v. Argentina*, ICSID Case No. ARB/04/01, Decision on Liability, 27 Dec. 2010, para. 125; *Valores Mundiales, S.L. and Consorcio Andino S.L. v. Venezuela*, ICSID Case No. ARB/13/11, Award, 25 Jul. 2017, para. 530; *Anglo American PLC v. Venezuela*, ICSID Case No. ARB(AF)/14/1, Award, 18 Jan. 2019, para. 439; *SAUR International v. Argentina*, ICSID Case No. ARB/04/4, Decision on Jurisdiction and Liability, 6 Jun. 2012, paras 491ff. (while the Tribunal does not formally take a position on the issue, its reasoning leaves no doubt that it did not consider that the clause was a reference to the MST or custom); *Infinito Gold Ltd. v. Costa Rica*, ICSID Case No. ARB/14/5, Award, 3 Jun. 2021, para. 332; *Arif, supra* n. 231, para. 529; *Perenco Ecuador Ltd. v. Ecuador and Empresa Estatal Petróleos del Ecuador (Petroecuador)*, ICSID Case No. ARB/08/6, Decision on Remaining Issues of Jurisdiction and on Liability, 12 Sep. 2014, para. 557 ('This particular formulation of the standard is not tethered to the international minimum standard of treatment under customary international law'); *Global Telecom Holding S.A.E. v. Canada*, ICSID Case No. ARB/16/16, Award, 27 Mar. 2020, para. 484. *See also*: *EDF International S.A., SAUR International S.A. and León Participaciones Argentinas S.A. v. Argentina*, ICSID Case No. ARB/03/23, Award, 11 Jun. 2012, para. 999, indicating that it 'need not decide whether Article 3 establishes an autonomous and independent standard of fairness or simply coincides with customary international minimum standard'. Yet it also said that the clause does not refer to the MST, but rather to 'principles of international law', and that the treaty 'thus invites consideration of a wider range of principles related to fairness and equity'. The Tribunal also rejected the relevance of NAFTA case law: 'Respondent's reliance on NAFTA jurisprudence is equally unavailing. The very title NAFTA Article 1105(1) is – Minimum Standard of Treatment. The Argentina-France BIT contains no such language' (para. 1003).
237. *Air Canada, supra* n. 232, para. 447.

> Article II(2)(b) refers to fair and equitable treatment in conformity with principles of international law; it does not refer to the minimum standard of treatment. The authentic French and Arabic texts of the BIT are identical to the English text. This Tribunal finds no support for Canada's endeavour to override the terms of the BIT and to draft into Article II(2)(b) a reference to the minimum standard that would limit the potential application of a wider range of international law principles than the minimum standard alone.[238]

The *Global Telecom* Tribunal also noted that in other international treaties to which Canada is a party, explicit reference is made to the MST. It explained that the concept 'was well known to Canada when negotiating and signing the BIT', but that 'the BIT does not make reference' to it.[239] As a result, the Tribunal said that it had to 'construe the FET obligation in accordance with principles of international law'.[240] Similarly, the *Suez* Tribunal explained that three views existed on the issue of the status of FET clauses:

> A survey of practice and scholarship on this question reveals three views: 1) that fair and equitable treatment must be measured only against the minimum standard required by customary international law; 2) that it must be measured against international law including all sources; and 3) that it must be measured against an independent self-contained treaty standard.[241]

The *Suez* Tribunal noted that the clause in the BIT referred to 'the principles of international law', not to the MST. It explained that the 'formulation' MST 'is so well known and so well established in international law that one can assume that if France and Argentina had intended to limit the content of fair and equitable treatment to the minimum international standard they would have used that formulation specifically'.[242] The Tribunal noted that the parties did not.[243] In his separate opinion, Nikken disagreed with this interpretation.[244]

Finally, reference should be made to the rather unique, and slightly confusing, reasoning of the *OKO Pankki Oyj* Tribunal. It first indicated that it must 'give effect to its reference to international law, which is expressed as a form of qualification to its FET standard', adding that 'this reference cannot here be disregarded by the Tribunal as meaningless or redundant as a matter of treaty interpretation'.[245] On the one hand, it said that the aim of the reference was that the FET standard would *not* be 'interpreted as a wholly autonomous concept, thereby enabling a tribunal (arguably) to apply its own subjective or impressionistic conclusions as to whether a respondent state had

238. *Global Telecom, supra* n. 236, paras 484-485.
239. *Ibid.*, para. 487.
240. *Ibid.*
241. *Suez, supra* n. 124, para. 184.
242. *Ibid.*
243. *Ibid.*
244. *Ibid.*, separate opinion, Nikken believing that the terms 'principles of international law...' found in the France-Argentina BIT is 'a clear reference to the minimum standard, the only standard on Treatment of aliens in general international law at the time when the treaty was concluded' (para. 8).
245. *OKO Pankki Oyj and others v. Estonia*, ICSID Case No. ARB/04/6, Award, 19 Nov. 2007, para. 236.

acted "fairly" or "equitably", but rather to ensure that their FET standard was a recognized and defined standard in international law'.[246] Yet, on the other hand, it also stated that the standard in question was *not* the MST.[247] While it noted that the FET standard was 'difficult to define, in the abstract, as a matter of international law', it also said that it 'clearly provides a greater protection for the foreign investor' than the MST, which the Tribunal seems to equate with the *Neer* case.[248] Later in the award, the Tribunal said that it was 'unnecessary for this Tribunal to resolve the debate over the exact content of the minimum standard under international law' because 'the issue here (...) relates to an *autonomous* FET standard providing greater protection to a covered investor than the minimum standard'.[249] At the end of the day, while the reasoning is rather ambiguous, it seems that, at the very least, the Tribunal did not consider that the clause was a reference to the MST.

In sum, the awards mentioned in the previous paragraphs have considered it 'appropriate' to follow 'the more liberal approach, which focuses on the broadly consistent elements of "fair and equitable"'.[250] For them, the requirement to conform with international law is just a floor. The FET standard therefore offers *better* protection than the MST, just like any stand-alone 'autonomous' FET clause.

2.1.1.2 Awards Downplaying the Importance of the Distinction

While the tribunals mentioned in the previous section clearly interpreted the FET clause as imposing a different standard than the MST, some have also, at the same time, downplayed the importance of the distinction. For instance, the *Arif* Tribunal was faced with a clause referring to 'public international law principles' and said that it was 'satisfied' that it was an 'autonomous standard'.[251] But it also indicated that 'neither party has raised the question of whether this language limits' the FET standard to the MST under custom and that it was 'increasingly of historic significance as the rapidly expanding practice on FET clauses in treaties accelerates the development of customary international law'.[252] This comment suggests that the Tribunal considered that the level of treatment was the same under both the FET treaty standard and the MST.

Importantly, the reasoning of these tribunals and others indicating that there is no difference between the two standards is based on a controversial assumption that the level of protection under the MST has evolved rapidly in recent decades and now provides for basically the same level as under an FET treaty standard (a point further discussed below).[253] For instance, the *SAUR* Tribunal said that this question was rather

246. *Ibid.*, para. 237.
247. *Ibid.*
248. *Ibid.*, para. 238.
249. *Ibid.*, para. 246, emphasis added.
250. *Air Canada, supra* n. 232, paras 446-447.
251. *Arif, supra* n. 231, para. 529.
252. *Ibid.*
253. *See*, Part III.

dogmatic[254] and that as a result of the evolution of the MST under custom, it was no longer relevant.[255] Similarly, the *Anglo-American* Tribunal said that 'today such a debate is somewhat sterile' given the evolution of the MST since the 1926 *Neer* case.[256] The *Valores* Tribunal took the same position.[257]

2.1.1.3 The Infinito Gold Award: A Clash of Ideas

The *Infinito Gold* award contains a very interesting analysis regarding the meaning of the expression 'principles of international law'. The majority of the Tribunal first explained that the FET clause did not refer to custom or the MST. It rejected the argument that the text of the FET clause was 'very similar' to that of NAFTA Article 1105(1) because that provision is expressly entitled MST, 'a reference that is absent from Article II(2)(a) of the BIT'.[258] In reference to the Notes of Interpretation issued in 2001 by the NAFTA parties (referring to the 'customary international law minimum standard of treatment of aliens'), the majority noted that no 'note of interpretation has been issued by the Contracting Parties to the BIT'.[259] The majority explained why the term used in the BIT was not a reference to the MST:

> Applying the general rule of interpretation set out in Article 31 of the VCLT, the majority of the Tribunal cannot conclude that the content of Article II(2)(a) of the BIT is limited to the MST under customary international law.
>
> Starting first with the ordinary meaning of the terms, there is nothing in the text of the BIT that limits the FET standard to customary international law. Article II(2)(a) provides that the Contracting Parties are required to accord to investments fair and equitable treatment 'in accordance with principles of international law'. (...)
>
> The Tribunal thus concludes that, in accordance with their ordinary meaning, the terms used by Article II(2)(a) cannot be interpreted as a reference to customary international law in general or to the MST in particular.
>
> There is likewise nothing in the context of the provision that would lead to restricting the FET standard to the MST. Neither the text of other provisions of the BIT, nor its preamble or annexes, limit the FET standard to customary international law. To the contrary, when chosing the applicable law, the Contracting Parties to the BIT made a distinction between 'rules of international law' and 'principles of international law', which distinction is unhelpful to decide whether

254. *SAUR, supra* n. 236, para. 491: 'En réalité, la question de savoir si le "traitement juste et équitable conformément aux principes du droit international" défini dans l'APRI coïncide ou non avec le niveau dit "minimal de traitement dû aux étrangers selon le droit international coutumier" constitue une discussion plutôt dogmatique et conceptualiste.'
255. *Ibid.*, para. 494.
256. *Anglo American, supra* n. 236, para. 442.
257. *Valores, supra* n. 236, para. 236: 'El Tribunal coincide con la apreciación de éste y otros tribunales que han llegado a la misma conclusión. En efecto, el concepto de "nivel mínimo de trato" se ha ampliado a tal punto que hoy otorga una protección muy similar a la acordada en virtud del estándar de tratamiento justo y equitativo. En consecuencia, la discusión planteada carece de efectos prácticos en este caso, toda vez que el nivel de protección otorgado a las inversiones protegidas bajo el Tratado es sustancialmente el mismo, independiente de cómo se interprete la referencia al 'Derecho Internacional' contenida en el Artículo IV(1) del APPRI.'
258. *Infinito Gold, supra* n. 236, para. 330.
259. *Ibid.*

> Article II(2)(a) refers to customary international law only or to international law in its entirety.[260]

Ultimately, the majority concluded that Article II(2)(a) of the BIT 'provides for an *autonomous FET standard* and is not limited to the MST under customary international law'.[261] This reference to an 'autonomous FET standard' was strongly rejected by Stern in her dissenting opinion. She said that this conclusion 'does not give any meaning, any effet utile to the reference in the BIT to the principles of international law, which are completely ignored'.[262] For her, 'international law has been eliminated, although it is mentioned in the BIT', adding that 'the result would have been exactly the same, in the absence of the expression "in accordance with principles of international law"'.[263] She also said that the scope of the FET as an autonomous standard 'is not defined in customary international law' and that this choice by the majority 'allowed' them 'to decide freely what are the sources of international law and what are the contours of concepts like FET or denial of justice, without any constraint coming from principles of international law, as required by the BIT, nor indeed from the general principles of international law referred to erroneously by the majority'.[264] For her, 'the FET standard is limited by the BIT to the Minimum Standard of Treatment under customary international law'.[265]

Coming back to the majority's reasoning in *Infinito Gold*, it rejected the argument raised by the respondent that there was an 'agreement' made by the contracting parties (under Article 31(2) VCLT) 'establishing that Article II(2)(a) of the BIT must be interpreted as limiting the FET standard to the MST under customary international law'.[266] The respondent had also argued that Costa Rica and Canada had 'confirmed in this arbitration that Article II(2)(a) of the BIT is limited to the MST', and that this constitutes a 'subsequent agreement between the parties' pursuant to Article 31(3) of the VCLT that 'demonstrates the intent of the Treaty's Contracting States'.[267] The majority of the Tribunal did not find that agreement convincing:

> Costa Rica's and Canada's concurrent positions in this arbitration do not amount to an agreement within the meaning of Article 31(3) of the VCLT. (...) Yet, the Contracting Parties must have agreed to a particular interpretation. This requires a joint manifestation of consent from the Contracting Parties, or at least an offer and acceptance, evidencing their common intention that Article II(2)(a) of the BIT reflects the MST under customary international law.
>
> No such consent is found here. The submissions made by Costa Rica and Canada in this arbitration reflect legal arguments put forward in the context of this

260. *Ibid.*, paras 331, 332, 334. 335.
261. *Ibid.*, para. 350, emphasis added.
262. *Ibid.*, dissenting opinion of Stern, para. 84.
263. *Ibid.*
264. *Ibid.*, para. 97.
265. *Ibid.*, paras 79, 81, 95, 98 ('I think that arbitrators have a mission to fulfil in the framework of the provision giving them jurisdiction. When they are required to interpret concepts in accordance with principles of international law, their power is limited by the content of these principles, i.e., by customary international law').
266. *Ibid.*, majority, para. 336.
267. *Ibid.*, para. 337.

> dispute to advance their respective interests. Although they happen to coincide, they do not reflect an agreement as just described over the interpretation of the BIT. Even if the Tribunal could infer an 'agreement' from the Contracting States' submissions, quod non, this agreement would postdate the commencement of this arbitration and the Tribunal could not take it into consideration in favour of one litigant to the detriment of the other without incurring the risk of breaching the latter's due process rights.[268]

The majority of the Tribunal also referred to arguments raised by both Canada (intervening as the non-disputing party) and Costa Rica in the context of *other* arbitral proceedings about the meaning to be given to Article II(2)(a) of the BIT. For the majority of the Tribunal, 'these sources reflect Canada's and Costa Rica's litigation posture, and do not qualify as means of treaty interpretation under Article 31 of the VCLT', adding that 'none of these cases was based on the Treaty and thus these statements cannot establish a "practice in the application of the treaty" within the meaning of Article 31(3)(b) of the VCLT'.[269] It should be added that the award also dealt with other material referred to by the parties regarding the meaning to be given to the FET clause.[270]

2.1.1.4 Awards Finding that 'International Law' Is a Reference to the MST

I have found only four cases where tribunals considered that the wording 'in accordance with international law' was a reference to custom.

In the *Koch Minerals* case, the Tribunal had to interpret Article 4(1) of the Switzerland-Venezuela BIT stating that the respondent has to 'provide, in accordance with the rules and principles of International Law, investments in its territory of investors of the other Contracting Party fair and equitable treatment'. The Tribunal stated that 'these words import the customary international law minimum standards, rather than any autonomous higher standards'.[271] For the Tribunal, the 'additional express wording' was considered 'conclusive in confirming the meaning of the FET and FPS standards as the duties imposed by customary international law and in precluding an independent or autonomous meaning'.[272] The Tribunal also referred to another award (*Flughafen v. Venezuela*) where that Tribunal had reached the same conclusion about this provision.[273]

268. *Ibid.*, paras 338-339.
269. *Ibid.*, para. 344.
270. In this context, the Tribunal made this interesting remark: 'Even accepting that the BIT was drafted on the basis of Canada's model FIPA, which in turn was based on or inspired by NAFTA Chapter 11, this does not necessarily mean that it offers investors identical protections as the NAFTA. Faced with a treaty provision, the Tribunal must interpret it in accordance with the rules of interpretation of the VCLT, in particular its text and context; it cannot dispense with doing so simply because a provision might have been inspired by another treaty.' (*Ibid.*, para. 349).
271. *Koch Minerals Sarl and Koch Nitrogen International Sarl v. Venezuela*, ICSID Case No. ARB/11/19, Award, 30 Oct. 2017, para. 8.42.
272. *Ibid.*, para. 8.44.
273. *Ibid.*, referring to *Flughafen Zürich A.G. and Gestión e Ingeniería IDC S.A. v. Venezuela*, ICSID Case No. ARB/10/19, Award, 12 Nov. 2014, para. 573, indicating that the provision is 'requiring

It should be added that the *Rusoro* Tribunal also stated that the words 'principles of international law' were meant to refer to MST. But it also said that this whole debate had 'become dogmatic' as a result of the evolution of custom and that now 'there is no substantive difference in the level of protection afforded by both standards' (they have 'converged').[274] Finally, in *Vannessa Ventures*, the Tribunal first 'recognize[d] that there are different formulations of the precise content of the FET standard', but added that what 'they all have in common' is that it 'requires that the treatment of investments not fall below a minimum standard of fairness and equitableness that all investors have a right to expect'.[275] The expression may be a reference to the MST under custom. This is a plausible reading given that the Tribunal used the wording 'minimum standard' elsewhere in its award and concluded that the treatment given to the investor 'cannot be regarded as falling below that minimum standard'.[276]

2.1.2 Very Few Tribunals Have Examined What Are the Sources of International Law

If the vast majority of tribunals have concluded that the term 'in accordance with international law' was not meant to be a reference to the MST, one question remains: what is the standard of protection under 'international law'? One of the perhaps surprising findings of this study is that very few tribunals have actually examined what the sources of 'international law' are.[277]

One rare example of an award doing the analysis is the majority in the *Total* case. It stated that the phrase FET 'in conformity with the principles of international law' 'could not be read as treatment required by the MST under international law'.[278] But it also mentioned that this was 'irrespective of the issue of whether today there really is a difference' between the MST and 'what international law generally requires as to treatment of foreign investors and their investments'.[279] More specifically, the majority said that it would have to look at 'general principles' (as well as 'public international

that FET be defined in accordance with International Law necessarily incorporates a reference to the level of protection that International Law provides to foreigners, that is, to what is known as the customary minimum standard'.

274. *Rusoro Mining Ltd. v. Venezuela*, ICSID Case No. ARB(AF)/12/5, Award, 22 Aug. 2016, paras 520-521, also indicating: 'But the incorporation of the CIM Standard into the definition of the FET does not provoke a major disruption in the level of protection: the CIS Standard has developed and today is indistinguishable from the FET standard and grants investors an equivalent level of protection as the latter.'
275. *Vannessa Ventures Ltd. v. Venezuela*, ICSID Case No. ARB(AF)04/6, Award, 16 Jan. 2013, para. 222.
276. *Ibid. See also*, for instance, at para. 227 ('The Tribunal does not consider that the delays in this case are of an order that constitute conduct that falls below the minimum standard demanded by the Treaty').
277. For instance, *see García Armas, supra* n. 226, para. 342, simply indicating that 'conforme al Derecho Internacional', significando que deben aplicarse los criterios desarrollados por el derecho internacional de las inversiones'.
278. *Total, supra* n. 236, para. 125. In his dissenting opinion Alvarez agreed with the majority on this point, paras 13ff.
279. *Total, supra* n. 236, para. 125.

law')[280] 'in a non-BIT context'.[281] For the Tribunal, these 'general principles' were good faith and legitimate expectations (applying a narrow approach of the concept[282]).[283]

Another example is the *Gold Reserve* award. The Tribunal said that to determine what the 'principles of international law' are, it 'must consider the present status of development of public international law in the field of investment protection'.[284] The Tribunal then mentioned this evolution of 'public international law principles',[285] which include 'general principles of law',[286] and referred to awards having 'underscored the central role of an investor's legitimate expectations' in the FET analysis and others which have stated that it 'requires that any regulation of an investment be done in a transparent manner'.[287] It referred to the protection of 'legitimate expectations' as one of the 'legal sources' of the FET standard.[288] It concluded that in this case, 'the number, variety and seriousness of the breaches make the FET violation by Respondent particularly egregious' and that compensation for such breaches 'should reflect the seriousness of the violation'.[289] It awarded USD 713 million in compensation. Similarly, the *Suez* Tribunal first noted that 'principles of international law' in the Argentina-France BIT 'means just what it says', i.e., that the Tribunal must examine 'all relevant sources of international law', not just the MST.[290] The Tribunal then said that 'to borrow the terminology of Hans Kelsen, it is no exaggeration to say that the obligation of a host State to accord fair and equitable treatment to foreign investors is

280. *Ibid.*, para. 131, indicating that 'unilateral acts, statements and conduct by States may be the source of legal obligations'.
281. *Ibid.*, para. 127.
282. *Ibid.*, para. 117, indicating that 'the expectation of the investor is undoubtedly "legitimate", and hence subject to protection under the fair and equitable treatment clause, if the host State has explicitly assumed a specific legal obligation for the future, such as by contracts, concessions or stabilisation clauses on which the investor is therefore entitled to rely as a matter of law'. *See also*, at paras 118ff., referring to 'specific commitments' and that this 'does not amount to a requirement for the host State to freeze its legal system for the investor's benefit' (adding that 'a general stabilization requirement would go beyond what the investor can legitimately expect').
283. *Ibid.*, indicating that 'since the concept of legitimate expectations is based on the requirement of good faith', it follows that 'a comparative analysis of the protection of legitimate expectations in domestic jurisdictions is justified at this point' (para. 128). The Tribunal used a 'comparative analysis' of a few domestic legal orders regarding the concept of legitimate expectations. The Tribunal stated that 'while the scope and legal basis of the principle varies, it has been recognized lately both in civil law and in common law jurisdictions within well-defined limits' (para. 128).
284. *Gold Reserve, supra* n. 226, para. 567, indicating that to determine the 'principles of international law', it 'must consider the present status of development of public international law in the field of investment protection'.
285. *Ibid.*
286. *Ibid.*, para. 575.
287. *Ibid.*, para. 570.
288. *Ibid.*, para. 576, adding that 'based on converging considerations of good faith and legal security, the concept of legitimate expectations is found in different legal traditions' under a 'comparative analysis of many domestic legal systems'.
289. *Ibid.*, para. 615.
290. *Suez, supra* n 124, para. 185, indicating that the ordinary meaning of the words is 'the legal principles derived from all sources of international law'. It then cited 'authoritative documents' employing the term 'international law', Art. 38 of the Statute of the ICJ, which 'contain no implication that the term is limited to' the MST.

the *Grundnorm* or basic norm of international investment law'.[291] It defined the concept of legitimate expectations rather broadly.[292]

The question of the identification of the sources of international law led to a very interesting debate in the *Infinito Gold* case (mentioned above) between the majority and one dissenting arbitrator. The majority of the Tribunal said that the terms used ('in accordance with principles of international law') could be 'understood as a reference to the general principles of law' or the 'various sources of international law' under Article 38(1)(c) of the Statute of the International Court of Justice (ICJ Statute), but not 'as a reference to customary international law, which is but one source of international law and is distinct from general principles'.[293] For them, the words 'cannot be interpreted as a reference to customary international law in general or to the MST in particular'.[294] Stern in her dissenting opinion disagreed. She first noted that the majority had 'add[ed] a word to Article II(2)(a) when they concentrate[d] their analysis on "general principles" of international law, while the text refers to "principles" of international law'.[295] In a very detailed analysis, she explained that 'general principles' of international law were not the same as 'principles' of international law.[296] For her, the expression 'principles of international law' 'can easily be understood as merely a reference to general international law' and to 'international law as applied among all nations, which is customary international law'. Accordingly, for her 'the FET standard is limited by the BIT to the Minimum Standard of Treatment under customary international law'.[297]

2.1.3 *Most Tribunals Have Interpreted the Provision in the Same Way as a Stand-Alone Clause Having an Autonomous Character*

As mentioned above, whether the MST includes an obligation to protect an investor's legitimate expectations and a general obligation of transparency is a controversial question. Many tribunals which have examined FET clauses linked to the MST have denied that the standard includes these two elements.[298] One of the most interesting features of awards that have examined 'in accordance with international law' clauses is that the vast majority did so in very much the same way as other tribunals which have considered stand-alone FET clauses to have an autonomous character.[299] They have considered that the FET standard includes a protection of investors' legitimate

291. *Ibid.*, para. 188, citing Hans Kelsen, *The Pure Theory of Law* (1934).
292. *Ibid.*, paras 222-223.
293. *Infinito Gold*, *supra* n. 236, para. 332.
294. *Ibid.*, para. 334 ('in accordance with their ordinary meaning, the terms used by Article II(2)(a) cannot be interpreted as a reference to customary international law in general or to the MST in particular').
295. *Ibid.*, Stern, dissenting opinion, para. 77.
296. *Ibid.*
297. *Ibid.*, paras 79, 81, 95, 98.
298. The question is further examined in Chapter III, below.
299. *See*, awards mentioned above in Chapter I, section 1.1. It should be added that some awards do not examine in detail the content of the FET standard: *Vivendi*, *supra* n. 233, paras 7.4.7ff.

expectations. Many have also recognised a general obligation of transparency, and some have also referred to proportionality.[300]

As mentioned above, *Tecmed* was the first award examining an 'in accordance with international law' clause. The Tribunal gave the broadest possible interpretation of the concepts of legitimate expectation and transparency.[301] Following in the footsteps of the *Tecmed* award, other tribunals have broadly defined the concept of legitimate expectations.[302] For instance, in *EDF* the Tribunal mentioned that the NAFTA Note of interpretation 'instructed' arbitral tribunals to 'take such a restrictive approach', but that 'nothing of that nature has been introduced in connection with the Argentina-France BIT'.[303] In other words, it considered that it could adopt a broader approach than the one adopted by NAFTA tribunals. For the Tribunal, this language 'invites consideration of a wider range of principles related to fairness and equity', including 'the duty to aim for respect of specific commitments, such calculation of tariffs in dollars'.[304] It also said that the 'delineation of the contours' of the FET standard under this clause 'depends on the factual context of the host state's actions, including the evolution of the prevalent economic and social conditions'.[305] In the *Allard* case, the Tribunal said that the debate about the status of the clause was 'not material for the outcome of the case' because the entire FET claim was based on allegation of non-respect of the investor's legitimate expectations. It affirmed that 'whether Article II(2)(a) creates an autonomous FET standard or corresponds to the minimum standard of treatment, in each case it includes the protection of an investor's legitimate expectations arising from a host State's representations, under certain conditions'.[306] In other words, it considered that an obligation to protect investors' legitimate expectations exists under the MST. It should be added that most tribunals examining this clause have nevertheless given a rather narrow definition of the concept of legitimate expectations.[307] A good example is the position of the *Rusoro* Tribunal:

300. *García Armas, supra* n. 226, paras 342, 342ff.
301. *Tecmed, supra* n. 28, paras 153-154.
302. *Vivendi, supra* n. 233, paras 222-223.
303. *EDF, supra* n. 236, para. 1003.
304. *Ibid.*, para. 1001.
305. *Ibid.*, para. 1004.
306. *Allard, supra* n. 227, paras 192-193.
307. *Arif, supra* n. 231, para. 531; *Crystallex, supra* n. 230, paras 546-547; *Total, supra* n. 236, para. 117; *Anglo American, supra* n. 236, paras 443, 467-469 (but it also included transparency and predictability as part of the FET standard), at paras 443, 461; *Global Telecom, supra* n. 236, paras 491, 539 (but at the same time, the Tribunal referred to transparency as part of the FET standard, at paras 491, 570, 571); *Infinito Gold, supra* n. 236, paras 355, 515, 519 (in her dissenting opinion, Stern does not refute these findings); *Allard, supra* n. 227, para. 194; *Saint-Gobain, supra* n. 227, para. 531; *Copper Mesa, supra* n. 226, paras 6.51, 6.61, 6.81; *Frontier Petroleum, supra* n. 226, paras 285ff.; *Air Canada, supra* n. 232, para. 448 (indicating that 'adopting a liberal FET approach does not lower the threshold for finding a violation' and using a rather narrow conception of legitimate expectations and transparency); *Perenco, supra* n. 236, paras 559ff.; *OKO Pankki Oyj, supra* n. 245, para. 246; *Koch Minerals, supra* n. 271, para. 8.47. *See also, Gold Reserve, supra* n. 226, paras 570, 571. The Tribunal underscored the 'central role of an investor's legitimate expectations' in the FET analysis, but it applied a nuance approach. On the one hand, it broadly defined the concept: 'Legitimate expectations are created when a State's conduct is such that an investor may reasonably rely on that conduct as being consistent.' On the other hand, it also indicated that such expectations are based on

The required threshold of propriety must be defined by the tribunal after a careful analysis of facts and circumstances, and taking into consideration a number of factors, including among others the following:

- whether there has been harassment, coercion, abuse of power or other bad faith conduct by the host State;
- whether the State had made specific representations to the investor, prior to the investment;
- whether the State's actions or omissions can be labelled as arbitrary, discriminatory or inconsistent;
- whether the State has respected the principles of due process and transparency when adopting the offending measures;
- whether the State has failed to offer a stable and predictable legal framework, breaching the investor's legitimate expectations.

In evaluating the State's conduct, the Tribunal must balance the investor's right to be protected against improper State conduct, with other legally relevant interests and countervailing factors. First among these factors is the principle that legislation and regulation are dynamic and that States enjoy a sovereign right to amend legislation and to adopt new regulation in the furtherance of public interest. The right to regulate, however, does not authorize States to act in an arbitrary or discriminatory manner or to disguise measures targeted against a protected investor under the cloak of general legislation. Other countervailing factors affect the investor: it is the investor's duty to perform an appropriate pre-investment due diligence review and to show a proper conduct both before and during the investment.[308]

2.1.4 *The Impact of Tribunals' Findings Regarding Matters of Liability and Compensation*

The question of how a tribunal analyses the status of an 'in accordance with international law' FET clause has had a direct impact on how it addresses matters of liability and compensation. In only one-third of awards, tribunals have not found a breach of the FET clause (11 awards out of 30).[309] In the majority of cases, about two-thirds of awards (19 out of 30), tribunals have concluded that the FET clause had been breached. Some have found a breach but decided not to award any compensation.[310] Most

'undertakings and representations made explicitly or implicitly by the host State'. *See also, PSEG Global, supra* n. 226, indicating that 'legitimate expectations by definition require a promise of the administration on which the Claimants rely to assert a right that needs to be observed' (para. 241), but also referring (at para. 253) to the fact that no investor 'may reasonably expect that the circumstances prevailing at the time the investment is made remain totally unchanged'.

308. *Rusoro Mining, supra* n. 274, paras 524-525.

309. *Anglo American, supra* n. 236, para. 443; *Global Telecom, supra* n. 236; *Allard, supra* n. 227, paras 192-193 (indicating that the debate was 'not material for the outcome of the case'); *Saint-Gobain, supra* n. 227; *Koch Minerals, supra* n. 271; *Rusoro Mining, supra* n. 274; *Vannessa Ventures, supra* n. 275, para. 232; *Frontier Petroleum, supra* n. 226, para. 547; *Eutelsat, supra* n. 226, paras 384-385, 405-409; *Louis Dreyfus, supra* n. 227, para. 369; *Tenaris, supra* n. 227, paras 423-424.

310. *Infinito Gold, supra* n. 236, para. 350, majority of the Tribunal; *PSEG Global, supra* n. 226, para. 256.

tribunals have awarded large compensations.[311] Some tribunals have awarded compensation for breaches of the FET clause and other provisions.[312] Other tribunals have awarded compensation for breach of the FET clause alone.[313]

2.1.5 Conclusion Regarding 'in Accordance with International Law' FET Clauses

Most awards which have taken a position on the status of an 'in accordance with international law' FET clause have concluded that this is *not* a reference to the MST under custom. They have considered that under this clause the FET standard offers better protection than under the MST and have, in practice, interpreted the clause in very much the same way as other tribunals have regarding stand-alone FET clauses having an autonomous character.[314] For instance, they have adopted broad interpretations, by including the concepts of legitimate expectations (often defined narrowly) and transparency. These broad interpretations led the majority of tribunals (two-thirds of awards) to find a breach of FET and to award compensation.

In fact, whether a breach of the FET obligation was found by the tribunal seems to be clearly connected to the way it considered the meaning of the clause. The vast majority of tribunals (13 out of 15 awards) which concluded that the clause 'in accordance with international law' is *not* a reference to the MST *have found* a breach of the FET clause.[315] In contrast, three of the four awards where the tribunal held that this clause *was* a reference to the MST came to the conclusion that *no* FET violation had been committed (and the amount of compensation in the only award which came to a different conclusion is rather low: USD 10 million[316]).[317] There is therefore a clear correlation between the way a tribunal interprets an FET clause (and its relation to the MST) and its findings in terms of liability. When a tribunal considers that the clause is *not* a reference to the MST, it is more likely to give it a broad interpretation and, in turn, to find that a violation has been committed.

311. *See*, *Dan Cake*, *supra* n. 226, where the Tribunal found a breach of the FET clause but the final award on quantum (21 Nov. 2017) is not publicly available.
312. *Vivendi*, *supra* n. 233 (USD 105 million); *Valores*, *supra* n. 236, para. 530 (USD 430 million); *Crystallex*, *supra* n. 230, paras 543, 546 (USD 1.2 billion); *EDF*, *supra* n. 236 (USD 136 million); *SAUR*, *supra* n. 236 (USD 40 million); *Tecmed*, *supra* n. 28 (the expropriation clause was also breached, USD 5 million); *Air Canada*, *supra* n. 232 (USD 20.7 million); *García Armas*, *supra* n. 226, para. 571 (USD 213 million); *Copper Mesa*, *supra* n. 226, paras 6.51, 6.61, 6.81 (USD 11.1 million); *Perenco*, *supra* n. 236, award on quantum, 27 Sep. 2019 (USD 449 million).
313. *Total*, *supra* n. 236, *see* Award, 27 Nov. 2013 (USD 269 million); *OKO Pankki Oyj*, *supra* n. 245 (USD 4.45 million, EUR 8.5 million); *Suez*, *supra* n. 124, para. 185, *see* Award, 9 Apr. 2015 (USD 405 million); *Flughafen Zürich*, *supra* n. 273, paras 599, 600ff. (examining a violation of denial of justice, USD 9.7 million); *Gold Reserve*, *supra* n. 226 (USD 713 million); *Arif*, *supra* n. 231 (USD 2.8 million).
314. *See*, awards examined in Chapter I.
315. The two exceptions are: *Anglo American*, *supra* n. 236, para. 443; *Global Telecom*, *supra* n. 236.
316. *Flughafen Zürich*, *supra* n. 273, paras 599, 600ff.
317. It should be added that about half of the awards which did not take a position on the status of the clause have held that a breach had been committed.

2.2 FET Clauses Where Treatment Must Be 'No Less' than That Required by International Law

According to the 2012 UNCTAD Report, under this formulation the FET obligation is 'not strictly linked to the stipulations of international law', instead, international law 'appears to set the floor of protection that can be claimed by an investor'.[318] The same view is held by many authors.[319] The UNCTAD Report also mentioned that this formulation 'would seem to give more room for interpreting FET as adding to the international law requirements', further specifying that the wording is 'effectively closer to the unqualified FET standard and gives arbitrators greater freedom of interpretation'.[320] Perhaps surprisingly, this approach has been followed by only half of the tribunals which have addressed the issue of the status of this type of clause and its relationship with the MST.

I have found 33 relevant awards.

A few words should first be said about 11 of these awards where the question of the status of a 'no less' clause was not raised by the parties and not discussed by the tribunals.[321] In one case, some passages suggest that the tribunal applied 'international law' without further exploring the issue.[322] In some awards, tribunals have applied a narrow definition of the concept of legitimate expectations and rejected the existence of any transparency obligation.[323] In another case, the question of the content of the FET

318. UNCTAD, *supra* n. 2, 23.
319. I. Laird, *Betrayal, Shock and Outrage - Recent Developments in NAFTA Article 1105*, in: T. Weiler (ed.), *NAFTA Investment Law and Arbitration: Past Issues, Current Practice, Future Prospects* (Transnational Publ. 2004) 51; R. Picherack, *The Expanding Scope of the Fair and Equitable Treatment Standard: Have Recent Tribunals Gone Too Far?*, 9(4) J. World Invest. & Trade, 260 (2008) DOI: 10.1163/221190008x00061; L. Paradell, *The BIT Experience of The Fair and Equitable Treatment Standard*, in: F. Ortino et al. (eds), *Investment Treaty Law, Current Issues II* (British IICL 2007) 123.
320. UNCTAD, *supra* n. 2, 23. *See also*, Islam, *supra* n. 14, 59 (these treaties 'imply that FET is not strictly linked to principles of international law. Rather international law here sets the floor of protection an investor can claim, and the standard may accommodate other requirements of the treaty itself').
321. *Mr. Hassan Awdi, Enterprise Business Consultants, Inc. and Alfa El Corporation v. Romania*, ICSID Case No. ARB/10/13, Award, 2 Mar. 2015 (concluding that the FET had been breached and awarding EUR 7.5 million); *Bosh International, Inc and B&P Ltd Foreign Investments Enterprise v. Ukraine*, ICSID Case No. ARB/08/11, Award, 25 Oct. 2012, paras 208ff.; *Link-Trading Joint Stock Company v. Department for Customs Control of Moldova*, UNCITRAL, Award, 18 Apr. 2002, para. 31.
322. *Big Sky Energy Corporation v. Kazakhstan*, ICSID Case No. ARB/17/22, Award, 1 Nov. 2012, para. 533, indicating that in the course of its detailed analysis as to whether the conduct amounted to a denial of justice, it 'also took into account whether decisions, actions and omissions were arbitrary, lacking in due process, lacking in good faith, etc.', and concluding that it 'failed to find any such conduct to be objectively wrongful as a matter of international law'. *See also*, para. 537: because it did not consider the relevant judicial conduct to be 'wrongful under international law, the Claimant's FET contention under Article II(2)(a) of the BIT fails'. The claim was rejected.
323. *Jan de Nul v. Egypt*, ICSID Case No. ARB/04/13, Award, 6 Nov. 2008, paras 187, 192-194. *See also, Rasia FZE and Joseph K. Borkowski v. Armenia*, ICSID Case No. ARB/18/28, Award, 20 Jan. 2023, indicating that there is 'no need to enunciate any overarching definition of the standard' (para. 641). The Tribunal explained that a violation of contract by the host State did 'not represent the kind of fundamental repudiation necessary to establish frustration of

was discussed by the parties but the majority of the tribunal said very little on the topic; it simply applied the concept of legitimate expectations and considered good faith to be part of the standard.[324] In the *LG&E* case, the Tribunal did not take a position on this debate but defined the FET in a very broad way just like an autonomous clause.[325] Overall, the claimants were successful in only 3 of these 11 cases.[326]

The reasoning of the tribunals which did take a position on this issue (22 awards) can be divided into two groups:

- Tribunals interpreting the provision *not* as a reference to the MST, but as offering *better* protection than under that standard (11 awards, section 2.2.1).
- Tribunals interpreting the provision as a reference to the MST under custom (11 awards, section 2.2.2).

I will also examine the question of the impact of these tribunals' findings on this point regarding matters of liability and compensation (section 2.2.3).

legitimate expectations under the fair and equitable treatment standard' (para. 645) and referred to 'objectively reasonable' expectations (para. 646). It also considered that the Tecmed's (*supra* n. 28) statement on transparency was 'one of aspiration, rather than a reflection of what international law actually requires' (para. 648). It concluded that 'Armenia's actions constitute a breach of contract, but they do not rise to the level of a due process failure capable of constituting a violation of FET' (para. 650). The claim was rejected. *See also, David Minnotte & Robert Lewis v. Poland*, ICSID Case No. ARB (AF)/10/1, Award, 16 May 2014, para. 193: 'while there may, arguably, be a general expectation that States will observe basic standards such as reasonable consistency and transparency, more specific expectations must be specifically created and proved'. The Tribunal held that the claimants had not shown that they had any legitimate expectations that were defeated by the conduct of the Respondent (para. 196). *See also, Manchester Securities Corporation v. Poland*, PCA Case No. 2015-18, Award, 7 Dec. 2018, paras 425ff., 492ff., indicating that 'for an investor's expectation to be considered as a legitimate expectation protected by international law, something more than the existence of a general legal framework is needed' (para. 495, quoting the narrow definition in the *El Paso* award, *supra* n. 137, at para. 375). The Tribunal found a breach of the FET standard and did not examine other allegations (para. 499). It awarded PLN 37.6 million.

324. *LSF-KEB Holdings SCA and others v. Korea*, ICSID Case No. ARB/12/37, Award, 30 Aug. 2022, para. 736, indicating that 'it makes no difference in this case whether good faith is considered a branch of FET or a stand-alone ground' and concluding that the Respondent failed to act in good faith towards these investors (para. 741). The majority awarded some USD 433 million in compensation. In her dissenting opinion, Stern does not discuss these points.

325. *LG&E Energy Corp., LG&E Capital Corp. and LG&E International Inc. v. Argentina*, ICSID Case No. ARB/02/1, Decision on Liability, 3 Oct. 2006, para. 131, indicating that FET 'consists of the host State's consistent and transparent behavior, free of ambiguity that involves the obligation to grant and maintain a stable and predictable legal framework necessary to fulfill the justified expectations of the foreign investor'. *See also, Noble Ventures, Inc. v. Romania*, ICSID Case No. ARB/01/11, Award, 19 May 2006, paras 181ff., referring to the standard as a 'more general standard which finds its specific application in inter alia the duty to provide full protection and security, the prohibition of arbitrary and discriminatory measures and the obligation to observe contractual obligations towards the investor'.

326. *Awdi, supra* n. 321 (awarding EUR 7.5 million); *Manchester, supra* n. 323, paras 425ff., 492ff. (awarding PLN 37.6 million); *LSF-KEB Holdings, supra* n. 324, para. 736 (awarding USD 433 million).

2.2.1 Tribunals Finding That the Clause Is Not a Reference to the MST

I have found 11 awards where tribunals have explicitly interpreted this clause to mean that the standard of treatment under the treaty is essentially the same as under an 'autonomous' stand-alone FET clause. Tribunals have however adopted different approaches to come to the same conclusion.

2.2.1.1 Awards Finding That the Clause Sets a Floor, Not a Ceiling; It Offers Better Protection than under the MST

Some tribunals dealing with 'no less' clauses have explicitly interpreted the provision to mean that the standard of treatment required is *better* than that offered under custom. The MST has been considered a floor rather than a ceiling in terms of the level of protection offered to investors. I have found 11 awards that adopted this approach.

It should be added that in some awards, the tribunal provides limited reasoning. In one award, the tribunal simply noted that a 'no less' clause provides for an autonomous FET standard that is 'different' from the MST, which, at least implicitly, means that it offers a better level of treatment.[327] The reasoning of the *Continental* Tribunal also suggests that the FET treaty standard is not the same as the MST and that it provides better protection.[328] But it also said that it was 'not necessary' to 'go more into that debate' regarding the relation between the two.[329]

Other awards contain a more detailed analysis. A good illustration is the *Lemire* award. The Tribunal referred to the issue as a 'classic debate in investment arbitration law',[330] the starting point of which is 'the very definition of the international minimum standard - a question which is fraught with difficulties'.[331] It explained that for claims 'arising from administrative or legislative acts of Governments - which are the type of claims typically submitted in investment dispute', the leading case is *Roberts,* decided in 1926 by the United States-Mexico General Claims Commission.[332] The Tribunal mentioned that the 'principle of assimilation' (i.e., that the FET treaty standard 'should be reduced to the customary international law minimum standard', such as in the 2004 (United States) US Model BIT) was not applicable to the FET clause contained in the

327. *Banco Bilbao Vizcaya Argentaria S.A. v. Bolivia*, ICSID Case No. ARB(AF)/18/5, Award, 12 Jul. 2022, para. 547.
328. *Continental Casualty Company v. Argentina*, ICSID Case No. ARB/03/9, Award, 5 Sep. 2008, para. 254 ('It does not follow that, whatever that wording, the Fair and Equitable Treatment standard should always be the lower minimum standard under customary international law').
329. *Ibid.*, paras 255-256.
330. *Joseph Charles Lemire v. Ukraine II*, ICSID Case No. ARB/06/18, Decision on Jurisdiction and Liability, 14 Jan. 2010, para. 247: 'A classic debate in investment arbitration law is whether the FET standard established by bilateral or multilateral investment treaties coincides with or differs from the international minimum standard of protection for aliens imposed by customary international law.'
331. *Ibid.*, para. 248.
332. *Ibid.*, referring to: *Harry Roberts (U.S.A.) v. United Mexican States*; 2 Nov. 1926; UNRIAA, vol. IV, 7.

BIT.[333] Later, it stated very clearly that 'the FET standard defined in the BIT is an *autonomous* treaty standard, whose precise meaning must be established on a case-by-case basis'.[334] For the Tribunal:

> What the US and Ukraine agreed when they executed the BIT, was that the international customary minimum standard should not operate as a ceiling, but rather as a floor. Investments protected by the BIT should in any case be awarded the level of protection offered by customary international law. But this level of protection could and should be transcended if the FET standard provided the investor with a superior set of rights.
>
> In view of the drafting of Article II.3 of the BIT, the Tribunal finds that actions or omissions of the Parties may qualify as unfair and inequitable, even if they do not amount to an outrage, to willful neglect of duty, egregious insufficiency of State actions, or even in subjective bad faith.[335]

The Tribunal stated that the FET standard is closely tied to the notion of legitimate expectations,[336] but it offered a balanced and nuanced picture of the scope of the FET standard. The Tribunal explained that a violation of the FET clause 'requires an action or omission by the State which violates a certain threshold of propriety' and that it must bear in mind a number of factors, including, *inter alia*, 'whether the State has failed to offer a stable and predictable legal framework', 'whether the State made specific representations to the investor', and 'whether there is an absence of transparency in the legal procedure or in the actions of the State'.[337] But, at the same time, the Tribunal stated that the 'evaluation of the State's action cannot be performed in the abstract and only with a view of protecting the investor's rights'.[338] Thus, the Tribunal 'must also balance other legally relevant interests, and take into consideration a number of countervailing factors, before it can establish that a violation of the FET standard' has been committed.[339] The Tribunal concluded that the measures were in breach of the FET standard[340] and subsequently awarded approximately USD 8.7 million in compensation.[341]

Other tribunals, like *Enron*, have interpreted a 'no less' clause (which it qualified as 'none too clear and precise')[342] to mean that the standard of treatment required was

333. *Lemire, supra* n. 330, paras 251-252.
334. *Ibid.*, para. 284, emphasis added.
335. *Ibid.*, paras 253-254.
336. *Ibid.*, paras 264ff.
337. *Ibid.*, para. 284.
338. *Ibid.*, para. 285.
339. *Ibid.*, listing a number of factors including 'the State's sovereign right to pass legislation and to adopt decisions for the protection of its public interests, especially if they do not provoke a disproportionate impact on foreign investors'.
340. *Ibid.*, para. 418.
341. *Ibid.*, Award, 28 Mar. 2011.
342. *Enron Creditors Recovery Corporation (formerly Enron Corporation) and Ponderosa Assets, L.P. v. Argentina*, ICSID Case No. ARB/01/3, Award, 22 May 2007, para. 256 ('The Tribunal notes that the Respondent is right in arguing that fair and equitable treatment is a standard none too clear and precise. This is because international law is not too clear and precise either on the treatment due to foreign citizens, traders and investors or with respect to the fact that the pertinent standards have gradually evolved over the centuries').

better than that offered under custom.[343] For the *Enron* Tribunal, 'the very fact that recent [NAFTA] FTC interpretations or investment treaties have purported to change the meaning or extent of the standard only confirms that those specific instruments aside, the standard is or might be a broader one'.[344] In other words, the FET standard must be interpreted broadly, beyond the level of protection existing under the MST, unless the parties have agreed otherwise in a treaty. The reasoning of the Tribunal in the *Sempra* award is rather confusing. It appears that the Tribunal was of the same view as the *Enron* award given that the language used is similar. It mentioned it was not excluding 'the possibility that the fair and equitable treatment standard imposed under a treaty can also eventually require a treatment additional to or beyond that of customary law', but added this rather ambiguous comment: 'such does not appear to be the case with the present dispute, however'.[345] It is not clear why the 'possibility' mentioned by the *Sempra* Tribunal was not applicable in this specific dispute.

2.2.1.2 *Awards Downplaying the Importance of the Issue Because the FET Treaty Standard and the MST Offer the Same Level of Protection*

Other tribunals have followed the 'not ceiling, but floor' perspective mentioned in the previous section, but have also said that, in any event, the level of protection was the same under both the FET treaty standard and the MST.

One example is the *Azurix* award. The Tribunal first said that the FET clause provides for a 'higher standard' 'than required by international law' and that the purpose of a 'no less' FET clause was 'to set a floor, not a ceiling, in order to avoid a possible interpretation of these standards below what is required by international law'.[346] The Tribunal also added that it did 'not consider' that this question was 'of material significance for its application' of the FET to the facts of the case.[347] Thus, 'the minimum requirement to satisfy this standard has evolved and the Tribunal considers

343. *Ibid.*, para. 258 ('It might well be that in some circumstances where the international minimum standard is sufficiently elaborate and clear, fair and equitable treatment might be equated with it. But in other more vague circumstances, the fair and equitable standard may be more precise than its customary international law forefathers. This is why the Tribunal concludes that the fair and equitable standard, at least in the context of the Treaty applicable to this case, can also require a treatment additional to, or beyond that of, customary law').
344. *Ibid.*
345. *Sempra Energy International v. Argentina*, ICSID Case No. ARB/02/16, Award, 28 Sep. 2007, para. 302. This is the full passage: 'It might well be that in some circumstances in which the international minimum standard is sufficiently elaborate and clear, the standard of fair and equitable treatment might be equated with it. But in other cases, it might as well be the opposite, so that the fair and equitable treatment standard will be more precise than its customary international law forefathers. On many occasions, the issue will not even be whether the fair and equitable treatment standard is different or more demanding than the customary standard, but only whether it is more specific, less generic and spelled out in a contemporary fashion so that its application is more appropriate to the case under consideration. This does not exclude the possibility that the fair and equitable treatment standard imposed under a treaty can also eventually require a treatment additional to or beyond that of customary law. Such does not appear to be the case with the present dispute, however.'
346. *Azurix, supra* n. 194, para. 361.
347. *Ibid.*

that its content is substantially similar whether the terms are interpreted in their ordinary meaning, as required by the Vienna Convention, or in accordance with customary international law'.[348] The Tribunal therefore concluded that the levels of treatment were the same based on the assumption that the MST had evolved rapidly. But it did so only on the basis of what another tribunal (*Mondev*) had previously said about that evolution. Importantly, neither the *Azurix* nor the *Mondev* tribunals have actually demonstrated such an evolution with concrete examples of State practice and evidence of *opinio juris*. Finally, the *Azurix* Tribunal rejected the relevance of some of the material put forward by the respondent (the 2001 NAFTA Free Trade Commission (FTC) Note, Free Trade Agreements (FTAs) entered by the US) which referred to the MST:

> The interpretation of the FTC or the examples of FTAs adduced by the Respondent may be evidence of a significant practice by one of the parties to the BIT, but the Tribunal has difficulty in reading it in the text of the BIT which governs these proceedings. The fact that the FTC interpreted Article 1105 in reaction to a tribunal's different understanding of this article and that, in recent agreements, the correlative clause has been drafted to reflect the FTC's interpretation show that the meaning of that article and similar clauses in other agreements could reasonably be understood to have a different meaning.[349]

The *Cargill* award is another example of a tribunal downplaying the importance of the question of the status of the FET clause.[350] The Tribunal stated that 'the Contracting States intended to adopt an autonomous standard'.[351] It also explained that 'the reference to international law in Article 11:6 clearly sets a flour and not a ceiling'.[352] But, at the same time, it also added that it 'tends to concur' with the position adopted by several tribunals which have said that the FET treaty standard 'is not materially different from the international law minimum as it has evolved under customary law'.[353] Interestingly, the Tribunal also referred to material put forward by the respondent to support its position (9 US BITs with other States) 'which include a provision identical or nearly identical to Article 11:6 of the Treaty'.[354] However, the Tribunal explained that in all cases, there was a Letter of Transmittal from the US government to the US Senate accompanying the BIT 'explicitly provid[ing] that the guarantee of fair and equitable treatment "sets out a minimum standard of treatment based on standards found in customary international law"', adding that 'no such mention appears in the Letter of Transmittal of this BIT' (the Poland-US BIT).[355] The

348. *Ibid.*, para. 361, *See also* at para. 364: 'The question whether fair and equitable treatment is or is not additional to the minimum treatment requirement under international law is a question about the substantive content of fair and equitable treatment and, whichever side of the argument one takes, the answer to the question may in substance be the same.'
349. *Ibid.*, para. 363.
350. *Cargill, Incorporated v. Poland*, ICSID Case No. ARB(AF)/04/2, Award, 5 Mar. 2009, para. 453.
351. *Ibid.*
352. *Ibid.*
353. *Ibid.*
354. *Ibid.*, para. 454.
355. *Ibid.*

Tribunal did not further explore the reason why that specific letter contained different wording nor what the consequences of such an omission were.

The same type of approach has also been adopted by tribunals in several other cases. One example is *Duke*.[356] The Tribunal explained that it was of the opinion that the 'discussion about the autonomous character of the standard is irrelevant given the circumstances of the case' and that 'it also appears overtaken by the evolution in the latest ICSID decisions'.[357] It concurred with the *Azurix* award's findings that the FET clause sets 'a floor and not a ceiling' and that the standards under the treaty and under customary international law were 'substantially similar'.[358] This conclusion led the Tribunal to affirm that 'a stable and predictable legal and business environment is considered an essential element of the fair and equitable treatment standard' which was 'directly linked to the investor's justified expectations'.[359] Yet, it also applied a narrow definition of the concept of legitimate expectations.[360]

The reasoning behind the *Occidental* award is interesting in many respects. The Tribunal acknowledged that the FET standard was not defined in the BIT but referred to the preamble indicating that the parties agreed that FET of investment 'is desirable in order to maintain a stable framework for investment and maximum effective utilization of economic resources'.[361] It concluded that 'the stability of the legal and business framework is thus an essential element of fair and equitable treatment'.[362] It then explained that 'various arbitral tribunals have recently insisted on the need for this stability', citing the *Metaclad* award.[363] It also cited the very broad interpretation given by the *Tecmed* award.[364] Based on the test set out in *Tecmed*, the *Occidental* Tribunal concluded that the FET clause had been breached.[365] After having already decided that a breach had been committed, the Tribunal said that there was 'still one aspect that [it] need[ed] to address': whether the FET standard 'mandated by the Treaty is a more demanding standard than that prescribed by customary international law'.[366] Without any explanation, the Tribunal said that it was of the 'opinion that in the instant case the Treaty standard is not different from that required under international law concerning both the stability and predictability of the legal and business framework of the investment'.[367] Importantly, the Tribunal added that the FET treaty

356. *Duke Energy Electroquil Partners and Electroquil S.A. v. Ecuador*, ICSID Case No. ARB/04/19, Award, 18 Aug. 2008.
357. *Ibid.*, para. 333.
358. *Ibid.*, para. 336-337 ('the standards are essentially the same').
359. *Ibid.*, paras 339-340.
360. *Ibid.*, para. 340.
361. *Occidental Exploration and Production Co v. Ecuador*, LCIA Case No. UN3467, Award, 1 Jul. 2004, para. 185.
362. *Ibid.*
363. *Ibid.*, citing *Metalclad Corporation v. Mexico*, ICSID No. ARB(AF)/97/1, Award, 30 Aug. 2000, para. 99, without however indicating the important fact that the reasoning of the Tribunal on transparency had been subsequently set aside by a BC Court: *Mexico v. Metalclad*, 2001 BCSC 664, Supreme Court of British Columbia, Judgment and Reasons for Decision, 2 May 2001.
364. *Ibid.*, para. 185, citing *Tecmed, supra* n. 28.
365. *Ibid.*, para. 187.
366. *Ibid.*, para. 189.
367. *Ibid.*, para. 190.

standard 'can be equated with that under international law as evidenced by the opinions of the various tribunals cited above' and that it was 'quite evident that the Respondent's treatment of the investment falls below such standards'.[368] The Tribunal concluded that the standard of protection under the FET treaty standard and under custom was the same based on an assumption. It assumed that there exists an obligation under international law for the host State to provide investors with the 'stability and predictability of the legal and business framework of the investment'.[369] The fact that the Tribunal fully endorsed this proposition is clear from another passage where it referred to the 'requirements of stability and predictability under international law'.[370] The only source that the Tribunal mentioned to support this broad affirmation was the *Tecmed* award. The Tribunal did not examine any element of State practice, let alone *opinio juris*, to support its affirmation that such an obligation was now a well-established rule of custom. As further discussed below,[371] the proposition is controversial and has been rejected by many other tribunals examining FET clauses being linked to the MST. In any event, given this very broad interpretation of the standard of treatment allegedly existing under international law, the question as to whether the FET treaty standard was 'more demanding' than that under custom simply did 'not arise in this case'.[372]

The reasoning of the *CMS* Tribunal is very similar. The Tribunal also mentioned that the preamble of the treaty stated that it was desirable 'to maintain a stable framework for investments and maximum effective use of economic resources' and said that 'there can be no doubt, therefore, that a stable legal and business environment is an essential element of fair and equitable treatment'.[373] The Tribunal added that a significant number of treaties 'that have dealt with this standard also unequivocally shows' that FET is 'inseparable from stability and predictability'.[374] Having concluded that a breach of the FET clause had been committed, the Tribunal then added that there was 'one additional aspect' it 'must examine'.[375] The Tribunal made this comment:

> While the choice between requiring a higher treaty standard and that of equating it with the international minimum standard might have relevance in the context of some disputes, the Tribunal is not persuaded that it is relevant in this case. In fact, the Treaty standard of fair and equitable treatment and its connection with the required stability and predictability of the business environment, founded on solemn legal and contractual commitments, is not different from the international law minimum standard and its evolution under customary law.[376]

368. *Ibid.*
369. *Ibid.*
370. *Ibid.*, para. 191. The Tribunal also indicated that 'there is certainly an obligation' under international law 'not to alter the legal and business environment in which the investment has been made'.
371. *See*, analysis of case law in Chapter III.
372. *Occidental, supra* n. 361, para. 192.
373. *CMS Gas Transmission Company v. Argentina*, ICSID Case No. ARB/01/8, Award, 12 May 2005, para. 274.
374. *Ibid.*, para. 276.
375. *Ibid.*, paras 281-282.
376. *Ibid.*, para. 284.

The Tribunal's conclusion that the level of treatment was 'not different' was entirely based on the controversial assumption that there exists a requirement for 'stability and predictability of the business environment' under the MST.

Awards where tribunals have affirmed (just like in the *Azurix* and *Cargill* cases mentioned above) that the level of treatment under both the FET treaty standard and the MST was essentially the same, have adopted the 'convergence theory'. Under this approach, the level of protection to be accorded to foreign investors under the MST is said to have rapidly evolved in recent decades and is, apparently, believed now to be the same as the one existing under BITs containing an unqualified FET clause. The approach, further discussed below,[377] is controversial and has been rejected by many tribunals and authors.[378] What matters for the present purposes is to point out that the approach taken by these tribunals has led them to significantly increase, or 'boost', the level of protection allegedly existing under custom. It can be argued that this 'boosting' is rather artificial given that these tribunals have offered no evidence of State practice or *opinio juris* to support the claim of such a rapid evolution.

A good illustration is the *Murphy* award, where the Tribunal said that the 'debate is more theoretical than substantial'.[379] The Tribunal first endorsed a broad interpretation of the role of FET clauses: 'the function of the FET clause in investment treaties is broadly the same: it ensures the stability and predictability of the legal and business framework in the State party subject to any qualifications otherwise established by the treaty and under international law'.[380] The Tribunal then referred to the 'constantly evolving international standard', and, perhaps more surprisingly, stated that 'protecting the stability and predictability of the host State's legal and business framework also underpins the modern customary international law standard'.[381] As mentioned above, this is a controversial statement. For instance, no tribunal assessing an FET clause expressly linked to the MST (such as in the context of NAFTA and CAFTA) has reached this conclusion.[382] Having interpreted the level of protection offered under custom in such a liberal and 'evolutive' fashion, the Tribunal had no difficulty in concluding that the MST and the FET treaty standard 'continue to influence each other' and that 'these standards are increasingly aligned'.[383] In other words, after having significantly 'boosted' the level of protection said to exist under the MST, it was easy for the Tribunal to conclude that there was 'no material difference between the customary international law standard and the FET standard under the present BIT'.[384] For that

377. *See*, analysis in Part III.
378. UNCTAD, *Investor-State Dispute Settlement and Impact on Investment Rulemaking* 75 (2007); Kill, *supra* n. 142, 853ff.
379. *Murphy Exploration and Production Company International v. Ecuador* II, PCA Case No. 2012-16 (formerly AA 434), Partial Final Award, 6 May 2016, para. 206.
380. *Ibid.* Later in the award (paras 247ff.), the Tribunal defined legitimate expectation rather narrowly.
381. *Ibid.*, para. 207.
382. *See*, Dumberry, *supra* n. 100.
383. *Murphy*, *supra* n. 379, para. 207.
384. *Ibid.*, para. 208.

reason, it considered that it was not 'necessary to determine' whether the FET standard 'reflects an autonomous standard above the customary international law standard'.[385]

The important point is that had these tribunals not followed this 'convergence' approach, they would have come to the same conclusion as other tribunals dealing with 'no less' clauses. Thus, they would have interpreted this clause to mean that the standard of treatment required under the FET clause was *better* than that offered under custom. In other words, they have come to the conclusion that the treatments are the same *only because* they have (artificially) boosted the level of protection that they believe now exists under the MST.

2.2.2 Tribunals Interpreting the Provision as a Reference to the MST under Custom

In the previous section, I examined the reasoning behind 11 awards where tribunals interpreted a 'no less' FET clause to mean that it offers *better* protection than under the MST. This section assesses 11 awards which have come to the opposite conclusion, i.e., that the words 'international law' in a 'no less' FET clause is a reference to the MST under custom.

Some of the awards contain limited analysis and the issue is dealt with in just one paragraph. This is the case in the following cases: *M.C.I. Power*,[386] *Genin*,[387] *Ulysseas*,[388] *Lauder*,[389] and *Díaz Gaspar*.[390] The *Burlington* award, which analysed the clause in the context of allegations of expropriation, could be added to this list.[391] In

385. *Ibid.*
386. *M.C.I. Power Group L.C. and New Turbine, Inc. v. Ecuador*, ICSID No. ARB/03/6, Award, 31 Jul. 2007, para. 369: 'The international law mentioned in Article II of the BIT refers to customary international law, i.e., the repeated, general, and constant practice of States, which they observe because they are aware that it is obligator.'
387. *Alex Genin, Eastern Credit Limited, Inc. and A.S. Baltoil Genin v. Estonia*, Award, 25 Jun. 2001, para. 367: 'the Tribunal understands it to require an 'international minimum standard' that is separate from domestic law, but that is, indeed, a *minimum* standard. Acts that would violate this minimum standard would include acts showing a wilful neglect of duty, an insufficiency of action falling far below international standards, or even subjective bad faith', emphasis in the original.
388. *Ulysseas, Inc v. Ecuador*, UNCITRAL, Final Award, 12 Jun. 2012, para. 245: 'As to the reference made by Article II (3)(a) of the BIT to the minimum standard of treatment required by international law, the Tribunal notes that the international minimum standard has evolved over time. What matters in our case is that the treatment of foreign investors do not fall below this minimum international standard, regardless of the protection afforded by the Ecuadorian legal order.'
389. *Ronald S. Lauder v. Czech Republic*, UNCITRAL, Final Award, 3 Sep. 2001, para. 292: 'Fair and equitable treatment is related to the traditional standard of due diligence and provides a "minimum international standard which forms part of customary international law"'.
390. *Alejandro Diego Díaz Gaspar v. Costa Rica*, ICSID Case No. ARB/19/13, Award, 29 Jun. 2022, para. 356: 'La referencia al derecho internacional que hace el Artículo III-1 es al derecho internacional consuetudinario. Es decir, el nivel de trato que le otorga al inversionista el Artículo III-1 del Tratado es el nivel mínimo de trato del derecho internacional consuetudinario'.
391. *Burlington Resources Inc. v. Ecuador*, ICSID Case No. ARB/08/5, Decision on Reconsideration and Award, 7 Feb. 2017. The Tribunal examined the FET clause in the context of the claim of expropriation (para. 166). The BIT provision indicates that an expropriation must be carried

Iberdrola, the Tribunal, dealing with a denial of justice claim, considered that the words 'international law' referenced customary international law.[392] In *Chevron*, while the Tribunal did not examine the question specifically, some passages suggest that it considered that the clause was linked to the MST.[393] In the *AMT v. Zaire* case, while the Tribunal did say that the 'no less' FET clause was a reference to the MST,[394] its analysis only focused on the full protection and security (FPS) protection contained in the clause.

It should be added that the reasoning of two tribunals examining the Argentina-US BIT seems to suggest that they have also considered that the clause was a reference to the MST. This is, for instance, the position taken by the *El Paso* Tribunal:

> The Tribunal considers this discussion to be somewhat futile, as the scope and content of the minimum standard of international law is as little defined as the BITs' FET standard, and as the true question is to decide what substantive protection is granted to foreign investors through the FET. The issue is not one of comparing two undefined or weakly defined standards; it is to ascertain the content and define the BIT standard of fair and equitable treatment.
>
> This being said, it is the view of the Tribunal that the position according to which FET is equivalent to the international minimum standard is more in line with the evolution of investment law and international law and with the identical role assigned to FET and to the international minimum standard. The Tribunal wishes to emphasise what is, in its view, the specific role played by both the general international minimum standard and the FET standard as found in BITs. The role of these similar standards is to ensure that the treatment of foreign

out, *inter alia*, in accordance with the general principles contained in Art. II(3) (the FET clause). The Tribunal said that the 'no less' FET clause was a reference to the MST (para. 165). It found that 'the expropriation was not carried out in accordance with the principle of fair and equitable treatment, which is a condition of a lawful expropriation under Article III(1) referring to Article II(3), even under a stringent interpretation of that standard' (para. 167). It awarded some USD 379 million for expropriation.

392. *Iberdrola Energia, S.A. v. Guatemala*, ICSID Case No. ARB/09/5, Award, 17 Aug. 2012, para. 427, rejecting the argument that 'the standard of denial of justice of the Treaty is broader than that of customary international law'. The Tribunal stated that 'based on the text of the Treaty, which sets as a minimum treatment that of customary international law, will refer to the concept of denial of justice in the current state of customary international law, which has been consistently dealt with in the decisions of the international arbitral tribunals'. The FET claim was rejected.
393. *Chevron Corporation and Texaco Petroleum Company v. Ecuador* (II), PCA Case No. 2009-23, Second Partial Award, Track II, 30 Aug. 2018. The Tribunal only examined allegations of denial of justice and said that 'denial of justice under the FET standard equates with denial of justice under customary international law, both as provided in Article II(3)(a) of the Treaty' (para. 8.25). The Tribunal did not examine the relationship between a 'no less' clause and the MST. But two passages suggest that it considered the FET clause as a reference to the MST: the 'conduct amounted to a failure of the Respondent's national system as a whole to satisfy minimum standards required under international law' (para. 8.60); 'wrongfully committed a denial of justice under the standards both for fair and equitable treatment and for treatment required by customary international law under Article II(3)(a) of the Treaty' (Part X, The Operative Part, paras 10.5, 10.6). It held that a breach had been committed and that the quantum would be determined in a subsequent award. In its decision (17 Nov. 2023), the Dutch Supreme Court has dismissed Ecuador's application to set aside the award. The case is still pending.
394. *American Manufacturing & Trading v. Zaire*, ICSID Case No. ARB/93/1, Award, 21 Feb. 1997, paras 6.60ff.

> investments, which are protected by the national treatment and the most-favoured investors' clauses, do not fall below a certain minimum, in case the two mentioned standards do not live up to that minimum. (...)
>
> In conclusion, it is the Tribunal's view that the FET is not to be viewed with reference to national law – in which case it could be lower than required by international law – but has to be interpreted with reference to international law, the result being that it cannot go below what is required by international law, which is the standard to be applied. But if national law or the treatment accorded to some foreigners exceeds this minimum international standard, it is one of the former that has to be applied. In a sense, it could be said that the foreign investor is entitled to the most favourable treatment, be it national law, rules applied to some foreigners or the international minimum standard embodied in FET. The Tribunal thus considers that the FET of the BIT is the international minimum standard required by international law, regardless of the protection afforded by the national legal orders.[395]

The *Mobil Exploration* Tribunal adopted the same view as the *El Paso* Tribunal about the 'position according to which the FET is equivalent' to the MST being 'more in line with the evolution of investment law and international law'.[396]

Following the approach adopted by the tribunals mentioned in this section, the requirement to offer investors a level of protection no less than that existing under international law sets a floor *and* a ceiling. In other words, the level of treatment is the same as the one existing under the MST, *not* better.

Interestingly, the findings of these tribunals on this issue seem to have had a direct consequence on how they defined the scope of the standard. They adopted a rather narrow definition of the standard. While the *M.C.I. Power* Tribunal does refer to the obligation to respect investors' legitimate expectations, using a narrow definition,[397] some other passages suggest that it did not consider this element to be part of the FET standard.[398] In any event, it concluded that no breach of the FET had been committed. In *Genin*, the Tribunal said that 'acts that would violate this minimum standard would include acts showing a wilful neglect of duty, an insufficiency of action falling far below international standards, or even subjective bad faith'.[399] The Tribunal seems to have adopted a definition close to the one mentioned in the *Neer* case. It is also noteworthy that the award contains no reference to legitimate expectations.[400] Arbitrary or

395. *El Paso, supra* n. 137, paras 331-337.
396. *Mobil Exploration and Development Inc. Suc. Argentina and Mobil Argentina S.A. v. Argentina*, ICSID Case No. ARB/04/16, Decision on Jurisdiction and Liability, 10 Apr. 2013, para. 911.
397. *M.C.I., supra* n. 386, paras 278, 349.
398. *Ibid.*, para. 371 ('The Tribunal concludes that the acts alleged by the Claimants (...) when evaluated individually or as a whole, they do not constitute unfair or inequitable, discriminatory or arbitrary treatment in violation of the parameters established by international law as reflected in the BIT'). In fact, in the decision section of the Award, para. 373, the Tribunal referred to the elements contained in the FET box, but does not mention legitimate expectations: 'Claimants have failed to prove violation of the standards of fair and equitable treatment, including the obligation to act in good faith, or the standards of non-discriminatory or nonarbitrary treatment that the BIT requires of Ecuador as a State party.'
399. *Genin, supra* n. 387, para. 367.
400. But that could be explained by the fact that back in 2001 when the award was rendered, the concept had not yet been a central feature of claimants' arguments.

discriminatory measures were covered by another clause (Article II(3)(b) of the BIT) and the Tribunal also applied a rather high threshold of gravity necessary to constitute a breach of the provision.[401] The *Genin* Tribunal did not find a breach of the BIT. The *Ulysseas* Tribunal referred to the *Occidental* award indicating that 'the stability of the legal and business framework is thus an essential element of fair and equitable treatment'.[402] But, at the same time, it adopted a rather narrow definition of legitimate expectations.[403] The Tribunal concluded that no FET breach had been committed. In *Lauder*, the Tribunal did not find any breach of the FET but said that some measures were arbitrary and discriminatory in violation of a separate provision of the BIT.[404] Yet, it held that the breach was 'too remote to qualify as a relevant cause for the harm caused' and awarded no compensation.[405] The *Díaz Gaspar* Tribunal did not refer to the obligation of transparency as part of the FET standard and narrowly defined the concept of legitimate expectations.[406] It found that some of the measures adopted were arbitrary, that they had been corrected by local courts and, consequently, that no FET violation had occurred.[407]

2.2.3 *The Impact of Tribunals' Findings Regarding Matters of Liability and Compensation*

One of the most important findings of my survey of awards dealing with 'no less' FET clauses is that the question of how a tribunal analyses the status of the clause and its relationship with the MST seems to have a direct impact on the interpretation (broad or narrow) it gives to the content of the standard and, in turn, on how it addresses matters of liability and compensation.

It is indeed remarkable that *all* tribunals which have interpreted a 'no less' FET clause as meaning that the standard of treatment under the treaty offers *better* protection than under the MST have come to the *same* conclusion in terms of liability. They have *all* held that the FET clause had been breached. Some tribunals awarded

401. *Genin, supra* n. 387, para. 371: 'in order to amount to a violation of the BIT, any procedural irregularity that may have been present would have to amount to bad faith, a wilful disregard of due process of law or an extreme insufficiency of action'.
402. *Ulysseas, supra* n. 388, para. 247, citing *Occidental, supra* n. 361, para. 183.
403. *Ulysseas, supra* n. 388, para. 247: 'The idea that legitimate expectations, and therefore FET, imply the stability of the legal and business framework, may not be correct if stated in an overly-broad and unqualified formulation,' citing *EDF, supra* n. 172, para. 217 (indicating that 'Except where specific promises or representations are made by the State to the investor, the latter may not rely on a bilateral investment treaty as a kind of insurance policy against the risk of any changes in the host State's legal and economic framework. Such expectation would be neither legitimate nor reasonable').
404. *Lauder, supra* n. 389, paras 222-232.
405. *Ibid.*, para. 235.
406. *Gaspar, supra* n. 390, paras 362-363, 365-366, citing the NAFTA *Thunderbird* award as the appropriate test.
407. *Ibid.*, para. 541. It also found that press statements by the health minister violated the FET standard, but awarded no damages.

compensation for breach of the FET and other clauses.[408] Others held that only the FET clause had been breached.[409]

The conclusions reached by these tribunals in terms of liability are in sharp contrast with the position taken by other tribunals which have taken the opposite view that a 'no less' FET clause is in fact a reference to the MST. How did these tribunals address matters of liability and compensation? At the outset, two awards should be excluded from the analysis because compensation was *not* awarded for a breach of the FET standard.[410] A third case (*Chevron*) is still pending. Out of the remaining eight cases, the vast majority of awards (six awards, i.e., 75%) that have considered that a 'no less' FET clause was a reference to the MST have come to the conclusion that *no violation* had been committed. The only awards which can truly be considered exceptions are the *Mobil Exploration* case (awarding USD 196.2 million),[411] and the *El Paso* case (USD 43 million), both decided under the Argentina-US BIT.[412]

2.2.4 *Conclusion Regarding 'No Less' FET Clauses*

There is a very clear link between the approach adopted by a tribunal regarding the status of a 'no less' FET clause and how it assesses matters of liability and compensation. Thus, all tribunals which considered 'no less' clauses in the same way as autonomous stand-alone FET clauses, i.e., as providing *better* protection than under custom, gave broad interpretations which led them to conclude that a breach had been committed. Contrarily, in the vast majority of cases where tribunals interpreted the clause as a reference to the MST, they adopted narrower approaches which led them to find no breach.

2.3 General Conclusion on FET Clauses Referring to 'International Law'

My findings on FET clauses referring to 'international law' can be summarised as follows:

408. *Occidental, supra* n. 361, paras 188-189 (USD 71 million); *Banco Bilbao, supra* n. 327, para. 547; *Cargill, supra* n. 350 (USD 1.9 million); *Duke Energy, supra* n. 356, para. 340 (USD 5.5 million); *Enron, supra* n. 342 (USD 106.2 million); *Sempra supra* n. 345 (USD 128 million); *Azurix, supra* n. 194 (USD 165 million); *CMS, supra* n. 373 (USD 133 million).
409. *Lemire, supra* n. 330, para. 418, and subsequent Award, 28 Mar. 2011 (USD 8.7 million); *Continental, supra* n. 328 (USD 2.8 million). *See also, Murphy, supra* n. 379, para. 294 (USD 19 million). Given its finding on the FET clause, the Tribunal did not examine other allegations of other treaty breach. In a subsequent award, Final Award, 17 Feb. 2017, the Tribunal calculated that the adjustment that should be made to the fair market value of the investment was USD 57.1 million.
410. *AMT, supra* n. 394, paras 6.60ff., the Tribunal awarded USD 9 million in compensation, but its analysis only focused on FPS (an element of protection which was contained in the same provision together with the FET standard). In *Burlington, supra* n. 391, the Tribunal examined the FET clause only in the context of a claim of expropriation and awarded some USD 379 million for that breach.
411. *Mobil Exploration, supra* n. 396, Award, 25 Feb. 2016.
412. *El Paso, supra* n. 137.

- The question of how a tribunal analyses the status of an FET clause containing a reference to 'international law' has a direct impact on the interpretation (broad or narrow) it gives to the content of the standard and, in turn, on how it addresses matters of liability and compensation.
- The vast majority of awards where tribunals took a position on the status of an 'in accordance with international law' FET clause concluded that this is *not* a reference to the MST under custom.
- They have considered that under this clause the FET standard offers better protection than under the MST. They have, in practice, interpreted the clause in very much the same way that other tribunals have regarding stand-alone FET clauses having an autonomous character. These broad interpretations led the majority of tribunals (two-thirds of awards) to find a breach of FET and to award compensation. It is noteworthy that this success rate is the same for tribunals which have expressly stated that a stand-alone FET clause has an 'autonomous' character.[413]
- Tribunals assessing 'no less' FET clauses have been evenly divided on the interpretation to be given to this clause and its relation to the MST.
- There is a clear link between the approach adopted by a tribunal regarding the status of a 'no less' FET clause and how it assesses matters of liability and compensation. Tribunals that have considered 'no less' clauses as offering better protection than under the MST have all concluded that a breach had been committed. On the contrary, tribunals which have interpreted 'no less' clauses as meaning that the level of protection is the same as the one existing under MST, have adopted narrower approaches which led the vast majority of them to find no breach.

Ultimately, what is clear is that a BIT that contains an FET clause with a reference to 'international law' (whether 'in accordance' or 'no less') does *not* provide any guarantee that a tribunal will interpret this wording as being synonymous with the MST under custom. My analysis of awards shows that a State simply cannot assume that the terms 'international law' contained in an FET clause will be interpreted as meaning the same thing as the MST. In fact, only a minority of tribunals have adopted this approach (15 out of 63 awards, i.e., 25%). It is much more likely that a tribunal will interpret such language similarly to a stand-alone FET clause containing no reference to 'international law' whatsoever.[414] In practical terms, the vast majority of tribunals that adopted this approach came to the conclusion that the FET clause had been breached and awarded compensation. This means that a reference to 'international law' in an FET clause offers limited protection for States against the possibility of tribunals adopting broad interpretations and finding liability.

413. *See*, awards examined in Chapter I, Section 1.1.
414. *Ibid*.

III FET CLAUSES LINKED TO THE MST OR CUSTOM

Introduction

A third category of FET clauses are those where the FET is expressly linked to the MST or 'customary international law'. Whether or not the clause refers to one concept and/or the other is not significant. As explained in Part I, when a clause mentions the MST, it is an obvious reference to the standard existing under custom. Similarly, when a clause indicates that the standard of treatment is the one under custom, there is no doubt that this is a reference to, *inter alia*, the MST. The 2023 OECD Report indicates that the FET standard is linked to the MST in 155 treaties. Given that the use of this approach is found in many plurilateral treaties, the reference to the MST is present in treaties covering 396 relationships.[415] Importantly, about half of all treaties concluded in the past decade which include an FET clause have adopted this approach. This is one example of a rather simple clause:

> Investments or returns of investors of either Contracting Party shall at all times be accorded treatment in accordance with the customary international law minimum standard of treatment of aliens, including fair and equitable treatment and full protection and security. (Canada-Czech Republic BIT, 2009, Art. 3).

Many recent treaties have adopted a very detailed FET clause based on the US Model BIT (2004). The OECD found 51 of these treaties, covering a total of 136 bilateral relationships.[416] As mentioned in Part I, under Article 5 of the US Model BIT, the standard is explicitly linked to the MST under custom, with three additional clarifications:

> Art. 5 Minimum Standard of Treatment[417]
> 1. Each Party shall accord to covered investments treatment in accordance with customary international law, including fair and equitable treatment and full protection and security.
> 2. For greater certainty, paragraph 1 prescribes the customary international law minimum standard of treatment of aliens as the minimum standard of treatment to be afforded to covered investments. The concepts of 'fair and equitable treatment' and 'full protection and security' do not require treatment in addition to or beyond that which is required by that standard, and do not create additional substantive rights. The obligation in paragraph 1 to provide:
>   (a) 'fair and equitable treatment' includes the obligation not to deny justice in criminal, civil, or administrative adjudicatory proceedings in

415. OECD, *supra* n. 9, 16.
416. *Ibid.*
417. A footnote is attached to the title of the provision, which indicates that 'Article 5 shall be interpreted in accordance with Annex A' (entitled 'Customary International Law'), which reads as follows: 'The Parties confirm their shared understanding that 'customary international law' generally and as specifically referenced in Article 5 and Annex B results from a general and consistent practice of States that they follow from a sense of legal obligation. With regard to Article 5, the customary international law minimum standard of treatment of aliens refers to all customary international law principles that protect the economic rights and interests of aliens.'

accordance with the principle of due process embodied in the principal legal systems of the world; and

(b) 'full protection and security' requires each Party to provide the level of police protection required under customary international law. (...).

Together, clauses where the FET standard is linked to MST or custom are found in 200 treaties, representing about 8% of all treaties.

How do tribunals interpret these clauses? In its 2012 Report, UNCTAD explained that an explicit link between the FET obligation and the MST is used by States to 'prevent overexpansive interpretations of the FET standard by arbitral tribunals' and to 'rein in the discretion of tribunals when considering its content'.[418] While interpreting a stand-alone FET clause based on the VCLT gives the arbitrators a significant margin of appreciation to assess what they consider to be unfair and unreasonable conduct, the same cannot be said when the clause is expressly linked to custom. By definition, the role of an arbitrator is more constrained. As explained in the Report, linking the FET standard to the MST 'send[s] out a message to arbitrators that the latter cannot go beyond what customary international law declares to be the content of the minimum standard of treatment'.[419] Rules of custom emerged with consistent State practice and the need to show that States consider that they have the obligation to adopt a certain conduct (*opinio juris*).[420] The quantity of this type of rule is limited because it takes years for them to develop and crystallise on the international plane. It is also more difficult for the parties in proceedings to demonstrate the existence of any such rule.[421] As noted by a recent OECD paper, the fact that this type of clause 'incorporates a body of law outside the treaty into the treaty' makes them 'fundamentally different from provisions that set autonomous treaty standards'.[422] Importantly, the UNCTAD Report noted that such linkage 'will likely lead tribunals to apply a higher threshold for finding a breach of the standard, as compared with unqualified FET clauses'.[423] In this chapter, I will demonstrate that this is indeed what tribunals have done.

The 2012 UNCTAD Report also noted that awards rendered by tribunals for this category of FET clauses did not 'share a common approach to the interpretation' of such clauses and that, therefore, 'a degree of unpredictability persists'.[424] Consequently, 'tribunals have interpreted the MST in a variety of ways, some more strict and conservative, others more creative and liberal'.[425] This is a correct assessment of what NAFTA tribunals did back then. At the time, NAFTA tribunals dealt with the 2001 Note

418. UNCTAD, *supra* n. 2, 28.
419. *Ibid.*
420. On this question, *see*, P. Dumberry, *The Formation and Identification of Rules of Customary International Law in International Investment Law* (Cambridge UP 2016).
421. UNCTAD, *supra* n. 2, 28: 'The process of establishing the content of customary international law (determining State practice and opinion juris) is methodologically difficult and puts an onerous burden on the claimants.' A similar assessment has been made by NAFTA tribunals: *Glamis*, *supra* n. 24; *Cargill, Inc. v. Mexico*, ICSID Case No. ARB(AF)/05/02, Award, 18 Sep. 2009.
422. Gaukrodger, *supra* n. 47, 20.
423. UNCTAD, *supra* n. 2, 29. For Islam, *supra* n. 14, 64, this argument is 'unconvincing'.
424. UNCTAD, *supra* n. 2, 29.
425. *Ibid.*, 45.

of Interpretation in different ways. As further explained in the next section, since then NAFTA case law has been much more consistent. The following sections examining CAFTA awards and the reasoning of other tribunals assessing FET clauses linked with the MST will show that in the last 10 years, tribunals have also adopted a restrictive approach which is generally in line with NAFTA case law.[426]

I have found 42 awards examining FET clauses linked to the MST. I will first examine awards rendered in the context of NAFTA (section 3.1), CAFTA (section 3.2), and then under other treaties (section 3.3).

3.1 NAFTA

I have found 27 awards dealing with NAFTA Article 1105(1).[427] The clause is entitled 'Minimum Standard of Treatment' and reads as follows:

> Each Party shall accord to investments of investors of another Party treatment in accordance with international law, including fair and equitable treatment and full protection and security.[428]

NAFTA case law is important for three reasons. First, the awards rendered after 2000 were the first ones to comprehensively address the scope and content of the FET standard which had found its way into most investment treaties in the previous decade. Second, the reaction of the States' parties to these awards has had wide-ranging and

426. My analysis of case law does not support the conclusion reached by Islam, *supra* n. 14, 64-65, for whom 'given that customary international law is itself highly indeterminate and its evolutionary nature contentious', 'it is clear that, in the vast majority of investment treaties, the host developing countries need to assume that a tribunal will interpret the FET standard as an independent and autonomous standard'.

427. *Metalclad, supra* n. 363; *S.D. Myers Inc. v. Canada,* UNCITRAL, First Partial Award, 13 Nov. 2000, para. 266; *Pope & Talbot Inc. v. Canada,* UNCITRAL, Award, the Merits of Phase II, 10 Apr. 2001; *Pope & Talbot Inc. v. Canada,* UNCITRAL, Award in Respect of Damages, 31 May 2002; *Mesa Power Group, LLC v. Canada,* UNCITRAL PCA Case No. 2012-17, Award, 24 Mar. 2016; *Lone Pine Resources Inc. v. Canada,* ICSID Case No. UNCT/15/2, Final Award, 21 Nov. 2022; *Windstream Energy LLC v. Canada,* UNCITRAL, Award, 27 Sep. 2016; *Mondev International Ltd. v. United States,* ICSID Case No. ARB(AF)/99/2, Award, 2 Oct. 2012; *Waste Management, Inc. v. Mexico ('Number 2'),* ICSID Case No. ARB(AF)/00/3, Award, 30 Apr. 2004; *Glamis, supra* n. 24; *Apotex Holdings Inc & Apotex Inc. v. United States,* ICSID Case No. ARB(AF)/12/1, Award, 25 Aug. 2014; *ADF Group Inc. v. United States,* ICSID Case No. ARB(AF)/00/1, Award, 6 Jan. 2003; *Cargill, supra* n. 421; *Merrill & Ring Forestry L.P. v. Canada,* UNCITRAL, Award, 31 Mar. 2010; *Eli Lilly and Company v. Canada,* UNCITRAL, Case No. UNCT/14/2, Final Award, 16 Mar. 2017; *Bilcon, supra* n. 22; *Mobil Investments, supra* n. 117; *Robert Azinian, Kenneth Davitian, & Ellen Baca v. Mexico,* ICSID No. ARB(AF)/97/2, Award, 1 Nov. 1999; *Loewen Group, Inc. and Raymond L. Loewen v. United States,* ICSID No. ARB(AF)/98/3, Award, 26 Jun. 2003; *Methanex Corporation v. United States,* UNCITRAL, Award, 3 Aug. 2005; *Thunderbird, supra* n. 23; *Chemtura Corporation v. Canada,* UNCITRAL, Award, 2 Aug. 2010; *Vento Motorcycles, Inc. v. Mexico,* ICSID Case No. ARB(AF)/17/3, Award, 6 Jul. 2020; *Jorge Luis Blanco, Joshua Dean Nelson and Tele Fácil México, S.A. de C.V. v. Mexico,* ICSID Case No. UNCT/17/1, Final Award, 5 Jun. 2020; *Grand River Enterprises Six Nations, Ltd., et al. v. United States,* UNCITRAL, Award, 12 Jan. 2011; *Gami Investments, Inc. v. Mexico,* UNCITRAL, Award, 15 Nov. 2004; *Lion Mexico Consoli, v. Mexico,* ICSID Case No. ARB(AF)/15/2, Award, 20 Sep. 2021.

428. For a general analysis, *see,* P. Dumberry, *The Fair and Equitable Treatment Standard: A Guide to NAFTA Case Law on Article 1105* (Wolters Kluwer 2013).

lasting repercussions beyond the NAFTA context. The clarifications adopted by the NAFTA parties regarding the scope of the FET standard were subsequently followed by numerous States. Third, NAFTA awards (those rendered after the 2001 Note) have mostly applied Article 1105 in a consistent way. Below, I will explain that while a few awards (*Merrill & Ring, Bilcon*) have adopted different views than the majority of awards on the scope and content of the clause, their influence has remained limited. They are considered 'outliers' among what can be qualified as a 'jurisprudence constante'. Importantly, this largely consistent case law has had a tremendous impact on how other tribunals (outside NAFTA) have interpreted treaties where the FET standard is also linked to the MST (such as CAFTA, further examined below). In fact, according to Alschner, NAFTA is by far the most cited treaty, as it holds 15% of all 'inward' citations.[429] He speaks of the 'unique position' of NAFTA which is 'by far the most influential IIA in the ISDS citation network'.[430]

Before examining NAFTA case law, it should be mentioned that NAFTA has been replaced by another treaty, the Canada-United States-Mexico Agreement (CUSMA).[431] The new treaty contains a detailed FET clause linked to the MST which is very similar to the US Model BIT.[432] Yet, it is likely that the new FET clause will not be frequently applied in the future.[433] Most importantly, as mentioned above in Part I, NAFTA case law on the FET has already had a tremendous impact on how States have drafted FET clauses in new treaties. The most prominent example is the Comprehensive Economic and Trade Agreement (CETA). NAFTA case law has also had a very important impact on the way tribunals have interpreted similarly-drafted FET clauses (a point further discussed below). Given that States are increasingly including FET clauses linked to the MST in their new BITs the legacy of NAFTA case law is likely going to be felt for decades to come.

429. Wolfgang Alschner, *Investment Arbitration and State-Driven Reform* (Oxford UP) 245. An 'inward' citation occurs when a tribunal set up under a certain treaty refers to a case decided under another treaty (such as NAFTA).

430. *Ibid.*, 246.

431. Agreement Between the United States of America, the United Mexican States, and Canada (CUSMA), adopted on 10 Dec. 2019, entered into force on 1 Jul. 2020.

432. *See*, Art. 14.6(1).

433. Annex 14-D of Ch. 14 on investor-State dispute settlement does not apply between Canada and the United States and between Canada and Mexico. It should be added that investors from Canada and Mexico will still be able to sue both States under the ISDS mechanism contained in another multilateral treaty: the Comprehensive and Progressive Agreement for Trans-Pacific Partnership (CPTPP). The implication of this important change from NAFTA is that Art. 14.6(1) on the FET only finds application in disputes involving an US or a Mexican investor against either the United States or Mexico. Yet, under Art. 14-D.3 of Annex 14.D (applicable between these two countries), only claims for breach of national treatment, most-favoured nation, and 'direct' (not indirect) expropriation can be submitted to arbitration. FET claims are therefore excluded. However, this exclusion does not apply to contracts which qualify as 'covered government contracts' (mentioned at Annex 14-E), which includes oil and gas production, power generation, transportation, telecoms and certain other infrastructure investments. It should be added that under the CUSMA, investors from all three States could still raise NAFTA Ch. 11 claims with respect to 'legacy' investments within three years after the termination of NAFTA.

In the following sections, I will examine the following points:

- Early case law and the 2001 Note of Interpretation (section 3.1.1).
- Since the 2001 Note, all tribunals have applied the MST under custom (section 3.1.2).
- Tribunals have narrowly defined the content of the FET standard and have applied a high threshold of gravity to find a breach (section 3.1.3).
- The restrictive approach adopted by tribunals has had an impact on their findings regarding liability and compensation (section 3.1.4).

3.1.1 Early Case Law and the 2001 Note of Interpretation

Early NAFTA case law was marked by the controversial rulings rendered by three tribunals in 2000-2001: *Metalclad, S.D. Myers* and *Pope & Talbot*. Their findings can be summarised as follows:

- The *Metalclad* Tribunal concluded that when interpreted in light of the NAFTA preamble, Article 1105 includes obligations of transparency and predictability.[434] The Tribunal found that Mexico had failed to ensure a transparent and predictable framework for the investor's investment and that this constituted a breach of Article 1105. The Tribunal awarded the investor USD 16.7 million in compensation for Mexico's breach of Articles 1105 and 1110.
- Soon after, the *S.D. Myers* Tribunal rendered its Partial Award awarding the investor CAD 6 million[435] in compensation for the breach of both Articles 1102 and 1105. In the award, two of the three tribunal members concluded that a finding of a breach of the national treatment provision (Article 1102) supported a claim for a breach of Article 1105.[436] This conclusion was rejected by the Parties.[437] Another controversial finding was the Tribunal's interpretation of the FET clause as an 'overriding' provision that covers other standards of protection, including the national treatment.
- The *Pope & Talbot* Tribunal released its Award on the Merits of Phase 2 concluding, *inter alia*, that Article 1105 requires the application of the FET *independently* (and *in addition*) to the MST under international law.[438] One important aspect of the case is that during the proceedings, all three NAFTA Parties had expressly rejected that interpretation. The Tribunal finally concluded that Canada had breached its obligations under Article 1105 regarding one aspect of the implementation of the 1996 bilateral Canada–United States Softwood Lumber Agreement (i.e., the 'verification review' process). In other

434. *Metalclad, supra* n. 363, paras 70, 76.
435. Around USD 4 million in 2000.
436. *S.D. Myers, supra* n. 427, para. 266. Arbitrator Chiasson dissented and considered that a breach of another provision cannot be the foundation for a violation of Art. 1105.
437. M. Kinnear, A. Bjorklund & J.F.G. Hannaford, *Investment Disputes under NAFTA: An Annotated Guide to NAFTA Chapter 11* (Kluwer Law 2006) 23.
438. *Pope & Talbot* (2001 award), *supra* n. 427.

ongoing NAFTA arbitration cases at the time, NAFTA Parties strongly rejected the reasoning of the *Pope & Talbot* Tribunal; the US affirmed (only *two days* after the award was rendered) that it was 'poorly reasoned and unpersuasive';[439] Canada stated that the Tribunal had 'arrived at an incorrect interpretation of fair and equitable';[440] and Mexico indicated that the Tribunal's 'refusal to adopt the Parties' shared view [on this point] can only be viewed as perverse'.[441]

- In the meantime, Mexico had commenced set-aside proceedings of the *Metalclad* award before the Supreme Court of British Columbia (the seat of the arbitration proceedings) to challenge, *inter alia*, the Tribunal's broad interpretation of Article 1105. Justice Tysoe issued his decision on 22 May 2001, a little over a month after the controversial *Pope & Talbot* award.[442] In his decision, Justice Tysoe rejected in rather strong terms, the reasoning behind the *Pope & Talbot* ruling on Article 1105 and concluded that the protection under this provision was limited to the MST. His conclusion reflected the position that had been advanced by NAFTA Parties in the proceedings.[443] Justice Tysoe rejected the *Metalclad* Tribunal's findings on the so-called transparency obligation and set aside the part of the award related to Article 1105.

In reaction to these developments, on 31 July 2001, under the aegis of the FTC,[444] the trade ministers of the three NAFTA Parties issued the 'Notes of Interpretation of Certain Chapter 11 Provisions' (hereinafter the 'Note') regarding two issues: access to documents and the relation between the FET standard and the MST. For the present purposes, the relevant part of the Note regarding Article 1105 reads as follows:

> 1. Article 1105(1) prescribes the customary international law minimum standard of treatment of aliens as the minimum standard of treatment to be afforded to investments of investors of another Party.
> 2. The concepts of 'fair and equitable treatment' and 'full protection and security' do not require treatment in addition to or beyond that which is required by the customary international law minimum standard of treatment of aliens.
> 3. A determination that there has been a breach of another provision of the NAFTA, or of a separate international agreement, does not establish that there has been a breach of Article 1105(1).

The ultimate goal of the NAFTA Parties when they put forward the Note was to 'correct' the interpretations given by previous NAFTA tribunals. For instance, the Note overruled *Pope & Talbot*'s holding that the FET standard of protection should be considered *in addition* to the MST. It was now clear to everyone that the FET clause was a reference to the MST under customary international law.

---

439. *Methanex, supra* n. 427, US Reply Memorial on Jurisdiction, Admissibility and the Proposed Amendment, 12 Apr. 2001, at 26.
440. *Ibid.*, Canada's Second Art. 1128 Submission, 30 Apr. 2001.
441. *Ibid.*, Mexico's Art. 1128 Submission, 30 Apr. 2001.
442. *Mexico v. Metalclad, supra* n. 363.
443. Kinnear, *supra* n. 437, 27.
444. The Commission is composed of one representative from each NAFTA Party (Art. 2001).

3.1.2 *Since the 2001 Note All Tribunals Have Applied the MST under Custom*

NAFTA Article 1131(2) makes it clear that the Note is binding for NAFTA tribunals. As a result, all tribunals (even *Bilcon*)[445] which have rendered awards after the Note have concluded that the FET under Article 1105 is a reference to the MST under custom. In the words of the *Bilcon* award, 'NAFTA Article 1105 is, then, identical to the minimum international standard.'[446] The *Mesa* Tribunal is also clear on this point:

> The FTC Note is clear that the Tribunal must apply the customary international law standard of the international minimum standard of treatment, and nothing else There is thus no scope for autonomous standards to impose additional requirements on the NAFTA Parties.[447]

Another similar example is the *Windstream* award:

> The Tribunal therefore considers that the treatment required under Article 1105(1) is fair and equitable treatment and full protection and security consistent with the minimum standard of treatment under customary international law. In other words, as stated by the FTC, the treatment required is not 'in addition to or beyond' that which is required by the customary international law standard, but one that is in accordance, or consistent, with the standard, while remaining 'fair and equitable' and providing 'full protection and security'.[448]

Yet, I have explained elsewhere[449] that some tribunals have challenged in the past the letter and the spirit of the FTC Note and thereby undermined its real effectiveness. These tribunals have basically used two distinct (yet closely related) sets of arguments, which can be summarised as follows.

On the one hand, some tribunals have interpreted customary international law as an evolving and flexible concept. In other words, faced with the binding FTC Note that *restricts* the extent of investors' rights, these tribunals have simply 'moved the goal post'. They have interpreted customary international law broadly by emphasising its evolutionary character. Under this interpretation, the level of protection offered to foreign investors under Article 1105 is (at least theoretically) *superior* to the treatment under the minimum standard. This reasoning was adopted by the *Pope & Talbot*

445. *Bilcon supra* n. 22, para. 432 ('In light of the FTC Notes and in the specific context of NAFTA Chapter Eleven in which this Tribunal operates, "fair and equitable treatment" and "full protection and security" cannot be regarded as "autonomous" treaty norms that impose additional requirements above and beyond what the minimum standard requires').
446. *Ibid.*, para. 433. *See also*, *Cargill*, *supra* n. 421, para. 268, 'the Tribunal joins all previous NAFTA tribunals in the view that Article 1105 requires no more, nor less, than the minimum standard of treatment demanded by customary international law'.
447. *Mesa Power*, *supra* n. 427, para. 502. *See also*, *Lone Pine*, *supra* n. 427, para. 613.
448. *Windstream*, *supra* n. 427, para. 356.
449. Dumberry, *supra* n. 428, 106ff.; P. Dumberry, *Moving the Goal Post! How Some NAFTA Tribunals have Challenged the FTC Note of Interpretation on the Fair and Equitable Treatment Standard under NAFTA Article 1105*, 8(2) World Arb. & Med. Rev. (2014); F. Jadeau & F. Gélinas, *CETA's Definition of the Fair and Equitable Treatment Standard: Toward a Guided and Constrained Interpretation*, 13(1) TDM 10-11 (2016) DOI: 10.2139/ssrn.2931503.

Tribunal in its 2002 ruling.[450] This position is even clearer in two subsequent NAFTA awards (*Mondev* and *ADF*). The *Merrill & Ring* Tribunal later took this 'evolutionary' approach to the extreme by adopting the theory of 'convergence'.[451] It held that the MST had evolved so rapidly in recent years to the point where it now (apparently) protects foreign investors 'against all such acts or behaviour that might infringe on a sense of fairness, equity and reasonableness'.[452] The adoption of this approach by the *Merrill & Ring* Tribunal is a direct challenge to the FTC Note.[453]

On the other hand, other tribunals (*Glamis, Cargill*) have taken a different approach. The *Glamis* Tribunal first noted that the 'fundamentals' of the *Neer* standard still apply today and therefore, in order to prove a violation of the MST, an investor must show that the conduct was 'egregious' and 'shocking'.[454] Yet, the Tribunal was quick to add that it was 'entirely possible, however that, as an international community, we may be shocked by State actions now that did not offend us previously'.[455] In other words, while the '*test*' may not have changed, it nevertheless remains that the *perception* regarding what is 'egregious' and 'shocking' has evolved over time. The type of State conduct that would have not been considered a breach of the MST in the past may be deemed so today. Whether this is the case is for each tribunal to determine. Nothing prevents a tribunal from adopting a very liberal interpretation of what it considers to be 'egregious' and 'shocking' State conduct. This is indeed what the *Bilcon* Tribunal did in its 2018 award (a point further discussed below). It should be added that in a more recent award, the *Windstream* Tribunal made comments suggesting that what really matters to determine the content of the MST standard is the wording used more than the 2001 FTC Note itself.[456]

---

450. *Pope & Talbot* (2002 award), *supra* n. 427.
451. The point is further examined below in Part III.
452. *Merrill & Ring, supra* n. 427, para. 210.
453. For a critical analysis of the award, *see*: Dumberry, *supra* n. 428, 117-122; UNCTAD, *supra* n. 2, 57 ('This appears, at first glance, to reaffirm a very expansive reading of the FET standard, while at the same time saying that this actually represents the customary minimum standard. The *Merrill & Ring* tribunal failed to give cogent reasons for its conclusion that the MST made such a leap in its evolution, and by doing so has deprived the 2001 NAFTA Interpretative Statement of any practical effect').
454. *Glamis, supra* n. 24, para. 616.
455. *Ibid.*
456. *Windstream, supra* n. 427, para. 355: 'The Tribunal has carefully analyzed the Parties' positions and considers that, when determining the content of the standard of treatment contained in Article 1105(1) of NAFTA, it cannot disregard the language of the provision. While the FTC in its Notes of Interpretation established that the rule contained in Article 1105(1) of NAFTA, bearing the heading "Minimum Standard of Treatment", is the customary international law minimum standard of treatment, it does not follow that the terms used in this provision have thereby become irrelevant; there is nothing in the FTC's Notes which would suggest that NAFTA tribunals should entirely disregard the relevant rules of treaty interpretation. Indeed, there can be no "plain reading" of a treaty provision that would involve no interpretation at all; "plain meaning" is in itself a result of interpretation. Consequently, when determining the content of the standard of treatment contained in Article 1105(1), the Tribunal must take into account both FTC's Notes of Interpretation, which establish that the standard contained in Article 1105(1) is indeed the customary international law minimum standard of treatment, and the general rule of treaty interpretation, as reflected in Article 31 of the Vienna

3.1.3 *Tribunals Have Narrowly Defined the Content of the FET Standard and Required a High Threshold of Gravity to Find a Breach*

As explained elsewhere by the present author,[457] two main conclusions emerge from NAFTA case law.[458]

NAFTA tribunals have recognised that the FET standard under Article 1105 contains only a *limited number* of specific elements of protection that must be accorded to investors. They have generally adopted (with one exception)[459] the 'shopping list' approach used by a number of authors whereby the FET standard is described as comprising a number of 'elements'.[460] The best example is the following passage from the *Waste Management* award which has since been endorsed by many tribunals:[461]

> Taken together, the *S.D. Myers, Mondev, ADF* and *Loewen* cases suggest that the minimum standard of treatment of fair and equitable treatment is infringed by conduct attributable to the State and harmful to the claimant if the conduct is arbitrary, grossly unfair, unjust or idiosyncratic, is discriminatory and exposes the claimant to sectional or racial prejudice, or involves a lack of due process leading to an outcome which offends judicial propriety – as might be the case with a manifest failure of natural justice in judicial proceedings or a complete lack of transparency and candour in an administrative process. In applying this standard it is relevant that the treatment is in breach of representations made by the host State which were reasonably relied on by the claimant.
>
> Evidently the standard is to some extent a flexible one which must be adapted to the circumstances of each case.[462]

Convention, which establishes that a treaty must be interpreted "in good faith in accordance with the ordinary meaning to be given to the terms of the treaty in their context and in the light of its object and purpose"'.

457. Dumberry, *supra* n. 428, 44ff.
458. The same conclusion was reached by the Tribunal in *Apotex, supra* n. 427, Part IX, paras 9.41, 9.47.
459. *Windstream, supra* n. 427, paras 347ff. The Tribunal also did not identify the elements to be considered within in the FET 'box'. This is noteworthy given that the parties had argued the case from this 'shopping' list perspective (*see*, para. 298). The Tribunal referred to *Mondev, supra* n. 427, where the Tribunal said that 'what is fair and equitable cannot be reached in the abstract', and added that: 'just as the proof of the pudding is in the eating (and not in its description), the ultimate test of correctness of an interpretation is not in its description in other words, but in its application on the facts' (para. 362). Instead, the Tribunal referred on several occasions to the requirement that conduct be 'unfair' and 'inequitable' (paras 376 and 379).
460. *See*, for instance (the list is not exhaustive), *Glamis, supra* n. 24, para. 627; *Cargill, supra* n. 421, para. 296; *Mobil Investments, supra* n. 117, para. 152; *Eli Lilly, supra* n. 427, para. 222; *Bilcon, supra* n. 22, para. 442; *Mesa Power, supra* n. 427, para. 502.
461. *Lone Pine, supra* n. 427, para. 608, noting that the dictum of the *Waste Management* Tribunal (*supra* n. 427) 'has been considered by almost every arbitral tribunal coming thereafter and has also been followed by many arbitral tribunals as describing the current customary international law minimum standard of treatment for FET'. *See also, Bilcon, supra* n. 22, para. 442 ('The formulation of the "general standard for Article 1105" by the Waste Management Tribunal is particularly influential, and a number of other tribunals have applied its formulation of the international minimum standard based on its reading of NAFTA authorities'); *Mesa Power, supra* n. 427, para. 501.
462. *Waste Management, supra* n. 427, para. 98.

Most recently, the *Mesa* award mentioned the following components of the FET under Article 1105:

> arbitrariness; 'gross' unfairness; discrimination; 'complete' lack of transparency and candor in an administrative process; lack of due process 'leading to an outcome which offends judicial propriety'; and 'manifest failure' of natural justice in judicial proceedings. Further, the Tribunal shares the view held by a majority of NAFTA tribunals that the failure to respect an investor's legitimate expectations in and of itself does not constitute a breach of Article 1105, but is an element to take into account when assessing whether other components of the standard are breached.[463]

In the following paragraphs, I will summarise NAFTA case law regarding the different elements of protection considered to fall into the FET 'box'.

All NAFTA tribunals have held that an obligation not to deny justice exists under Article 1105.[464] They have also consistently recognised the existence of a due process obligation.[465] NAFTA tribunals have also required a high threshold of gravity or seriousness to find a breach. They have, for instance, referred to a 'complete' lack of due process.[466] In contrast, the majority of the *Bilcon* Tribunal mentioned that 'the imprudent exercise of discretion or even outright mistakes [by administrative authorities] do not, as a rule, lead to a breach' of the FET standard.[467] The reasoning suggests that a much lower threshold was actually applied by the majority.[468] In his dissenting opinion, McRae emphasised the existence of a high threshold ('the NAFTA standard is not the domestic law standard'),[469] adding that 'whether Canadian law has been complied with is a relevant consideration in deciding whether there has been a violation of Article 1105 NAFTA, it is not of itself sufficient to establish such a violation'.[470]

463. *Mesa Power, supra* n. 427, para. 502.
464. *See*, for instance (the list is not exhaustive): *Azinian, supra* n. 427, paras 102ff.; *Metalclad, supra* n. 363, paras 91, 93; *Pope & Talbot* (2001 award), *supra* n. 427, para. 181; *Pope & Talbot* (2002 award), *supra* n. 427, para. 68; *Mondev, supra* n. 427, paras 96, 126-127; *Loewen, supra* n. 427, paras 54ff., 87, 119, 122, 124-137; *Glamis, supra* n. 24, para. 22; *Waste Management, supra* n. 427, paras 95, 97ff.; *Thunderbird, supra* n. 23, para. 194; *Methanex, supra* n. 427, Part IV, Ch. C, p. 8, para. 15; *S.D. Myers, supra* n. 427, para. 134; *Mobil Investments, supra* n. 117, para. 152; *Apotex, supra* n. 427, Part IX, para. 9.16.
465. *See, inter alia, Glamis, supra* n. 24, para. 22; *Waste Management, supra* n. 427, para. 98; *Thunderbird, supra* n. 23, para. 85; *Chemtura, supra* n. 427, para. 145; *Apotex, supra* n. 427, Part IX, paras 9.41ff., 9.49; *Vento, supra* n. 427, paras 302ff.
466. *Glamis, supra* n. 24, para. 627; *See also*: *Cargill, supra* n. 421, para. 296 (referring to 'an utter lack of due process so as to offend judicial propriety'); *Eli Lilly, supra* n. 427, paras 222ff.; *Mesa Power, supra* n. 427, para. 502 (referring to 'gross' unfairness, 'complete' lack of transparency and candour in an administrative process; lack of due process 'leading to an outcome which offends judicial propriety'; and 'manifest failure' of natural justice in judicial proceedings); *Loewen, supra* n. 427, para. 132 (referring to 'manifest injustice in the sense of a lack of due process leading to an outcome which offends a sense of judicial propriety'); *Blanco, supra* n. 427, paras 359, 363, 361 (indicating that a 'lack of due process can be established only if the administration has *entirely* disregarded the procedural rules that it must follow within a particular process', emphasis in the original).
467. *Bilcon, supra* n. 22, para. 437.
468. *Ibid.*, paras 590ff.
469. *Ibid.*, Dissenting opinion of McRae, para. 42.
470. *Ibid.*, para. 31.

All NAFTA tribunals that have examined the concept of transparency have come to the conclusion that it is *not* a stand-alone element of the FET standard and that it does not impose any obligation on host States under Article 1105.[471] This position is in line with the approach adopted by UNCTAD in its 2012 Report.[472] Two NAFTA awards have adopted a rather nuanced approach on this point.[473] The only exception is the *Metalclad* award,[474] which was set aside in judicial review before a B.C. Court precisely with regards to this point.[475] All other tribunals have endorsed the position taken by the *Waste Management* Tribunal, which considered the concept of transparency relevant to assess whether the due process obligation had been breached.[476] NAFTA tribunals have consistently denied the existence, as a stand-alone obligation under Article 1105, of a broader obligation to maintain a stable legal and business environment for investments.[477] There is only one exception to this line of awards.[478] The *Windstream* award could possibly be considered another exception.[479] Tribunals have also denied that there is a stand-alone obligation of 'proportionality' under NAFTA.[480]

471. *Glamis, supra* n. 24, para. 561; *Cargill, supra* n. 421, para. 294.
472. UNCTAD, *supra* n. 2, 90 concluding that 'transparency, consistency, legality and stability of regulatory framework' are not part of custom.
473. *See, Merrill & Ring, supra* n. 427, para. 231, noting that a 'requirement for transparency may not at present be proven to be part of the customary law standard, as the judicial review of *Metalclad* rightly concluded, but that it is nonetheless approaching that stage'. *See also, Mesa Power, supra* n. 427, referring to 'complete' lack of transparency (para. 502) and mentioning (para. 595) that 'the existence of an obligation of transparency under international law and under Article 1105 of the NAFTA in particular is a controversial issue', but deciding that it was not 'necessary to enter into the merits of this debate in the context of this dispute'.
474. *Metalclad, supra* n. 363, paras 70, 76. 88, 99.
475. *Mexico v. Metalclad, supra* n. 363, paras 68, 72.
476. *Waste Management, supra* n. 427, para. 98.
477. For instance, *Mobil Investments, supra* n. 117, para. 153.
478. *Merrill & Ring, supra* n. 427, para. 232, indicating that 'the stability of the legal environment is also an issue to be considered in respect of fair and equitable treatment' and that 'State practice and jurisprudence have consistently supported such a requirement (...)'.
479. *Windstream, supra* n. 427. The Tribunal noted that although the conduct of the government of Ontario leading to its decision to impose a moratorium on the development of offshore wind 'could have been more transparent' (because the claimant 'was kept in the dark as to the evolving policy position of the Government while [it] continued to invest in the Project'), this was not wrongful in itself, since it was 'at least in part driven by a genuine policy concern' about the scientific impact of such a project (paras 376-377). But for the Tribunal, the government had failed to undertake appropriate scientific studies on offshore wind (adding that those studies undertaken had not led to any changes to the regulatory framework, para. 378), and, most importantly, it 'did little to address the legal and contractual limbo in which Windstream found itself after the imposition of the moratorium' (para. 379). The Tribunal concluded that such conduct was 'unfair and inequitable' (para. 379). It also stated that the failure of the Government 'to take the necessary measures (...) within a reasonable period of time after the imposition of the moratorium to bring clarity to the regulatory uncertainty surrounding the status and the development of the Project created by the moratorium, constitutes a breach of Article 1105(1) of NAFTA' (para. 380). This passage seems to suggest that the Tribunal recognised the existence of a much broader obligation to maintain a stable legal and business environment for investments.
480. *Resolute Forest Products Inc. v. Canada*, PCA Case No. 2016-1, Award, 25 Jul. 2022, para. 757: 'With one tenuous exception, tribunals have not accepted proportionality as a stand-alone criterion to assess whether the host State has afforded fair and equitable treatment. Instead, investment tribunals – including those referred to by the Claimant – apply a proportionality test

Several NAFTA tribunals have held that a prohibition of arbitrary conduct exists under the MST;[481] all of them have listed it as a stand-alone element of the FET standard under Article 1105. The threshold of severity applied by NAFTA tribunals regarding arbitrary conduct has consistently been high. They have referred to treatment that 'rises to the level that is unacceptable from the international perspective',[482] to '*wholly* arbitrary' conduct,[483] and to 'manifest arbitrariness falling below international standards'.[484] For instance, the *Glamis* Tribunal stated that Article 1105 'requires something greater than mere arbitrariness, something that is surprising, shocking, or exhibits a manifest lack of reasoning'[485] and sets the threshold of liability at 'manifest arbitrariness'.[486] In *Cargill,* the Tribunal said that 'arbitrariness may lead to a violation of a State's duties under Article 1105, but only when the State's actions move beyond a merely inconsistent or questionable application of administrative or legal policy or procedure to the point where the action constitutes an unexpected and shocking repudiation of a policy's very purpose and goals, or otherwise grossly subverts a domestic law or policy for an ulterior motive'.[487] NAFTA tribunals have consistently stated that 'something more' than simple illegality is required to constitute an arbitrary conduct. In *Bilcon,* the majority of the Tribunal adopted a much lower threshold.[488] It is noteworthy that only one tribunal (*Cargill*) found that an arbitrary conduct had been committed. The Tribunal held that Mexico had deliberately and intentionally targeted the US investor in retaliation for a US trade policy.

With one exception,[489] NAFTA tribunals have held that nationality-based discrimination is *not* covered by Article 1105 and that custom does not contain any general prohibition of discrimination against foreign investors.[490] Some tribunals have examined allegations of discrimination within the broader context of arbitrariness.[491]

---

as part of their appraisal of other manifestations of the fair and equitable treatment standard, such as due process or arbitrariness.'

481. *See*, Dumberry, *The Prohibition against Arbitrary Conduct and the Fair and Equitable Treatment Standard under NAFTA Article 1105*, 15 J. World Invest.& Trade 117ff. (2014) DOI: 10.1163/22129000-01502004, examining several cases.
482. *S.D. Myers, supra* n. 427, para. 263.
483. *Waste Management, supra* n. 427, para. 115, emphasis added.
484. *Thunderbird, supra* n. 23, para. 194. *See also, Lone Pine, supra* n. 427, para. 612.
485. *Glamis, supra* n. 24, para. 617.
486. *Ibid.*, paras 626ff. *See also, Eli Lilly, supra* n. 427, paras 222ff.
487. *Cargill, supra* n. 421, para. 293.
488. *Bilcon, supra* n. 22, para. 591, concluding that the 'The JRP [Joint Review Panel] effectively created, without legal authority or fair notice to Bilcon, a new standard of assessment [i.e. the "community core values" factor] rather than fully carrying out the mandate defined by the applicable law.' In his dissenting opinion, McRae paras 36-37 disagreed. On this point, *see*, M. Carfagnini, *Too Low a Threshold: Bilcon v. Canada and the International Minimum Standard of Treatment*, Canadian YIL 274-276 (2016) DOI 10.1017/cyl.2016.17.
489. *Merrill & Ring, supra* n. 427, para. 208.
490. *Methanex, supra* n. 427, Part IV, Ch. C, p. 8, paras 14-27; *Grand River, supra* n. 427, paras 208ff.; *Glamis, supra* n. 24, para. 542, fn. 1087; *Mercer International Inc. v. Canada*, ICSID Case No. ARB(AF)/12/3, Award, 6 Mar. 2018, paras 7.58, 7.86ff. (Orrego Vicuna dissenting on this point); *Vento, supra* n. 427, paras 324ff.
491. *Gami, supra* n. 427, paras 24, 98.

The reasonings of other tribunals[492] can be interpreted as suggesting that Article 1105 covers some types of specific ('targeted')[493] 'discrimination' (*other* than nationality-based), such as 'sectional or racial prejudice'.[494]

A few words should be mentioned about the controversial concept of legitimate expectations. Thus far, only one NAFTA tribunal (*Bilcon*)[495] has found that a host State stood in violation of the obligation to protect an investor's legitimate expectations under Article 1105. Until recently, only the *Glamis* award[496] (and to some extent the *Thunderbird* award)[497] could be considered supporting the view that the concept of legitimate expectations is a stand-alone element of the FET standard under Article 1105.[498] The *Bilcon* award,[499] however, fully endorsed this controversial proposition which had been prominent among many tribunals outside NAFTA.[500] Other NAFTA tribunals have instead followed the approach adopted by the *Mobil* Tribunal.[501] They have held that the host State's failure to respect an investor's legitimate expectations does *not* constitute a breach of the FET standard by itself, but is rather a 'factor' to be taken into account when assessing whether or not *other well-established* elements of the standard have been breached.[502] These tribunals have thus followed the NAFTA Parties' position that such an 'obligation' is not a component of the MST under custom. NAFTA tribunals have also repeatedly qualified the concept of legitimate expectations narrowly in order to significantly reduce its scope of application. They have endorsed the four-element definition adopted by the *Thunderbird* Tribunal: (1) conduct or representations must have been made by the host State; (2) the claimant must have

492. *Waste Management, supra* n. 427, para. 98, endorsed by *Mobil Investments, supra* n. 117, para. 152; *Mesa Power, supra* n. 427, para. 502; *Eli Lilly, supra* n. 427, paras 416, 431ff.
493. *Cargill, supra* n. 421, para. 300 (indicating that 'willful targeting, by its nature, to be a manifest injustice' in breach of FET, para. 550); *Blanco, supra* n. 427, para. 351.
494. The terms are mentioned in *Waste Management, supra* n. 427, para. 98. The question is examined in UNCTAD, *supra* n. 2, 81-82.
495. *Bilcon, supra* n. 22.
496. *Glamis, supra* n. 24, para. 627. The Tribunal in *Eli Lilly, supra* n. 427, para. 381, endorsed the reasoning of the *Glamis* award on this point, but decided not to take a position on the question.
497. *Thunderbird, supra* n. 23, para. 147. *See also*, the separate opinion of Wälde, para. 37, stating that the legitimate expectations principle is a 'self-standing subcategory and independent basis for a claim under the 'fair and equitable standard' as under Art. 1105 of the NAFTA'.
498. Dumberry, *supra* n. 22.
499. *Bilcon, supra* n. 22, paras 444-445, 448-449, 455ff., 470, 589. *See*, however, the dissenting opinion of McRae, paras 5, 33, 39.
500. *See*, analysis in: F. Dupuy & P.M. Dupuy, *What to Expect from Legitimate Expectations? A Critical Appraisal and Look into the Future of the 'Legitimate Expectations' Doctrine in International Investment Law*, in: M.A. Raouf, P. Leboulanger & N.G. Ziadé (eds), *Festschrift Ahmed Sadek El-Kosheri: From the Arab World to the Globalization of International Law* (Kluwer 2015) 280, noting and explaining the differences between NAFTA and non-NAFTA case law. *See also*, 285 ('almost all NAFTA tribunals share a restrictive vision of the expectations principle. (...) This conclusion is in clear contrast with the position adopted in a number of non-NAFTA awards interpreting the host state's obligations under a BIT or a multilateral treaty such as the ECT').
501. *Waste Management, supra* n. 427, para. 98; *Cargill, supra* n. 421, para. 296 (where the Tribunal does not list the concept of legitimate expectations among the elements of the FET standard under Art. 1105); *Mesa Power, supra* n. 427, para. 502. The Tribunal in *Lone Pine, supra* n. 427, para. 614, did not take a position on this issue because no representation had been made.
502. *Mobil Investments, supra* n. 117, para. 152.

relied on such conduct or representations to make its investment; (3) such reliance by the claimant on these representations was 'reasonable'; and (4) the host State subsequently repudiated these representations, therefore, causing damage to the investor.[503] Another manifestation of the narrow approach favoured by NAFTA tribunals is the fact that they have continued to further restrictively *qualify* these four requirements in subsequent awards. Thus, the *Glamis* award (subsequently endorsed by other tribunals)[504] required that an investor's expectations be based on 'definitive, unambiguous and repeated'[505] specific 'commitments'[506] (or 'assurances')[507] made by the host State which have 'purposely and specifically induced the investment'[508] by the investor.[509] It should be added that NAFTA tribunals have held that legitimate expectations *cannot* simply be based on the host State's existing domestic legislation on foreign investments at the time when the investor makes its investment.[510] In contrast, the majority in *Bilcon* adopted a much broader interpretation of the concept of legitimate expectations.[511]

In sum, NAFTA case law is in sharp contrast with the position adopted by non-NAFTA tribunals which have been increasingly willing to recognise new requirements as components of the ever-enlarged concept of the FET standard.[512] The recent

503. *Thunderbird, supra* n. 23, para. 147.
504. *Cargill, supra* n. 421, para. 290; *Mobil Investments, supra* n. 117, paras 152, 170; *Grand River, supra* n. 427, para. 141.
505. *Glamis, supra* n. 24, para. 802.
506. *Ibid.*, para. 767.
507. *Ibid.*, paras 800ff.
508. *Ibid.*, para. 766. *See also*, para. 767.
509. It should be added that the majority of the Tribunal in *Bilcon, supra* n. 22, adopted a much broader approach on the issue. See, however, the dissenting opinion of McRae, paras 5, 33, 39.
510. *Glamis, supra* n. 24, paras 620, 766; *Mobil Investments, supra* n. 117, paras 153, 620; *Mesa Power, supra* n. 427, para. 619.
511. *Bilcon, supra* n. 22. The award referred to the need for 'specific representations, rather than abstract references to the general legal framework in relation to an investment or general statements about the attractiveness of an investment destination' (para. 589). Yet, the majority of the Tribunal has nevertheless interpreted the concept in a much broader and very *different* way than other tribunals by consistently referring to 'specific encouragements' (*see*, for instance, paras 448, 470). As rightly noted by McRea, in his dissenting opinion, any such 'assurances or encouragement' by officials have 'nothing to do with the expectation that an investor will have Canadian law applied properly to it' (adding 'that is an expectation that an investor would have independently of any assurances or encouragement') (para. 5). For him, such encouragements are therefore of 'no assistance' (para. 33) in the instant case because the 'failure to treat someone in accordance with Canadian law does not of itself constitute a breach of Article 1105' (para. 39).
512. Picherack, *supra* n. 319, 270: 'In contrast to the conservative rulings of the NAFTA and other tribunals discussed in the previous section, the decisions of a number of recent arbitral tribunals outside of the NAFTA context have arguably pushed the bounds of the minimum standard and the fair and equitable treatment standard to well past their previous contours. Underlying many of these recent decisions is a re-conceptualization of the standard away from a traditional interpretation that imposes obligations on States not to treat investors unfairly or inequitably understood in accordance with the minimum standard as traditionally applied, and towards a belief that the standard imposes additional and stricter obligations on States to act proactively in favour of the investor in order to promote, stimulate and ensure the investor's investment'. *See also* at 271: 'As part of this re-conceptualization, tribunals have been increasingly willing to identify a number of new requirements as essential or core elements to the standard of fair and equitable treatment. Recent additional requirements popular with

Bilcon award (majority) seems to be an outlier in this respect.[513] It is noteworthy that its reasoning has been contested by all three contracting parties in subsequent proceedings.[514] Since then, no NAFTA tribunal has followed the broad approach adopted by the *Bilcon* award.

Finally, it should be mentioned that (almost all) NAFTA tribunals have consistently required proof of a high (or 'very high')[515] threshold of severity or gravity to conclude that the host State has breached any of the elements contained within the FET standard under Article 1105.[516] Even the *Bilcon* Tribunal agreed with other awards on this point.[517] As pointed out by the *Glamis* and *Cargill* tribunals, the existence of such a high threshold is clear given NAFTA tribunals' consistent use of qualifiers such as 'manifest', 'gross', 'evident', 'blatant', and 'complete'.[518] This is indeed one aspect that clearly differentiates NAFTA case law from awards rendered by other tribunals which have often used a lower threshold of liability when applying a stand-alone FET clause.[519] One example, mentioned above, is the *Saluka* award.[520]

In practice, the majority in *Bilcon*[521] and, to some extent, the *Windstream* award[522] did not apply the same high threshold. The *Merrill & Ring* Tribunal also

---

tribunals include provision at all times of a stable and predictable business environment, the respect of the legitimate substantive expectations of foreign investors, and the requirement of total transparency as central to fair and equitable treatment and the minimum standard'.

513. On this question, Carfagnini, *supra* n. 488, 273-274; E.B. Barrera, *The Case for Removing the Fair and Equitable Treatment Standard from NAFTA*, CIGI Papers No. 128, 6ff. (2017).

514. *Mesa Power, supra* n. 427, Canada Observations on the *Bilcon* Award, 14 May 2015; *Mesa Power*, Mexico Submission on the *Bilcon* Award, 12 Jun. 2015; *Mesa Power*, US Submission on the *Bilcon* Award, 12 Jun. 2015.

515. *Lone Pine, supra* n. 427, para. 626 ('The Tribunal recalls that the standard to be met for a breach of NAFTA Article 1105 is a very high one') and using the term 'high threshold' elsewhere (paras 611, 623, 629, 631, 633).

516. *Glamis, supra* n. 24, para. 627; *Mesa Power, supra* n. 427, paras 504, 512; *Cargill, supra* n. 421, paras 285, 296; *Waste Management, supra* n. 427, para. 115; *ADF, supra* n. 427, para. 190; *Thunderbird, supra* n. 23, para. 194; *Eli Lilly, supra* n. 427, paras 222-223; *Apotex, supra* n. 427, Part IX, paras 9.47-9.49; *Blanco, supra* n. 427, para. 323; *Lone Pine, supra* n. 427, para. 611.

517. *Bilcon, supra* n. 22, para. 441 ('The Tribunal in the present case agrees that there is indeed a high threshold for Article 1105 to apply') para. 444 (noting that the list of elements covered by the FET obligation mentioned in the dictum by the *Waste Management* award, *supra* n. 427, 'conveys that there is a high threshold for the conduct of a host state to rise to the level of a NAFTA Article 1105 breach').

518. *Cargill, supra* n. 421, para. 616; *Glamis, supra* n. 24, para. 616. *See also*: *Blanco, supra* n. 427, para. 323 ('The Tribunal notes that the use of language such as "gross", "manifest", and "complete lack" indicates that the threshold for showing a breach of this obligation is particularly high'); *Eli Lilly, supra* n. 427, paras 222-223; *Lone Pine, supra* n. 427, para. 612 (putting the bar at 'manifestly or demonstrably arbitrary, grossly unfair, inherently unjust, or idiosyncratic').

519. *See*, UNCTAD, *supra* n. 2, 90 indicating that 'the difference between the two expressions of the standard is that the liability threshold under an unqualified FET standard will be somewhat lower than under the qualified one'.

520. *Saluka, supra* n. 51, para. 293, indicating that in the context of an autonomous FET clause, 'in order to violate the standard, it may be sufficient that States' conduct displays a relatively lower degree of inappropriateness' while in contrast, under the minimum standard, 'in order to violate that standard, States' conduct may have to display a relatively higher degree of inappropriateness' (para. 292).

521. *Bilcon, supra* n. 22. While the majority of the Tribunal referred to the existence of a high threshold (paras 440-444), it added that 'there is no requirement in all cases that the challenged

adopted a lower threshold. It held that the FET standard provides protection 'against all such acts or behaviour that might infringe on a sense of fairness, equity and reasonableness'[523] and that it 'provides for the fair and equitable treatment of alien investors within the confines of reasonableness'.[524] This approach however had no impact on liability and compensation as the Tribunal found no breach of Article 1105.

3.1.4 *The Restrictive Approach Adopted by Tribunals Has Had an Impact on Their Findings Regarding Liability and Compensation*

In sum, NAFTA tribunals have consistently (with very few exceptions) considered that only a limited number of elements of protection are within the FET 'box'. They have also required that a high threshold of seriousness be present to find a breach. This approach has had direct consequences in terms of finding liability. Very few NAFTA tribunals have concluded that the host State violated Article 1105. Ultimately, the number of awards finding breaches is limited to six cases:

- *Pope & Talbot*, only the FET breached: USD 461,566.
- *S.D. Myers*, violations of Articles 1102 and 1105: CAD 6 million.
- *Cargill*, breach of Articles 1102, 1105 and 1106: USD 77.3 million.
- *Bilcon* (majority), breach of Articles 1102, 1105: USD 7 million.
- *Windstream;* only the FET breached: CAD 25 million.
- *Lion Mexico*, only the FET breached (denial of justice): USD 47 million.

It is undeniable that the narrow interpretations adopted by (almost) all NAFTA tribunals have had some direct consequences in terms of findings on liability. Tribunals have found a breach in only 25% of claims (6 out of 27 awards). The amount of compensation awarded has also been relatively modest, with the exception of a few awards (*Lion Mexico, Cargill*). The success rate of claimants under NAFTA is significantly lower than that of other investors filling claims under stand-alone FET clauses or provisions referring to 'international law'.[525]

---

conduct reaches the level of shocking or outrageous behaviour' (para. 444). *See*, the reasoning of McRae in his dissenting opinion, para. 2, indicating that the Tribunal applied 'the standard in a way that it is met simply by an allegation of a breach of Canadian law'.

522. *Windstream, supra* n. 427. In the general discussion on Art. 1105, the Tribunal did not mention the existence of a high threshold of severity. It held that its task was to determine whether a conduct could be 'considered "unfair" or "inequitable" in accordance with the customary international law minimum standard of treatment' (para. 358). This passage suggests that the Tribunal concretely applied a relatively lower threshold of severity in that case.
523. *Merrill & Ring, supra* n. 427, para. 210.
524. *Ibid.*, para. 213. *See also, Pope & Talbot* (2001 award), *supra* n. 427, para. 118, which however was rendered *before* the 2001 Note.
525. *See* awards examined in Chapters I and II. For the same conclusion, *See*, Gaukrodger, *supra* n. 47, 55.

3.2 CAFTA

The Central America-Dominican Republic Free Trade Agreement (CAFTA-DR) (hereinafter simply referred to as 'CAFTA')[526] contains an FET clause (Article 10.5) entitled 'MST' which reads as follows:

> 1. Each Party shall accord to covered investments treatment in accordance with customary international law, including fair and equitable treatment and full protection and security.
> 2. For greater certainty, paragraph 1 prescribes the customary international law minimum standard of treatment of aliens as the minimum standard of treatment to be afforded to covered investments. The concepts of 'fair and equitable treatment' and 'full protection and security' do not require treatment in addition to or beyond that which is required by that standard, and do not create additional substantive rights. The obligation in paragraph 1 to provide:
>   (a) 'fair and equitable treatment' includes the obligation not to deny justice in criminal, civil, or administrative adjudicatory proceedings in accordance with the principle of due process embodied in the principal legal systems of the world; and
>   (b) 'full protection and security' requires each Party to provide the level of police protection required under customary international law.
> 3. A determination that there has been a breach of another provision of this Agreement, or of a separate international agreement, does not establish that there has been a breach of this Article.

A footnote is attached to the title of the clause indicating that 'Article 10.5 shall be interpreted in accordance with Annex 10-B.'[527]

The language of CAFTA Article 10.5 is the same as Article 5 of the 2004 US Model BIT. The provision contains the same three clarifications: (1) identifying the customary rule at stake as 'the customary international law minimum standard of treatment of aliens'; (2) providing a definition of custom; and (3) explicitly stating that the FET obligation includes: denial of justice and due process. As mentioned in Part I, the text of the 2004 US Model BIT reflects how NAFTA tribunals have interpreted Article 1105, taking into account the Note of Interpretation of 2001. As Gantz puts it, the language of the CAFTA FET clause reflects the NAFTA experience regarding how to interpret the standard.[528] Given that these three clarifying elements were clearly the result of the

526. The Dominican Republic-Central America FTA (CAFTA-DR), signed on 5 Aug. 2004, and entered into force on 1 Jan. 2009, is a FTA between the United States, Costa Rica, El Salvador, Guatemala, Honduras, Nicaragua, as well as the Dominican Republic containing a chapter on investment protection.
527. Annex 10-B (entitled 'Customary International Law') indicates that 'The Parties confirm their shared understanding that 'customary international law' generally and as specifically referenced in Articles 10.5, 10.6, and Annex 10-C results from a general and consistent practice of States that they follow from a sense of legal obligation. With regard to Article 10.5, the customary international law minimum standard of treatment of aliens refers to all customary international law principles that protect the economic rights and interests of aliens.'
528. D.A. Gantz, *Settlement of Disputes under the Central America-Dominican Republic-United States Free Trade Agreement*, 30 B.C. Int'l & Comp. L. Rev. 357 (2007).

NAFTA experience, it is not surprising that CAFTA tribunals have systematically followed NAFTA case law.[529]

As noted by the *Lopez* Tribunal, 'the starting point of any analysis of the content of the MST and its relationship with FET is the language of the applicable instrument and, in particular, the degree of linkage it establishes between FET, on the one hand, and customary international law and MST on the other'.[530] For the Tribunal, 'by stating that the Parties must accord investors "treatment in accordance with customary law, including fair and equitable treatment", Article 10.5.1 of the Treaty indicates that FET is considered part of customary international law'.[531] The Tribunal also noted the position of 'a significant body of case-law based on treaties with similar language' which had stated that a 'strict' MST clause, such as the one found in the US–Oman FTA, identical to the CAFTA FET clause, 'cannot be interpreted in the expansive fashion' like other treaties' autonomous FET provisions have been interpreted.[532] Similarly, all other CAFTA tribunals have applied the MST. None have considered that the FET clause should be given an autonomous character.

The first CAFTA tribunal to examine Article 10.5 was in the *RDC* case.[533] The Tribunal endorsed the content of the MST standard definition as it had been laid out by the NAFTA *Waste Management* Tribunal.[534] It indicated that this award 'persuasively integrates the accumulated analysis of prior NAFTA Tribunals and reflects a balanced description of the minimum standard of treatment'.[535] Importantly, it also applied the same test as the *Waste Management* Tribunal (and used the exact same wording by referring to the 'arbitrary, grossly unfair, and unjust nature of the process')[536] when it concluded that the 'lesivo' process had been abused by Guatemala and used arbitrarily to extract concessions from the investor in breach of Article 10.5.[537] Both parties had referred to the *Waste Management* award and other cases regarding the content of the minimum standard.[538] Another example of a CAFTA tribunal explicitly adopting the *Waste Management* definition is the *TECO* award involving 'an allegation of abuse of power by the regulator and disregard of the regulatory framework in the context of an administrative tariff review process'.[539] The Tribunal defined the conduct in breach of

529. Dumberry, *supra* n. 100.
530. *Lopez, supra* n. 21, para. 407, referring to R. Dolzer, U. Kriebaum & C. Schreuer, *Principles of International Investment Law* (Oxford UP 2022) para. 200.
531. *Lopez, supra* n. 21, para. 408.
532. *Ibid.*, referring to *Adel A Hamadi Al Tamimi v. Oman*, ICSID Case No. ARB/11/33, Award, 27 Oct. 2015, para. 382.
533. *Railroad Development Corporation v. Guatemala*, ICSID Case No. ARB/07/23, Award, 29 Jun. 2012, para. 219.
534. *Waste Management, supra* n. 427, para. 98.
535. *RDC, supra* n. 533, para. 219. It should be added that Prof. James Crawford was sitting as a panel member in both the *Railroad* and the *Waste Management* cases.
536. *Ibid.*, para. 235.
537. *Ibid.*, para. 234.
538. *Ibid.*, Claimant (para. 156, referring to *Tecmed, supra* n. 28) and Respondent (para. 162, referring to the *GAMI*, *Thunderbird* and *Genin* awards).
539. *TECO Guatemala Holdings LLC v. Guatemala*, ICSID Case No. ARB/10/23, Award, 19 Dec. 2013, para. 454, *see also*, para. 492: 'State's regulatory powers cannot amount to condoning behaviors that are manifestly arbitrary, idiosyncratic, or that show a complete lack of candor in the conduction of the regulatory process.'

Article 10.5 as one that is 'arbitrary, grossly unfair or idiosyncratic, is discriminatory or involves a lack of due process leading to an outcome which offends judicial propriety'.[540]

The reason why the *RDC* Tribunal only referred to NAFTA case law, to define the content of Article 10.5, is apparent from the pleadings. The Respondent stated that the 'Claimant may not rely on the definition of fair and equitable treatment provided by international tribunals that were not similarly bound by the minimum standard of treatment of customary international law.'[541] In other words, the case law (outside NAFTA) dealing with autonomous FET clauses is not relevant when interpreting CAFTA. The Claimant (and El Salvador)[542] agreed: it observed that 'the terms of CAFTA and NAFTA are essentially the same in describing the fair and equitable obligation' and considered that 'arbitral awards in NAFTA cases are particularly relevant to this Tribunal'.[543] While the *RDC* Tribunal did not explicitly take a position on this point, the fact that it only referred to NAFTA awards shows that it essentially agreed with the position of the parties. The parties in other CAFTA cases have also followed the same approach. As the *Lopez* Tribunal noted, 'Claimants and Respondent rely heavily on case-law, predominantly on NAFTA.'[544]

CAFTA tribunals have also defined the content of the standard in the exact same way as NAFTA awards did.[545] They have also referred to the high threshold of gravity or seriousness required to find a breach.[546] Their findings are summarised in the following paragraphs.

CAFTA tribunals have considered that arbitrariness is a stand-alone element of the FET standard. The *Spence* Tribunal also endorsed the high threshold of severity that has been applied by NAFTA tribunals.[547] El Salvador in its Non-Disputing Party

540. *Ibid.*, para. 454. *See also*, paras 454, 465, 587, 465, 492. In support of this definition, the Tribunal cited (at para. 455) two NAFTA awards (*Waste Management* and *Glamis*) and two authors.
541. *Ibid.*, para. 159. The important distinction between stand-alone and NAFTA-style FET clauses would also subsequently become paramount in the context of the annulment proceedings in the *TECO* case, *supra* n. 539.
542. *RDC, supra* n 533, para. 208.
543. *Ibid.*, para. 177. *See also*, para. 187 on arbitrary conduct.
544. *Lopez, supra* n. 21, para. 405.
545. Denial of justice is the only element of the FET standard regarding which CAFTA tribunals have not systematically referred to NAFTA case law. *See*, Dumberry, *supra* n. 100. As further examined below, the *Lopez* Tribunal, *supra* n. 21, adopted a different view on whether the concept of legitimate expectations is a stand-alone element of the FET.
546. *Lopez, supra* n. 21, paras 413, 428, 415 (indicating that 'The choice of words' of the NAFTA *Waste Management* Tribunal 'and particularly the adjectives "*gross*" and "*manifest*"' 'underscores the stringency of the standard') 416 ('whilst malicious intention, willful neglect of duty or bad faith are not required elements of the MST under customary international law, there must be some aggravating factor such that the acts of the State in question consist of more than a minor derogation from what is deemed to be internationally acceptable').
547. *Spence International Investments, Llc, Berkowitz, et al, v. Costa Rica*, ICSID case No. UNCT/13/2, Interim Award, 30 May 2017, agreeing with the NAFTA *Glamis* award speaking of treatment being 'sufficiently egregious and shocking so as to fall below accepted international standards' (para. 282) and adding that 'such conduct includes' 'manifest arbitrariness and blatant unfairness' (para. 282). The Tribunal also explained that the Respondent could only be held liable at the merits stage if it could be shown that the property valuations adopted by the

Submission[548] also referred to 'manifest arbitrariness'.[549] In contrast, the US did not mention arbitrary conduct at all as part of the MST.[550] It should be added that other tribunals (*RDC*,[551] *Aven*,[552] and *Lopez*)[553] simply mentioned the adjective 'arbitrary' without using any qualifier. The *TECO* award used both terminologies.[554]

The *Lopez* Tribunal noted that the FET clause 'anchors MST to customary international law' and that the obligation of transparency does not constitute an 'autonomous requirement under the MST', but it added that 'lack of transparency becomes relevant if it adversely impacts due process or propriety of process'.[555] Just like NAFTA awards, CAFTA tribunals have applied a high gravity threshold to find a breach of due process.[556]

Similarly to the position adopted by the majority of NAFTA awards, two CAFTA tribunals have not referred to the concept of legitimate expectations as a stand-alone element of the FET standard, but rather as being only relevant in the context of the assessment of whether or not a certain State conduct is arbitrary, unfair, etc.[557] It should be added that the US[558] and El Salvador[559] have consistently taken the same position in their non-disputing submissions. In *Kappes*, all four intervening States

courts were 'manifestly arbitrary, blatantly unfair or were otherwise in breach' of the MST requirement (para. 156, also paras 86, 88, 135).

548. *Ibid.*, para. 156.
549. *Ibid.*, paras 86, 88, 135.
550. *Ibid.*, para. 360, referring to the Non-Disputing Party Submission of the United States indicating that 'the obligation to provide fair and equitable treatment, which includes, for example, a denial of justice, which could arise, illustratively, when a State's judiciary administers justice to aliens in a notoriously unjust or egregious manner that offends a sense of judicial propriety'.
551. *RDC, supra* n. 533, para. 235.
552. *David R. Aven and Others v. Costa Rica*, ICSID Case No. UNCT/15/3, Final Award, 18 Sep. 2018, para. 585, making one single reference to the term.
553. *Lopez, supra* n. 21, para. 428.
554. *TECO, supra* n. 539, using no qualifier at paras 454, 465, 587, but referring to 'manifestly arbitrary' at para. 492.
555. *Lopez, supra* n. 21, paras 426-427, 532 ('the standard of treatment of Article 10.5 of the Treaty does not incorporate a general duty of transparency, and lack of transparency is only relevant if it reaches the threshold of a serious breach of due process'). This was also the position adopted by the US in its Non-Disputing Party Submission (para. 402).
556. *TECO, supra* n. 539, paras 458 (referring to 'willful disregard of the fundamental principles upon which the regulatory framework is based, a complete lack of candor or good faith on the part of the regulator in its dealings with the investor, as well as a total lack of reasoning, would constitute a breach of the minimum standard') 465, 457 (indicating that to assess whether there is a breach of due process, 'it is relevant that the Guatemalan administration entirely failed to provide reasons for its decisions or disregarded its own rules'); *Lopez, supra* n. 21, paras 428 (speaking of conduct that is 'grossly unreasonable and disproportionate or manifestly fails to respect procedural propriety and due process') 532 (referring to 'serious breach of due process'), 520 (referring to procedural irregularities that are 'grave enough to shock a sense of judicial propriety' and that 'the threshold to establish a breach of due process is high').
557. *RDC, supra* n. 533, paras 50. 172. 189, 235; *Spence, supra* n. 547, para. 283 ('there is insufficient support for the proposition' that the MST includes a 'stand-alone protection of the expectations of the investor').
558. *See*, for instance: US' position, in *Lopez, supra* n. 21, para. 402; *Spence, supra* n. 547, para. 160; *Michael Ballantine and Lisa Ballantine v. Dominican Republic*, PCA Case No. 2016-17, Final Award, 3 Sep. 2019, para. 416.
559. *See*, *RDC, supra* n. 533, para. 210; *Spence, supra* n. 547, para. 156; *TECO, supra* n. 539, para. 621.

(Costa Rica, the Dominican Republic, El Salvador and the US) adopted the same view.[560] CAFTA tribunals also qualified the concept of legitimate expectations narrowly in order to reduce its scope of application.[561] The reasoning of the *Lopez* Tribunal is however different. It first dismissed the relevance of one passage of the ICJ *Bolivia v. Chile* case on legitimate expectations in the specific context of investment arbitration.[562] The *Lopez* Tribunal mentioned that 'many investment treaty tribunals' had 'brought the concept of legitimate expectations within the purview of provisions on the treatment of aliens under the MST'.[563] It nevertheless added that 'the requirements for a finding of a violation by a State of an investor's legitimate expectation are stringent'.[564] Expectations need to be 'reasonable and objective in light of the circumstances and the State's conduct'.[565] The Tribunal found no violation of the FET standard.

Perhaps surprisingly, the application of the MST and the NAFTA-style narrow definition of the scope of the FET standard did not seem to have had a direct impact in terms of liability and compensation. Thus, some of the tribunals that examined the clause[566] held that the FET clause had not been breached (*Lopez, Aven*). Others did find a violation of this specific head of damages (*RDC, TECO*).[567] The compensations awarded were relatively modest (*RDC*, USD 10 million; *TECO,* USD 21 million) compared to awards rendered under different FET clauses mentioned above in Chapters I and II.

3.3 Other Tribunals Examining FET Clauses Where the Standard Is Expressly Linked to the MST

In this section, I will examine the reasoning of other tribunals which have assessed FET clauses with wording similar, or identical, to the provision found in the US Model BIT (2004), where the standard is expressly linked to the MST. I have found 10 awards

560. *Daniel W. Kappes and Kappes, Cassiday & Associates v. Guatemala*, ICSID Case No. ARB/18/43. The (unpublished) submissions are discussed in: IAReporter, 16 Mar. 2021. The case is pending.
561. *TECO, supra* n. 539, paras 611, 617-618, 621.
562. *Lopez, supra* n. 21, para. 419. In *Obligation to Negotiate Access to the Pacific Ocean (Bolivia v. Chile)*, Judgment, 1 Oct. 2018, ICJ Rep. 2018, para. 162, the Court said that from many references to legitimate expectations found in arbitral awards, it does not follow 'that there exists in general international law a principle that would give rise to an obligation on the basis of what could be considered a legitimate expectation'. For the *Lopez* Tribunal, the Court's dictum 'is to be understood simply as denying that such awards can be invoked as evidence of the existence of a rule of customary international law on legitimate expectations applicable to the relations between States'. The Tribunal believes that 'is not dispositive' to infer from this dictum the existence of any rule of custom 'denying effects to legitimate expectations engendered by States in the specific context of their relations with foreign investors'.
563. *Lopez, supra* n. 21, para. 420.
564. *Ibid.*, para. 422.
565. *Ibid.*, para. 423.
566. In *Spence, supra* n. 547, the case was discontinued, and no final decision was rendered.
567. The award was partially annulled in set aside proceedings started by the investor regarding the evaluation of the amount of compensation. *See, TECO, supra* n. 539, Annulment Proceedings, Decision on Annulment, 5 Apr. 2016. The claim was resubmitted, and the award rendered on 13 May 2020, awarded more than USD 26 million.

where the tribunals examined the status of the FET clause and its relationship with the MST.[568]

3.3.1 *Awards Adopting a NAFTA-Style Restrictive Approach*

The first example is the *Al Tamimi v. Oman* case. It interpreted the US-Oman FTA, which contains the same FET language as the US Model BIT. The Tribunal stated that a 'strict' MST provision 'cannot be interpreted in the expansive fashion in which some autonomous fair and equitable treatment or full protection and security provisions of other treaties have been interpreted'.[569] It also noted that tribunals have 'continued to employ descriptions which emphasise the high threshold for breach', adding that a breach of the MST 'requires more than a minor derogation from the ideal standard of perfectly fair and equitable treatment'.[570] The Tribunal cited NAFTA awards and applied the same standard. Interestingly, it referenced the standard articulated in the *Tecmed* award, which necessitates establishing a breach 'merely if a State fails to act "in a consistent manner, free from ambiguity and totally transparently in its relations with the foreign investor"'.[571] The Tribunal explained that the *Tecmed* standard was not applicable in the present case where the FET clause 'imposes a higher threshold for breach'.[572] This is the relevant passage:

> The Tribunal does not accept the Claimant's contention, citing Tecmed v. Mexico, that the standard will be breached merely if a State fails to act 'in a consistent manner, free from ambiguity and totally transparently in its relations with the foreign investor'. That standard may be consistent with an 'autonomous' treaty standard for fair and equitable treatment, which was the relevant standard before

568. Three other cases should be briefly mentioned. *Bay View Group LLC and The Spalena Company LLC v. Rwanda*, ICSID Case No. ARB/18/21, Award, 30 Mar. 2022, was decided under the US-Rwanda BIT, which contains the same clause as in the US Model BIT. The Tribunal did not examine the meaning or scope of this provision. It examined allegations regarding legitimate expectations. It referred to the position of the US in its third-party submission, indicating that the concept 'is not a component element of "fair and equitable treatment" under customary international law that gives rise to an independent host State obligation', but sided with the respondent's narrow definition of the concept. Ultimately, the Tribunal held that it did not have jurisdiction over the case. In *Bridgestone Licensing Services, Inc. and Bridgestone Americas, Inc. v. Panama*, ICSID Case No. ARB/16/34, Award, 14 Aug. 2020, the clause contained in the US-Panama Trade Promotion Agreement was the same as the US Model BIT. The Tribunal did not examine the scope of the clause insofar as the case only involved allegations of denial of justice. It only stated that 'there is no doubt that, when considering whether there has been a denial of justice under the TPA, the standard of customary international law has to be applied' (para. 178). In *Bear Creek Mining Corporation v. Peru*, ICSID Case No. ARB/14/21, Award, 30 Nov. 2017, para. 533, decided under the Canada-Peru FTA, whose FET clause is also similar to the US Model BIT, the Tribunal concluded that one decree adopted by Peru constituted an unlawful indirect expropriation and that there was, therefore, 'no need to examine whether it also constituted a breach of a duty to afford Claimant' FET. Yet the award contains a very detailed analysis of the position of the parties on the scope of the standard.
569. *Al Tamimi, supra* n. 532, paras 382, 384, 386.
570. *Ibid.*, paras 383-384.
571. *Ibid.*, para. 386, citing *Tecmed, supra* n. 28, para. 154.
572. *Ibid.*, para. 386.

> the Tribunal in Tecmed. The minimum standard of treatment in customary international law, to which Article 10.5 is expressly linked by virtue of Article 10.5.2, as well as Annex 10-A, imposes a higher threshold for breach. The language of Article 10.5.2 makes it very clear that the State Parties intended to impose only the minimum standard of treatment under customary international law. Whether other treaties impose a different standard of requisite treatment is not the concern of the present Tribunal.[573]

Based on these findings, the Tribunal said that establishing a breach of the FET clause requires evidence of a 'gross or flagrant disregard for the basic principles of fairness, consistency, even-handedness, due process, or natural justice expected by and of all States under customary international law'.[574] It held that no violation of the FET standard had been committed.

The second example is the *Elliott v. Korea* case. It was decided under the US-Korea FTA, which contains the same FET clause as the US Model BIT.[575] The Tribunal stated that the provision 'makes clear that the applicable standard is that of customary international law rather than an autonomous standard of fairness and equity'.[576] The Tribunal then explained that the claimant had to show that the act or omission '(i) constitutes a breach of a fundamental rule of procedure of customary international law governing treatment of aliens; or (ii) is incompatible with a substantive rule (or norm) of customary international law governing the treatment of aliens'.[577] The Tribunal mentioned that denial of justice and due process were illustrations of procedural standards of conduct. The Tribunal referred to the Parties' agreement that 'the content of the MST obligation was authoritatively described' in the NAFTA *Waste Management* award. It also referred to similarities and differences between NAFTA Article 1105 and the FET clause in the BIT.[578] Given that the claimant neither allege any breach of the investor's legitimate expectations nor any lack of transparency, the Tribunal did not address them. The Tribunal found that the Respondent's conduct was 'unjust' and amounted to (using the *Neer* case wording) a 'willful neglect of ... duties' and 'a pronounced degree of improper action' which was 'incompatible with a rule of customary international law prohibiting such conduct that forms part' of the MST.[579] In practice, the Tribunal applied a high threshold of seriousness to find a breach. The

573. *Ibid.*
574. *Ibid.*, para. 390, adding: 'Such a standard requires more than that the Claimant point to some inconsistency or inadequacy in Oman's regulation of its internal affairs: a breach of the minimum standard requires a failure, wilful or otherwise egregious, to protect a foreign investor's basic rights and expectations.'
575. *Elliott Associates L.P. v. Korea*, PCA Case No. 2018-51, Award, 20 Jun. 2023.
576. *Ibid.*, para. 568.
577. *Ibid.*, para. 569.
578. *Ibid.*, para. 573: 'The Waste Management II award was not based on the Treaty, but on Article 1105 of NAFTA. Nevertheless, although the wordings of Article 11.5 of the Treaty and Article 1105 of NAFTA are not identical, they are similar, in particular when Article 1105 of NAFTA is considered in light of its interpretation by the NAFTA Free Trade Commission.' The Tribunal also noted some differences between the two provisions.
579. *Ibid.*, para. 603.

Tribunal found that the FET clause had been breached and awarded USD 54 million in compensation.[580]

In *Gramercy*, the Tribunal examined the FET clause contained in the US-Peru Trade Promotion Agreement which includes very similar language to the US Model BIT. The Tribunal mentioned at the outset that 'a classic debate in investment arbitration law' is whether the FET standard in a treaty 'coincides with or differs from the MST' under custom. It stated that 'there is no single answer to this question because there is diversity in the way the FET standard is formulated in investment treaties: certain agreements do not make any reference to the MST and customary international law, while others do'.[581] The Tribunal did not hesitate to say that the treaty 'provides clear rules incardinating the FET standard under the Treaty within customary international law and the MST'.[582] It did not further discuss the scope and content of the MST given that only arbitrariness was alleged. It also 'acknowledge[d] that the threshold for proving that State conduct is arbitrary or unjust is high', but explained that 'in the present case, this high threshold is met'.[583] It held that some measures were arbitrary in breach of the clause and awarded USD 33.2 million in compensation.

The *Kenon* award examined the FET clause in the Peru-Singapore FTA which contains the exact same clarifications as the US Model BIT.[584] At the time of writing, the award was not publicly available, but its content has been reported. The Tribunal apparently stated that the expression 'treatment in accordance with customary law, including fair and equitable treatment' could 'only be understood as acknowledging that FET is now part of the MST under customary international law'. It also stated that the phrase 'in addition to or beyond that which is required' by custom was meant to 'prevent an overbroad interpretation of the MST/FET, setting a higher threshold for a finding of breach than under an autonomous FET clause not tethered to customary international law'.[585] The fact that the clause was providing for a higher threshold than under an autonomous FET provision meant that 'both arbitrariness and discrimination must be sufficiently serious', meaning that 'only sufficiently blatant instances of arbitrariness and discrimination may justify a finding of breach'. The Tribunal found that one measure adopted by the State was 'seriously arbitrary' in breach of the FET clause. It also stated that 'as part of their broader customary international law obligation to act in good faith, host States must also protect an investor's legitimate expectations', adding, however, that the requirements for finding a breach of legitimate expectations 'must be stringent'. The Tribunal held that the standard does not offer a guarantee of a stable and predictable legal and regulatory environment. The Tribunal awarded USD 110.7 million in compensation.

580. To this amount should be added some USD 28 million in costs. In a subsequent rectification Award, 1 Sep. 2023, the amount of compensation was reduced by USD 5.1 million.
581. *Gramercy Funds Management LLC and Gramercy Peru Holdings LLC v. Peru*, ICSID Case No. UNCT/18/2, 6 Dec. 2022, para. 823.
582. *Ibid.*, para. 824.
583. *Ibid.*, para. 987.
584. *Kenon Holdings Ltd and IC Power Ltd v. Peru*, ICSID Case No. ARB/19/19, 3 Oct. 2023 Award, reported in: IARep, 11 Oct. 2023.
585. *Ibid.*

I have found two cases dealing with the FET clause (entitled 'MST') contained in the Mexico-Spain BIT.[586] In *Abengoa*, the Tribunal had no difficulty recognising that this clause referred to the MST under custom.[587] It endorsed the high threshold of severity mentioned in the NAFTA *Glamis* and *Cargill* awards.[588] It found that some of the actions taken were arbitrary and contrary to legitimate expectations[589] and that an expropriation took place. It awarded a total of MXN 491 million. The case was later settled between the parties. In the *Del Valle Ruiz* case, the Tribunal stated that 'a textual interpretation of the clause, including its title, leaves no doubt that the standard contained in Article IV of the Treaty is the minimum standard of treatment in accordance with customary international law'.[590] The Tribunal added that the awards invoked by the Claimants were 'equally unhelpful' because they dealt with BITs which referred to either 'international law' or 'principles of international law', and not to MST or custom.[591] Based on the dictum of the NAFTA *Waste Management* award, the Tribunal listed a limited number of conducts prohibited by the FET clause using the same qualifying adjectives[592] typical of NAFTA case law.[593] Importantly, the Tribunal also agreed with the view held 'by a majority of tribunals acting under a treaty where the FET clause was confined to the minimum standard of treatment' that the failure to respect an investor's legitimate expectations 'in and of itself does not constitute' a breach of the MST under custom, adding that it 'is an element to take into account when assessing whether other components of the standard are breached'.[594] The Tribunal held that the FET clause had not been breached.

In the *Rand Investments* case,[595] the Tribunal examined the FET clause (entitled 'MST') in the Canada-Serbia BIT.[596] The majority of the Tribunal had no hesitation in finding that the clause 'unequivocally limits FET to' the MST.[597] The majority of the

586. The clause reads as follows: 'Each Contracting Party shall accord to investments of investors of the other contracting party treatment in accordance with customary international law, including Fair and Equitable Treatment and full protection and security.'
587. *Abengoa S.A. y COFIDES S.A. v. Mexico*, ICSID Case No. ARB(AF)/09/2, Award, 18 Apr. 2013, para. 640.
588. *Ibid.*, para. 641.
589. *Ibid.*, referring to the *Waste Management* dictum, para. 98, where the expectations are not considered a stand-alone element of the FET standard.
590. *Antonio Del Valle Ruiz and others v. Spain*, PCA Case No. 2019-17, Final Award, 13 Mar. 2023, para. 513.
591. *Ibid.*, para. 515.
592. *Ibid.*, para. 518, noting that 'the use in Waste Management II of intensifying adjectives or adverbs such as "manifest", "complete" or "grossly" for certain characteristics of non-conforming conduct makes it clear that acts or omissions constituting a breach must be of a serious nature'.
593. *Ibid.*, para. 519.
594. *Ibid.*
595. *Rand Investments ltd., William Archibald Rand, Kathleen Elizabeth Rand, Allison Ruth Rand, Robert Harry Leander Rand and Sembi Investment Limited v. Serbia*, ICSID case no. Arb/18/8, Award, 29 Jun. 2023.
596. The clause provides for 'treatment in accordance with the customary international law minimum standard of treatment of aliens, including fair and equitable treatment and full protection and security' with the additional clarification that the concept of FET does 'not require treatment in addition to or beyond that which is required by' the MST under custom.
597. *Rand Investments, supra* n. 595, para. 599.

Tribunal cited the NAFTA *Waste Management* award which had 'correctly identified the content of the standard'.[598] It also referred to the NAFTA *Mesa* award which said, *inter alia*, that 'the failure to respect an investor's legitimate expectations in and of itself does not constitute a breach of Article 1105, but is an element to take into account when assessing whether other components of the standard are breached'.[599] The majority also said that 'the threshold for breaching the customary international law minimum standard of treatment is high'.[600] The majority held that some of the conduct and measures breached the FET clause and awarded EUR 14.5 million in compensation.

Finally, in other awards, the Tribunal's reasoning is much more limited. One illustration is the *PACC Offshore* case, where the Tribunal examined the FET clause in the Mexico-Singapore BIT which includes very similar language to the US Model BIT. The Tribunal recognised that the FET obligation under this provision did not extend 'beyond the MST'.[601] The Tribunal then asked this question: 'what does it mean FET when the Treaty links it to the minimum standard of treatment'? The Tribunal simply referred to the dictum of the *Waste Management* Tribunal without providing any other explanation. It concluded that the measure adopted by Mexico 'was arbitrary, grossly unfair and unjust' in breach of the clause[602] and awarded USD 6.7 million in compensation.

What these awards all have in common is that they have largely followed NAFTA case law in terms of defining the content of the FET standard narrowly and in applying a high threshold of severity to find a breach. Only one award (*Kenon*) recognised that the concept of legitimate expectations was a stand-alone element of the FET standard.

3.3.2 *Eco Oro v. Colombia*: Divergence of Opinion

One very interesting recent case where the question of the status of the FET clause was examined in detail is *Eco Oro v. Colombia*,[603] which was decided under the Canada-Colombia FTA. The FTA contains the same three elements of clarification found in the US Model BIT.[604] The majority of the Tribunal noted that the provision was not an

598. *Ibid.*, para. 601.
599. *Ibid.*, para. 603, citing: *Mesa Power, supra* n. 427, para. 502.
600. *Ibid.*, para. 604.
601. *PACC Offshore Services Holdings v. Mexico*, ICSID Case No. UNCT/18/5, 11 Jan. 2022, para. 255.
602. *Ibid.*, para. 259.
603. *Eco Oro Minerals Corp. v. Colombia*, ICSID Case No. ARB/16/41, Decision on Jurisdiction, Liability and Directions on Quantum, 9 Sep. 2021.
604. It should be added that although the provision does contain a clarification about the meaning of the term 'custom' in a footnote (and not in an annex), the definition is slightly different insofar as it indicates that this is a reference to 'international custom, as evidence of a general practice accepted as law, in accordance with subparagraph 1(b) of Article 38 of the Statute of the International Court of Justice'. Importantly, the Joint Commission set up under the FTA issued its Decision No. 6 on 24 Oct. 2017 whereby it further clarified, *inter alia*, that 'the investor has the burden of proving all elements of its claim [filed under Art. 805], consistent with general principles of international law applicable to international arbitration', adding that

autonomous FET and that, therefore, the obligation should not be interpreted expansively: 'The Tribunal also accepts that Colombia is under no obligation to exceed this standard and, as it is not considering an autonomous treaty standard of FET but a "minimum" standard, the Tribunal further accepts the obligation should not be interpreted expansively.'[605] Sands, in his dissenting opinion, agreed with the majority on this point:

> This language makes clear – as the Majority recognises – that the standard of protection which has been granted to the investor is the Minimum Standard of Treatment ('MST'), the one that exists in customary international law. The standard to be applied by the Tribunal is not the Fair and Equitable Treatment ('FET') standard, one that is to be found and applied in other investment protection agreements. The parties to the FTA have reinforced the distinction between the two different standards by the authoritative interpretation of Article 805 and MST adopted in 2017 by the Joint Commission established under the FTA; this confirms that the investor has 'the burden to prove a rule of customary international law invoked under Article 805'.[606]

The majority of the Tribunal then made this comment:

> The Tribunal does not, however, accept that footnote 2 to Article 805 limits it as to what sources the Tribunal may refer to as evidence in analysing the meaning of MST under customary international law; the concept has been considered by several tribunals and where the Tribunal finds it to be of assistance in ascertaining what is the current meaning of MST under customary international law, it considers those decisions which it finds to be relevant. As stated by the tribunal in Merrill 'State practice and opinio juris will be the guiding beacons of this evolution'.[607]

The passage is rather confusing. On the one hand, the majority cited the *Merrill & Ring* case[608] to affirm that the meaning of the MST should be discovered by examining State practice and *opinio juris*. But, on the other hand, the majority indicated that its analysis would *not* be limited to an examination of the two elements of custom. It explicitly said that it would also look at what other awards have said on the matter. But, as rightly pointed out by the Respondent, 'investment treaty tribunal decisions are not acceptable sources, at best they only reflect State practice and opinio juris'.[609] There is no doubt that arbitral awards cannot be considered evidence of *State* practice for the formation of rules of custom.[610] The NAFTA *Glamis* Tribunal stated that awards 'do not constitute State practice and thus cannot create or prove customary international law',[611] and added that awards can also 'serve as illustrations of

'This includes the burden to prove a rule of customary international law invoked under Article 805, through evidence of the elements of customary international law referred to in footnote 2 of Chapter Eight'.

605. *Eco Oro, supra* n. 603, para. 745.
606. *Ibid.*, dissenting opinion, para. 5.
607. *Ibid.*, para. 745.
608. *Merrill & Ring, supra* n. 427.
609. *Eco Oro, supra* n. 603, para. 731.
610. Dumberry, *supra* n. 420, 283.
611. *Glamis, supra* n. 24, para. 605.

customary international law if they involve an examination of customary international law'.[612] The same conclusion was reached by the NAFTA *Cargill* Tribunal stating that awards 'do not create customary international law but rather, at most, reflect customary international law'.[613] In other words, awards play an essential role in 'revealing' or determining whether such a rule exists.[614] The NAFTA *Lone Pine* award is the most recent tribunal to recognise this important point.[615] In another NAFTA award, the Tribunal said that it would have to rely on 'indirect' evidence, including awards, when the parties have failed to present evidence of the existence of a rule of custom.[616] At any rate, the passage in the majority's decision seems to be in contradiction with what the FET clause explicitly requires the Tribunal to do, i.e., only look at State practice and *opinio juris*.[617] Sands reached the same conclusion in his dissenting opinion:

> As with all rules of customary international law, the crucial issue is whether there is sufficient evidence of state practice and opinio juris to support the conclusion of the existence of a rule of customary law. As noted below, the majority has made no effort to address that evidentiary requirement, ignoring the explicit requirement of the FTA drafters that the Claimant must prove the content of the rule of customary international law invoked under Article 805.[618]

In the *Eco Oro* case, the arbitrators also fundamentally disagreed on whether or not a NAFTA-style approach should be followed regarding the interpretation of the FET

612. *Ibid. See also*, at para. 603 where the Tribunal does not list 'arbitral decisions' among the potential 'authoritative sources' of State practice which can demonstrate the existence of a rule of custom.
613. *Cargill, supra* n. 421, para. 277.
614. J. Crawford, *Brownlie's Principles of Public International Law* (8th ed. Oxford UP 2012) 19. It should be added that a decision by a tribunal identifying a given rule of custom is, of course, not per se conclusive as to the customary nature of such a rule. The actual weight to be a given to such a decision will depend on the authoritative stature of the court which has rendered the decision as well as the quality of the reasoning. *See, Cargill, supra* n. 421, para. 277.
615. *Lone Pine, supra* n. 427, para. 600: 'the Tribunal clarifies that arbitral awards rendered by international arbitral tribunals do not constitute State practice or opinio juris and, as such, do not create customary international law. Having said that, arbitral awards may serve as illustrations of custom, particularly those awards containing an examination of customary international law. Furthermore, whether an arbitral tribunal's articulation of the standard of customary international law has been consistently followed by later arbitral tribunals and is also relied on by States in other proceedings is a relevant guiding consideration in the analysis of the current standard of customary international law'.
616. *Windstream, supra* n. 427, para. 351: 'The Tribunal further agrees with the Respondent that in principle the content of a rule of customary international law such as the minimum standard of treatment can best be determined on the basis of evidence of actual State practice establishing custom that also shows that the States have accepted such practice as law (opinio juris). However, the Tribunal notes that neither Party has produced such evidence in this arbitration. In the circumstances, the Tribunal must rely on other, indirect evidence in order to ascertain the content of the customary international law minimum standard of treatment; the Tribunal cannot simply declare non liquet. Such indirect evidence includes, in the Tribunal's view, decisions taken by other NAFTA tribunals that specifically address the issue of interpretation and application of Article 1105(1) of NAFTA, as well as relevant legal scholarship'.
617. Footnote 2 to Art. 805 of the FTA provides that '[i]t is understood that the term "customary international law" refers to international custom, as evidence of a general practice accepted as law, in accordance with subparagraph 1(b) of Article 38 of the Statute of the International Court of Justice'.
618. *Eco Oro, supra* n. 603, dissenting opinion, para. 6.

clause. The majority of the Tribunal held that 'transparency, stability and the protection of the investor's legitimate expectations play a central role in defining the FET standard'.[619] The majority defined the FET standard broadly. But, at the same time, the majority also referred to the NAFTA-style high threshold of gravity required to find a breach.[620] They further explained that if Colombia were to breach the investor's legitimate expectations or 'failed to provide at all times a stable and transparent investment environment', the Tribunal would then have to examine whether such actions were 'unacceptable from an international law perspective'.[621] The majority found that Colombia had breached these expectations and that its 'conduct amounts to gross unfairness or manifest arbitrariness falling below acceptable standards'.[622] At the time of writing, the quantum phase of the arbitration proceedings was still pending.

In contrast, in his dissenting opinion, Sands explained that while the notion of legitimate expectations 'has become a recognized element of the FET standard', 'its role in the context of an MST inquiry is not yet established'.[623] He noted the above-mentioned specific requirements which have been developed by NAFTA case law to narrow the concept[624] and argued that 'the Majority's analysis fails to acknowledge or address this requirement, and in so doing has in effect conflated the FET and MST'.[625] Sands also noted that 'the obligation to provide stability or predictability has no foundation in the FTA or in the case law on the MST'.[626] He further explained that such an obligation 'only exists where the FET provision in question explicitly mentions stability' and that 'the decision of treaty parties – as in this FTA – not to include a

619. *Ibid.*, Award, para. 754.
620. *Ibid.*, para. 755: 'Having reviewed the relevant decisions, whilst malicious intention, wilful neglect of duty or bad faith are not requisite elements of MST under customary international law, there must be some aggravating factor such that the acts identified comprise more than a minor derogation from that which is deemed to be internationally acceptable. The conduct in question must engender a sense of outrage or shock, amount to gross unfairness or manifest arbitrariness falling below acceptable standards, or there must have been a lack of due process which has led to an outcome which offends a sense of judicial propriety. The treatment complained of must therefore be unacceptable from an international perspective whilst set against the high measure of deference that international law extends to States to regulate matters within their own borders.'
621. *Ibid.*, para. 762. *See also* at para. 806, where the Tribunal explained that it would 'consider whether Colombia's frustration of Eco Oro's legitimate expectations is unacceptable from an international law perspective', adding that 'Colombia will be in breach of Article 805 if it has acted in an unjust or arbitrary manner as understood under customary international law.'
622. *Ibid.*, paras 820-821.
623. *Ibid.*, dissenting opinion, Sands, para. 12.
624. *Ibid.*, para. 14, indicating that 'the limited jurisprudence that exists (in the NAFTA context) indicates inter alia that a claimant must be able to establish a "quasi-contractual" relationship or expectation, in the sense that the state must have made "explicit" or "specific" encouragements or representations on which the investor has placed reliance'.
625. *Ibid.*, para. 14.
626. *Ibid.*, para. 19. *See also*; 'the Majority explicitly states that the Respondent is not under an obligation to provide a stable legal framework. Yet when it comes to the application of the MST standard to the facts of the case, out of nowhere the obligation of stability suddenly emerges, as though magically concocted out of thin air, with no reference to be found either to the Claimant's evidentiary burdens (on state practice or opinio juris in relation to the customary law standard) or any legal authority'.

stability clause in an international agreement is one that a Tribunal must take seriously, as it represents a deliberate choice of the drafters to preserve a greater degree of regulatory discretion'.[627] In a rather forceful passage, he asked: 'Where is the authority for the proposition that a failure to provide stability or predictability can give rise to a violation of the MST standard? The Majority has cited none. I am aware of none.'[628] For him, 'the Majority has effectively engaged in judicial law-making; it has invented a new element for the identification of the customary standard which no state has appeared to have articulated, in the total absence of any evidence of state practice or opinio juris'.[629] His overall conclusion is that 'the Majority's analysis undercuts the plain meaning of the FTA and well-established principles of customary law' and that 'the effect of its approach is to significantly lower the bar, and in effect rewrite the FTA and the content and effect of MST'.[630] He added that 'a finding that a state has breached the MST will be rare and extraordinary'.[631]

3.3.3 One Exception: *OI European Group* Award

Apart from the *Eco Oro* award (majority), another award has adopted a less restrictive approach. The *OI European Group* Tribunal had to interpret a very unique FET clause contained in the Additional Protocol to the Netherlands-Venezuela BIT which essentially referred to FET and the MST.[632] The Tribunal said that the Spanish and English versions did not contain the same wording. It interpreted this peculiar clause as meaning that, 'as a general rule', 'the FET guaranteed by the BIT' 'shall equate to the

627. *Ibid.*, para. 21.
628. *Ibid.*, para. 22.
629. *Ibid.*, para. 22. He added: 'Despite the fact that the drafters of the FTA have made it clear that in relation to Article 805 and MST a claimant must prove the customary rule, with all that implies for evidence of state practice and opinio juris, the Majority makes no mention of these elements in relation to the facts of stability or predictability. Without evidence of opinion juris or state practice, the claim to a customary standard does not get off the ground.'
630. *Ibid.*, para. 36. *See also*, at para. 11, indicating that the threshold for finding a breach of the MST 'remains very high, such that a finding that it has been breached must be based on facts which are truly exceptional'.
631. *Ibid.*, para. 36.
632. *OI European Group B.V. v. Venezuela*, ICSID Case No. ARB/11/25, Award, 10 Mar. 2015, para. 477. The clause indicates that the parties have to provide treatment considered 'to be fair and equitable' (which was already mentioned in Art. 3(1)) 'if it conforms to the treatment accorded to investments of their own nationals, or to investments of nationals of any third State, whichever is more favorable to the national concerned, as well as to the minimum standard for the treatment of foreign nationals under international law'. In another case, *ConocoPhillips Petrozuata B.V., ConocoPhillips Hamaca B.V. and ConocoPhillips Gulf of Paria B.V. v. Venezuela*, ICSID Case No. ARB/07/30, Decision on Jurisdiction and the Merits, 3 Sep. 2013, para. 294, the Tribunal examined the same clause (but provided limited analysis on its scope and meaning). The Tribunal referred to the 'Explanatory Statement for the Dutch Treaty presented to the Congress of the Republic of Venezuela,' 19 Nov. 1991, indicating that this 'minimum required by International Law for the treatment of foreign nationals' is 'by definition, a pre-existing obligation of the Parties, independently of the Agreement' and therefore a reference to the MST under custom and that it 'specifies' the expression FET 'and thus limits the discretion of eventual arbitrators when examining the behaviour of any of the Parties'.

minimum customary standard', 'unless the investor is able to prove that the treatment guaranteed for the investments of nationals or third States is superior'.[633]

The Tribunal then examined an argument by the claimant invoking the MFN clause to import a 'better' FET clause contained in another BIT. The Tribunal mentioned that an 'in accordance with international law' FET clause[634] does not offer superior treatment to an investor compared with a clause mentioning the MST (which the Tribunal referred to as the 'minimum customary standard').[635] The Tribunal then examined the MST and stated that 'it is quite possible that currently the minimum customary standard and the FET envisaged in the treaties have converged, according the investor with substantially equivalent levels of protection'.[636] This statement led the Tribunal to affirm that the FET 'represents an indeterminate legal concept, which imposes a minimum standard of conduct on all States with respect to foreign nationals', adding that 'a State violates it when it takes an action or a chain of actions that are demonstrably unlawful or fail to recognize the basic requirements of the rule of law'.[637] It also stated that the standard is breached both by administrative and judicial actions as well as 'by means of general legislative actions, enacted by the State, if the new regulation contradicts the investor's legitimate expectations'.[638] The Tribunal therefore used a very broad definition of the FET standard. The Tribunal concluded that the FET had been breached, but its analysis suggests that this was, at least in part, because the acts of expropriation were arbitrary and in violation of due process.[639] It awarded USD 372.4 million in compensation.

3.3.4 Conclusion

In sum, all these awards (except for *OI European Group*) have adopted similar approaches. They have all closely followed the language of the clause and applied the MST. The fact that the *OI European Group* Tribunal was faced with a rather unique type of clause may possibly explain why it interpreted it differently and gave such a broad interpretation to the MST. The other tribunals have not adopted broad interpretations of the standard. The position of the majority of the Tribunal in *Ero Oro* is an exception, but Sands' strong dissenting opinion exposed some of that analysis' shortcomings. Two awards have considered that the failure to respect an investor's legitimate expectations does not in and of itself constitute a breach of the MST under custom, but only an element to be taken into account when assessing whether other components of the standard are breached. The *Kenon* award took a different approach. Similarly, tribunals

633. *Ibid.*, para. 480.
634. *See*, awards examined in Chapter II, Section 2.1.
635. *OI European*, *supra* n. 632, para. 482.
636. *Ibid.*, para. 489.
637. *Ibid.*, para. 491.
638. *Ibid.*
639. *Ibid.*, para. 560, indicating that Venezuela 'subjected Claimant's investments to unfair or inequitable treatment and to arbitrary measures in violation of Article 3(1) of the Netherlands-Venezuela BIT because the expropriation violated due process and the takeover of the Plants by INDEPABIS was arbitrary'.

have also applied a high threshold to find a breach. In both respects, they have generally followed the reasoning of NAFTA tribunals.[640]

What is perhaps surprising is that the NAFTA-style interpretation followed by the vast majority of tribunals does not seem to have had a direct impact on their assessment regarding matters of liability. The majority of tribunals found a breach of the FET clause and awarded compensation. Importantly, they did so based on the application of a threshold of gravity higher than under an autonomous stand-alone FET clause. It is noteworthy that the only award which did not (*OI European Group*) awarded the largest amount of damages.

3.4 Conclusion on FET Clauses Linked to the MST or Custom

The following conclusions can be reached about this type of clause.

First, all tribunals examining FET clauses expressly linked to the MST (or custom) have followed the clear intention of the contracting parties and have applied a strict standard. I have found no award[641] interpreting this type of clause as a stand-alone 'autonomous' FET clause.[642]

Second, interpreting the clause in accordance with the MST leads tribunals to define the content of the FET standard narrowly. For instance, the vast majority of tribunals have not considered legitimate expectations to be a stand-alone element, but rather as a factor to be taken into account when assessing other elements. I have only found three exceptions outside NAFTA (the *Lopez,*[643] *Kenon,*[644] and *Eco Oro*[645]

640. These findings contradict the position adopted by Islam, *supra* n. 14, 76 arguing that 'nobody of a minimum standard of international law or customary international law can be clearly and predictably applied to a modern and rapidly evolving standard like FET'. She also added that 'Apart from NAFTA Article 1105 and the CETA Article 8.10, it is clear that even the treaties that construct the FET standard in combination with international law or the minimum standard under customary international law, may not be clearly limiting the scope of the standard.'

641. The *OI European Group* award, *supra* n. 632, may be considered, to some extent, as one such exception.

642. My analysis of case law does not support the affirmation by Islam, *supra* n. 14, 66, referring to the 2012 UNCTAD study (*supra* n. 2) which 'argues that from the host country's perspective, combining FET with customary international law may be a progressive step, given that the tribunals will likely interpret the standard as a higher threshold for finding a breach of the standard as compared to unqualified FET clauses'. She rejects this approach for the following reasons: 'However, this view fails to reflect the drawback of such a construction, which is that no clear set of principles constitutes the minimum standard under customary international law. Given that customary international law is itself highly indeterminate and its evolutionary nature contentious, and that establishing the precise obligations to which it gives rise, tribunals will be unlikely to adhere to this view. The UNCTAD study's argument is therefore unconvincing.' For her, 'it is clear that, in the vast majority of investment treaties, the host developing countries need to assume that a tribunal will interpret the FET standard as an independent and autonomous standard' (65). My detailed examination of case law clearly shows that this statement is incorrect. Tribunals have *not* interpreted these clauses just like any other stand-alone FET clauses. It should be added that later she acknowledges, in reference to FET clauses modelled after the US Model BIT, that 'this appears to be a clearway of limiting the scope of the FET standard' and that 'Clauses like this therefore can potentially provide much clearer limits to the scope of the FET than invocation of international law or customary international law' (66).

643. *Lopez, supra* n. 21.

awards). In any event, almost all tribunals have systematically followed NAFTA case law and have applied a high threshold of severity to find a breach. The *OI European Group* award is one exception.[646]

Third, as a result of this narrow interpretation, NAFTA tribunals have come to the conclusion that the host State had violated the FET clause in a limited number of cases. The success rate of NAFTA claims (25%) is significantly lower when compared with awards interpreting other types of FET clauses.[647] It should be added that for non-NAFTA tribunals interpreting treaties containing similar wording, the success rate is similar to that of awards assessing stand-alone FET clauses.

IV GENERAL CONCLUSION ON THE ANALYSIS OF CASE LAW

As mentioned at the outset of this Part, in a 2012 Report, UNCTAD noted a significant statistical difference between the lower success rate of FET claims under NAFTA when compared to the much higher one under BITs (which at the time included essentially stand-alone FET clauses and provisions containing a reference to 'international law').[648] My findings confirm the same patterns and trends as those mentioned in the UNCTAD Report some 10 years ago. A stand-alone FET clause provides very limited protection for States against the possibility that a tribunal adopts a broad interpretation and concludes that a breach has been committed. The same is true for clauses containing a reference to 'international law'. In most cases, tribunals have interpreted them in pretty much the same way as stand-alone 'autonomous' FET clauses. An FET clause explicitly linked to the MST is the only type of provision which can significantly reduce the possibility of a tribunal giving a broad interpretation of the FET standard and, in turn, finding that a breach occurred.[649]

644. *Kenon, supra* n. 584.
645. *Eco Oro,* majority, *supra* n. 603.
646. *OI European Group, supra* n. 632.
647. *See,* awards examined in Chapters I and II.
648. UNCTAD, *supra* n. 2, para. 61.
649. My findings contradict the following affirmation by Islam, *supra* n. 14, 65: 'combining the FET standard with the minimum standard does not create any secure guarantee for developing countries that the ambit of the FET obligation will be significantly restricted'.

PART III

'The Analysis of Case Law Does Not Support the Theory of "Convergence Theory"'

The analysis of close to 300 awards rendered in the last 25 years in Part II shows that the specific language of Fair and Equitable Treatment (FET) clauses matters a great deal in terms of how tribunals address the relationship between the standard of treatment and the Minimum standard of treatment (MST). The specific wording of an FET clause also has a significant impact on how a tribunal interprets the scope and content of the standard and affects its findings regarding matters of liability and compensation.

I MY ANALYSIS CONFIRMS THE FUNDAMENTAL IMPORTANCE OF THE SPECIFIC WORDING OF EACH FET CLAUSE

In a book published in 2011, Kläger spoke of some 'misconceptions' which are 'based on simplistic premises and a false perspective in addressing fair and equitable treatment'.[1] He referred to the following 'misconception': 'the dichotomy is presented as a struggle between a presumably restrictive and clear-cut minimum standard and a far reaching fair and equitable treatment obligation that is at the disposal of arbitrators'.[2] He believes that the FET 'should be construed as representing only one single concept', adding that 'any division into distinct constructions of the standard – such as a presumably lower customary minimum standard and a presumably higher self-contained standard – would threaten consistency in international investment law'.[3]

1. R. Kläger, *Fair and Equitable Treatment in International Investment Law* (Cambridge UP 2011) 86.
2. *Ibid.*
3. *Ibid.*, 87.

My analysis of case law shows that this 'dichotomy' is far from being simply a 'misconception'. Tribunals do analyse stand-alone FET clauses and provisions linked to the MST differently. There is empirical evidence that tribunals examining FET clauses linked to the MST have adopted a much more 'restrictive' approach regarding the scope and content of the standard compared to those assessing stand-alone clauses having an autonomous character. The 'restrictive' approach they have adopted has led them to find fewer breaches of the FET clause in comparison to tribunals examining other types of clauses. In this context, one can hardly deny the existence of a real and concrete 'dichotomy' between different FET clauses. In fact, my analysis shows that this dichotomy even exists among tribunals examining the *same* type of FET clause. This is, in fact, one of the most surprising findings of my survey regarding FET clauses referring to 'international law'. On the one hand, tribunals which have considered 'no less' FET clauses in the same way as autonomous stand-alone clauses have given broad interpretations which led *all of them* to conclude that a breach had been committed. On the other hand, tribunals which have interpreted 'no less' clauses as providing the same level of protection as under MST, have adopted narrower approaches which led the vast majority of them to not find a breach.

Importantly, my comprehensive survey of awards shows that there is no empirical support for the so-called theory of convergence,[4] which has been supported by some scholars.[5] The question is further examined in the following sections.

II AN OVERVIEW OF THE REASONING OF TRIBUNALS SUPPORTING THE THEORY OF 'CONVERGENCE'

In the context of Bilateral investment treaty (BIT) arbitration *outside* the North American Free Trade Agreement (NAFTA), some tribunals have concluded that the long-standing debate on the differences between the protection offered to investors under the MST and a stand-alone FET clause had minimal practical relevance.[6] For instance, the *Saluka* Tribunal noted that 'it appears that the difference between the Treaty standard laid down in Article 3.1 [of the BIT] and the customary minimum standard, when applied to the specific facts of a case, may well be more apparent than real'.[7] This situation results from the fact that the level of protection offered to foreign investors under the MST has apparently increased in recent years. As a result of this

4. *Ibid.*, 86, describing the theory as follows: 'by emphasising the evolutionary character of the customary minimum standard, the tribunals have usually declared that there was no necessity to decide whether fair and equitable treatment diverges from an evolved minimum standard. To this extent, irrespective of the pertinent investment treaty formulation, a real difference as regards the practical outcome between the two approaches when considering the facts of a specific case seems to be non-existent'.
5. A. Newcombe & L. Paradell, *Law and Practice of Investment Treaties: Standards of Treatment* (Kluwer 2009) 274 ('even if it were accepted that in principle the standards are different, the trend appears to be towards convergence, not divergence').
6. *See*, analysis in P. Dumberry, *The Fair and Equitable Treatment Standard: A Guide to NAFTA Case Law on Article 1105* (Wolters Kluwer 2013) 260ff.
7. *Saluka Investments BV (The Netherlands) v. Czech Republic*, PCA Case No. 2001-04, Partial Award, 17 Mar. 2006, para. 291.

alleged rapid evolution, the level of protection is now said to be the same as the one existing under BITs containing a stand-alone FET clause.[8] I have found many tribunals which have come to this conclusion.[9] For instance, the *Rusoro* Tribunal stated that this whole debate had 'become dogmatic' as a result of the evolution of custom and that now 'there is no substantive difference in the level of protection afforded by both standards'.[10] Both standards have apparently 'converged'.[11] Tribunals that have adopted this approach were either examining stand-alone FET clauses or provisions referring to 'international law'.[12] None of the awards addressing FET clauses expressly linked to the MST have adopted this approach.[13] One exception is the *Merrill & Ring* award, examined in the following paragraphs.

8. *Azurix Corp. v. Argentina*, ICSID No. ARB/01/12, Award, 14 Jul. 2006, para. 361.
9. In a recent award, *The Lopez-Goyne Family Trust and Others v. Nicaragua*, ICSID Case No. ARB/17/44, Award, 1 Mar. 2023, para. 413, the Tribunal referred to the following list of awards which had adopted this approach: *Rusoro Mining Ltd v. Venezuela*, ICSID Case No. ARB (AF)/12/5, Award, 22 Aug. 2016, paras 519-521; *Merrill & Ring Forestry LP v. Canada*, ICSID Case No. UNCT/07/1, Award, 31 Mar. 2010, paras 208, 210-213; *Union Fenosa Gas S.A. v.* ICSID Case No. ARB/14/4, Award, 31 Aug. 2018, para. 9.51; *Rumeli Telekom A.S. and Telsim Mobil Telekomunikasyon Hizmetleri A.S. v. Kazakhstan*, ICSID Case No. ARB/05/16, Award, 29 Jul. 2008, para. 611; *Duke Energy Electroquil Partners and Electroquil S.A. v. Ecuador*, ICSID Case No. ARB/04/19, Award, 18 Aug. 2008, paras 332-337; *Murphy Exploration & Production Company International v. Ecuador II*, PCA Case No. 2012-16 (formerly AA 434), Partial Final Award, 6 May 2016, para. 208; *Occidental Exploration and Production Company v. Ecuador*, LCIA Case No. UN 3467, Final Award, 1 Jul. 2004, para. 190; *Deutsche Bank, AG v. Sri Lanka*, ICSID Case No. ARB/09/2, Award, 31 Oct. 2012, paras 419-420; *Saluka, supra* n. 7. The following passages are illustrative of the approach adopted by these tribunals: *CMS Gas Transmission Company v. Argentina*, ICSID No. ARB/01/8, Award, 12 May 2005, paras 282-284 ('While the choice between requiring a higher treaty standard and that of equating it with the international minimum standard might have relevance in the context of some disputes, the Tribunal is not persuaded that it is relevant in this case. In fact, the Treaty standard of fair and equitable treatment and its connection with the required stability and predictability of the business environment, founded on solemn legal and contractual commitments, is not different from the international law minimum standard and its evolution under customary law'); *Biwater Gauff (Tanzania) Limited v. Tanzania*, ICSID Case No. ARB/05/22, Award, 24 Jul. 2008, para. 592 ('the Arbitral Tribunal also accepts, as found by a number of previous arbitral tribunals and commentators, that the actual content of the treaty standard of fair and equitable treatment is not materially different from the content of the minimum standard of treatment in customary international law'); *Duke Energy Electroquil Partners and Electroquil SA v. Ecuador*, ICSID No. ARB/04/19, Award, 18 Aug. 2008, para. 333 ('the Tribunal is of the opinion that the discussion about the autonomous character of the standard is irrelevant given the circumstances of the case. It also appears overtaken by the evolution in the latest ICSID decisions'), para. 337 ('The Tribunal concurs with this statement [made by the *Azurix* tribunal] and with the conclusion that the standards are essentially the same'); *Rumeli, Ibid.*, para. 611 ('[this tribunal] shares the view of several ICSID tribunals that the treaty standard of fair and equitable treatment is not materially different from the minimum standard of treatment in customary international law').
10. *Rusoro, supra* n. 9, paras 520-521, also indicating: 'But the incorporation of the CIM Standard into the definition of the FET does not provoke a major disruption in the level of protection: the CIS Standard has developed and today is indistinguishable from the FET standard and grants investors an equivalent level of protection as the latter.'
11. *Ibid.*
12. *See*, Part II, Chapters I and II.
13. One possible exception is *OI European Group B.V. v. Venezuela*, ICSID Case No. ARB/11/25, Award, 10 Mar. 2015, 489, stating that 'it is quite possible that currently the minimum customary standard and the FET envisaged in the treaties have converged, according the investor with substantially equivalent levels of protection'.

The *Merrill & Ring* Tribunal first stated that the 2001 Free Trade Commission (FTC) Note had the 'effect of linking fair and equitable treatment with customary law'.[14] Yet, while the Tribunal indicated that it was 'mindful' of the FTC Interpretation 'which understood Article 1105 as a minimum standard of treatment under customary law',[15] it nevertheless added that the Note may not 'necessarily reflect[] the present state of customary and international law'.[16] This comment suggests that custom had somehow evolved in the last ten years since the Note was issued. Thus, as a result of custom's alleged rapid evolution, the Note's linkage of Article 1105 to the MST would now (in 2010) be outdated. On this point, the Tribunal observed that 'Canada has maintained that, to the extent that an evolution might have taken place, it must be proven that it has occurred since 2001, when the FTC Interpretation was issued, and this almost certainly has not happened.'[17] In response to this perfectly valid argument, the Tribunal simply stated that 'such a view is unconvincing',[18] without providing any explanation. The Tribunal held that 'the evolutionary nature' of custom 'provides scope for the interpretation of Article 1105, *even in the light of the Free Trade Commission's 2001 interpretation*'.[19] The Tribunal's objective was clearly to evaluate how custom had evolved in recent years *in spite* of what the Parties had enunciated in the 2001 FTC Note.

The Tribunal characterised the *Neer* and *ELSI* cases, 'dealing with situations concerning due process of law, denial of justice and physical mistreatment',[20] as 'the first track of the evolution' of the MST.[21] By the 1960s, State practice was apparently 'increasingly seen as being inconsistent' with the first track concept of the standard as set out in these older cases.[22] In this context, the Tribunal explained that a 'second track' of the evolution of the MST had emerged which dealt specifically with the 'treatment of aliens in relations to business, trade and investments'.[23] This 'new' standard was 'more liberal', as it did not require demonstrating 'outrageous' treatment in order to establish a breach of the standard.[24] Yet, all cases referred to by the Tribunal in support of this so-called new standard actually date back to the 1920s.[25]

The *Merrill & Ring* Tribunal observed that custom had evolved since the 1920s: 'today's minimum standard is broader than that defined in the *Neer* case and its

14. *Merrill & Ring, supra* n. 9, para. 189.
15. *Ibid.*, para. 191.
16. *Ibid.*, para. 192.
17. *Ibid.*, para. 194.
18. *Ibid.*
19. *Ibid.*, para. 192, emphasis added.
20. *Ibid.*, para. 197.
21. *Ibid.*, para. 201.
22. *Ibid.*, para. 204.
23. *Ibid.*, para. 205. *See also*, para. 201.
24. *Ibid.*, para. 205.
25. *Ibid.*, para. 206, referring to the following cases: *Case Concerning Certain German Interests in Polish Upper Silesia* (Merits), PCIJ, Series A. No. 7, at 19 (1926); *German Settlers in Poland*, PCIJ, Series B., No. 6, 19-20, 35-38 (1923); *Aboilard* (Haiti, France), 9 UNRIAA, 71, at 79-81 (1925); *Robert E. Brown* (United Kingdom, United States), 6 UNRIAA, 120, at 129-130 (1923); *George W. Cook* (Mexico, United States), 4 UNRIAA, 213, at 214-215 (1927); *Hopkins* (Mexico, United States), 4 UNRIAA, 41, at 46-47 (1926); *Lalanne and Ledoux* (France, Venezuela), 10 UNRIAA, 17, at 18 (1902).

progeny'.[26] For the Tribunal, the MST now 'provides for the fair and equitable treatment of alien investors within the confines of *reasonableness*'.[27] In other words, the MST had apparently evolved to the point where it now protects all foreigners against State conduct that is 'unreasonable'. Thus, any 'unreasonable' act would have to be considered in breach of international law. The *Merrill & Ring* Tribunal also noted that 'in the end, the name assigned to the standard does not really matter'.[28] Thus, the MST and a stand-alone FET clause offer the *same* level of protection to foreign investors. For the tribunal, '[w]hat matters is that the standard protects against all such acts or behavior that might infringe a sense of fairness, equity and reasonableness'.[29]

These are very controversial findings. It is true that these findings may not have had any *practical effect* on the host State's liability; the Tribunal ruled that Canada did not breach Article 1105. Yet, and importantly, the endorsement of the 'convergence' theory by the *Merrill & Ring* Tribunal completely 'deprived the 2001 NAFTA Interpretative Statement of any practical effect'.[30]

III REASONS TO REJECT THE THEORY

There are good reasons to believe that the MST under custom has in fact *not* converged with the free-standing FET standard contained in BITs. This is the position adopted by the United Nations Conference on Trade and Development (UNCTAD).[31] Scholars have also followed this approach.[32] They have rightly pointed out that tribunals adopting this approach do not make any attempt to actually *demonstrate* the rapid evolution of the minimum standard under customary international law.[33] They simply affirm, *en passant* in one or two sentences, that this is the case without examining the issue.[34] As rightly pointed out by UNCTAD, 'the *Merrill & Ring* tribunal failed to give cogent reasons for its conclusion that the MST made such a leap in its evolution'.[35] In fact,

26. *Merrill & Ring, supra* n. 9, para. 213. *See also*, para. 193 ('in spite of arguments to the contrary, there appears to be a shared view that customary international law has not been frozen in time and that it continues to evolve in accordance with the realities of the international community').
27. *Ibid.*, para. 213, emphasis added.
28. *Ibid.*, para. 210.
29. *Ibid.*
30. UNCTAD, *Fair and Equitable Treatment*, UNCTAD Series on Issues in International Investment Agreements II (2012) 57.
31. UNCTAD, *Investor–State Dispute Settlement and Impact on Investment Rulemaking* (2007) 57 ('some arbitral decisions had the effect of equating the minimum standard under customary international law with the plain meaning approach to the text. However, it is not self-evident that customary international law has evolved to such a degree').
32. *See*, for instance, T. Kill, *Don't Cross the Streams: Past and Present Overstatement of Customary International Law in Connection with Conventional Fair and Equitable Treatment Obligations*, 106 Mich. L. Rev. 853 (2008).
33. *Ibid.*, 865; M.C. Porterfield, *An International Common Law of Investor Rights?*, 27 U. Pa. J. Int'l Econ. L. 81-82 (2006); J.R. Picherack, *The Expanding Scope of the Fair and Equitable Treatment Standard: Have Recent Tribunals Gone Too Far?*, 9(4) J. World Invest. & Trade, 271, 287, 285 (2008) DOI: 10.1163/221190008x00061; G. Van Harten, *International Treaty Arbitration and Public Law* 89 (Oxford UP 2007).
34. Kill, *supra* n. 32, 866.
35. UNCTAD, *supra* n. 30, 57.

earlier in the award, the *Merrill & Ring* Tribunal mentioned that one important issue consisted of 'establish[ing] in which direction customary law has evolved' and added that 'State practice and *opinio juris* will be the guiding beacons of this evolution'.[36] Yet, the Tribunal did not cite *a single* example of State practice in support of its convergence thesis.[37] No arbitral decision is mentioned to illustrate its position that custom has evolved rapidly in recent years. The old arbitration cases from the 1920s that the Tribunal referred to in support of its claim of the existence of a so-called second-track evolution of the MST do not demonstrate such an evolution. The theory of 'convergence' has been put forward by many claimants in NAFTA proceedings. All NAFTA Parties have strongly rejected this line of argumentation.[38] The *Glamis* Tribunal summarily rejected the convergence theory as 'an overstatement'.[39] The *Merrill & Ring* ruling is the only case where a NAFTA tribunal adopted the convergence theory.

As noted by one writer, the convergence approach 'leads tribunals to the inevitable, but untenable, conclusion that as a matter of customary law, states owe duties to foreign corporations, including the maintenance of stable, predictable, and transparent regulatory environments that do not frustrate the legitimate expectations of the foreign investors', adding that 'such a conclusion overstates the protections afforded to investors under customary international law'.[40]

In the following sections, I will briefly examine some of the shortcomings associated with the convergence theory.

3.1 Tribunals' Failure to Properly Identify Rules of Custom

The *Merrill & Ring* Tribunal is not the only one that has failed to properly identify rules of custom. This is a very common problem among investment tribunals. They have generally failed in their task to properly reveal the existence of these rules based on an analysis of the 'double requirement'.[41] A good example is the *Glamis* Tribunal which entirely relied on the findings of previous NAFTA tribunals to 'reveal' the existence of

36. *Merrill & Ring, supra* n. 9, para. 193.
37. On this point, *see* J. Sharp, 'The Minimum Standard of Treatment, Glamis Gold, and Neer's Enduring Influence,' in: M. Kinnear et al. (eds), *Building International Investment Law: The First 50 Years of ICSID* (Kluwer 2015), 278.
38. *See*, for instance: *Cargill, Inc. v. Mexico*, ICSID Case No. ARB(AF)/05/02, Award, 18 Sep. 2009, para. 244; *Methanex Corporation v. United States*, UNCITRAL, US Post-Hearing Submissions on FTC Notes, 26 Oct. 2001, paras 5, 6; *Chemtura v. Canada*, UNCITRAL, Canada's Rejoinder, 10 Jul. 2009, para. 155; *Merrill & Ring, supra* n. 9, Canada's Rejoinder, 27 Mar. 2009, para. 168. For a recent analysis, *see* D. Gaukrodger, *Addressing the Balance of Interests in Investment Treaties; The Limitation of Fair and Equitable Treatment Provisions to the Minimum Standard of Treatment under Customary International Law*, OECD Working Papers on International Investment (2017) 33.
39. *Glamis Gold Ltd v. United States*, UNCITRAL, Award, 8 Jun. 2009, para. 609 ('Claimant has agreed with this distinction between customary international law and autonomous treaty standards but argues that, with respect to this particular standard, BIT jurisprudence has "converged with customary international law in this area". The Tribunal finds this to be an over-statement').
40. Kill, *supra* n. 32, 866.
41. The question is examined in detail in P. Dumberry, *The Formation and Identification of Rules of Customary International Law in International Investment Law* (Cambridge UP 2016), 47ff.

the prohibition of arbitrary conduct as a customary rule.[42] This example is not isolated. A number of other NAFTA tribunals (*Thunderbird*,[43] *Waste Management*,[44] and *Mobil*)[45] also came to the same conclusion about the customary nature of the prohibition against arbitrary conduct being part of the MST without actually examining State practice and *opinio juris*. One exception to this line of doctrinally disappointing awards is the *UPS* Tribunal which ultimately concluded that there was 'no rule of customary international law prohibiting or regulating anticompetitive behaviour'[46] based on an examination of the 'double requirement'. Tribunals have almost never examined States' *opinio juris*.[47] Instead, they consistently rely on the findings of the International Court of Justice (ICJ) or on the reasoning of *other tribunals* when 'revealing' the customary nature of rules.[48]

One example is the CAFTA *RDC* award.[49] The Tribunal addressed Guatemala's position (which was shared by three other CAFTA Parties – the United States, El Salvador and Honduras – in their non-disputing Party submissions) that the claimant had the burden of demonstrating the relevant standard under custom based on State practice and *opinio juris* rather than arbitral awards.[50] The Tribunal agreed that awards do not constitute evidence of State practice.[51] Yet, the award has also been criticised for not examining State practice at all and instead relying on the broad formulation used by the *Waste Management* Tribunal, which had itself failed to examine State practice.[52]

42. *Glamis*, *supra* n. 39, paras 607, 625-626.
43. *International Thunderbird Gaming Corporation v. Mexico*, UNCITRAL, Award, 26 Jan. 2006, para. 194.
44. *Waste Management, Inc. v. Mexico ('Number 2')*, ICSID Case No. ARB(AF)/00/3, Award, 30 Apr. 2004, para. 98.
45. *Mobil Investments Canada Inc. and Murphy Oil Corporation v. Canada*, ICSID Case No. ARB(AF)/07/4, Decision on Liability and on Principles of Quantum, 22 May 2012, para. 152.
46. *United Parcel Service of America Inc. v. Canada*, UNCITRAL, Award on Jurisdiction, 22 Nov. 2002, para. 92.
47. One rare exception is *Mondev International Ltd. v. United States*, ICSID Case No. ARB(AF)/99/2, Award, 2 Oct. 2012, para. 111, acknowledging that 'letters of submittal' by which the US government introduces draft legislation in Congress should be considered a manifestation of that State's *opinio juris*.
48. *Lone Pine Resources Inc. v. Canada*, ICSID Case No. UNCT/15/2, Final Award, 21 Nov. 2022, 597: 'International arbitral tribunals routinely refer to prior arbitral decisions as illustrations of custom,' citing the following cases: *Waste Management*, *supra* n. 44; *Cargill*, *supra* n. 38; *Glamis*, *supra* n. 39; *William Ralph Clayton, William Richard Clayton, Douglas Clayton, Daniel Clayton and Bilcon of Delaware, Inc. v. Canada*, UNCITRAL PCA Case No. 2009-04, Award on Jurisdiction and Liability, 17 Mar. 2015; *Mesa Power Group LLC v. Canada*, PCA Case No. 2012-17, Award, 24 Mar. 2016; *Thunderbird*, *supra* n. 43.
49. *Railroad Development Corporation v. Guatemala*, ICSID Case No. ARB/07/23, Award, 29 Jun. 2012, para. 216.
50. *Ibid.*, paras 159-160, 192, 207-211.
51. *Ibid.*, para. 217. The Tribunal also noted that 'parties in international proceedings use [arbitral awards] in their pleadings in support of their arguments of what the law is on a specific issue' and that it was 'an efficient manner for a party in a judicial process to show what it believes to be the law'.
52. M. Porterfield, 'A Distinction Without a Difference? The Interpretation of Fair and Equitable Treatment Under Customary International Law by Investment Tribunals,' *Investment Treaty News*, 22 Mar. 2013, indicating that the Tribunal 'accept[ed], without any evidence of state practice or opinio juris, the pronouncements of previous tribunals as definitive evidence of the standard under CIL'.

Interestingly, the *RDC* Tribunal criticised the *Neer* award precisely on that point by making this rather ironic statement: 'by the strict standards of proof of customary international law applied in Glamis Gold, Neer would fail to prove its famous statement (...) to be an expression of customary international law'.[53] The same can arguably be said about the *RDC* award. As noted by Alschner, 'the tribunal chose to substitute the findings by a different tribunal under a different treaty for its own analysis' of State practice and *opinio juris*.[54] He further noted that this is, in fact, what Article 10.5 and its Annex, 'had urged the tribunal *not* to do'.[55]

For that reason, a 2017 Organisation for Economic Co-operation and Development (OECD) paper noted that 'even the vigorous attention of some governments to making clear that MST-FET must be defined by state practice and opinio juris has not been successful in restraining arbitral tribunals from relying solely on arbitral precedents in defining MST-FET standards under customary international law in some cases'.[56] For Porterfield, this interpretation 'renders linkage of FET to CIL largely meaningless'.[57] In any event, scholars have long identified similar shortcomings in the decisions of the ICJ, which very rarely contain detailed analysis of the 'double requirement' of custom.[58] In fact, it has been argued that the 'main method employed by the Court is neither induction nor deduction but, rather, assertion'.[59]

3.2 Tribunals' Failure to Demonstrate the Evolution of the MST

The failure by tribunals (and claimant investors)[60] to actually demonstrate with evidence of State practice and *opinio juris* the evolution of the MST is the main reason

53. *RDC, supra* n. 49, para. 216.
54. W. Alschner, *Investment Arbitration and State-Driven Reform* (Oxford UP), 202.
55. *Ibid.*, emphasis in the original.
56. Gaukrodger, *supra* n. 38, 56.
57. Porterfield, *supra* n. 52.
58. J. Crawford, *The Identification and Development of Customary International Law*, ILA British Branch Conference (2014), 8; A. Pellet, *Shaping the Future of International Law: The Role of the World Court in Law-Making*, in: M.H. Arsanjani et al. (eds), *Looking to the Future: Essays on International Law in Honor of W. Michael Reisman* (Martinus Nijhoff 2011) 1076; R.H. Geiger, *Customary International Law in the Jurisprudence of the International Court of Justice: A Critical Appraisal*, in: U. Fastenrath et al. (eds), *From Bilateralism to Community Interest: Essays in Honour of Judge Bruno Simma* (Oxford UP 2011) 673, 674; O. Yasuaki, *Is the International Court of Justice an Emperor Without Clothes?*, 81 International Legal Theory, 16 (2002).
59. S. Talmon, *Determining Customary International Law: The ICJ's Methodology Between Induction, Deduction and Assertion*, 26(2) EJIL 417-443 (2015) DOI: 10.1093/ejil/chv020. For a rebuttal, *see*: O. Sender & M. Wood, 'The International Court of Justice and Customary International Law: A Reply to Stefan Talmon', EJIL Talks!, 30 Nov. 2015.
60. *See*, for instance, this passage in *Eco Oro Minerals Corp. v. Colombia*, ICSID Case No. ARB/16/41, Decision on Jurisdiction, Liability and Directions on Quantum, 9 Sep. 2021, dissenting opinion Sands, para. 7: 'In the present case, the Claimant has not met the burden of showing sufficient state practice, independent of the mere existence of FET provisions in modern investment treaties, to establish that the customary standard has evolved so as to be identical (or similar) to the FET standard. Nor has the Claimant offered any plausible evidence on the requisite opinio juris. In so proceeding, the Claimant has not engaged with the deliberate and explicit drafting choice made by the parties to the FTA, one that is premised on the customary standard (MST) continuing to have its own identity, autonomy and component element.'

undermining the theory of convergence.[61] As mentioned in a recent OECD paper, these awards 'appear to be rarely based on significant analysis of government action and views (state practice and opinio juris)'; 'instead, they appear to be based primarily on a comparison of arbitral and commentator views about FET and arbitrator and commentator views about MST-FET'.[62] In a very convincing article, Kill explained that one of the flaws of the convergence approach is that these tribunals 'have "cross the streams" by looking to the jurisprudence of tribunals that have applied' stand-alone autonomous FET clauses.[63] He further explains that the convergence theory should be rejected because it is based on an 'inaccurate or careless readings of previous tribunals, leading to confusion regarding the substantive content of customary international law':[64]

> In implementing their convergence approach, these tribunals have looked to the jurisprudence of tribunals that interpret fair and equitable treatment clauses to require a higher standard of treatment than that imposed by the minimum standard to inform the standard of treatment in the cases before them. Having defined the applicable standard with reference to the jurisprudence of the tribunals adopting an additive approach, the convergence tribunals then simply announce that the standard articulated is in fact equal to the minimum standard required under customary international law. This 'crossing of the streams' is pernicious because it blurs the line between conventional and customary international law, provides inconsistent jurisprudence to future tribunals, and decreases the ability of potential parties to an investment dispute to predict whether or not a claim for violation of fair and equitable treatment is valid.[65]
>
> The tribunals in *CMS* and *Occidental*, for example, relied on the *Tecmed* tribunal's articulation of the fair and equitable treatment standard, which both *CMS* and *Occidental* subsequently pronounced to be binding as a matter of customary international law. Yet the *Tecmed* tribunal stated that 'the scope of the undertaking of fair and equitable treatment under [the Treaty] described above is that resulting from an *autonomous interpretation*'. In other words, the *Tecmed* tribunal went out of its way to clarify that the standard it was enunciating was *not* customary international law but rather a conventional standard based on a reading of the specific terms of the treaty that applied only as between the two parties. *Tecmed* tried to warn future tribunals not to cross the streams.[66]

The other reasons to reject this theory are examined below in the next sections.

61. Kill, *supra* n. 32, 865-866.
62. Gaukrodger, *supra* n. 38, 12.
63. Kill, *supra* n. 32, 865. *See also*, at 880: 'The convergence approach suffers from the fatal flaw of "crossing the streams". While purporting to articulate the international minimum standard of treatment for aliens, these tribunals in fact rely upon a stream of jurisprudence developed under a plain meaning interpretation of the fair and equitable treatment treaty provisions. This approach incorrectly states the content of customary international law and should not guide future tribunals'.
64. *Ibid.*, 865.
65. *Ibid.*, 857-858.
66. *Ibid.*, 865, emphasis in the original.

3.3 There Is No 'Cross-Fertilisation' Between Awards Assessing Different Types of FET Clauses

One argument mentioned by the *Cairn* Tribunal in support of this 'convergence' is the 'cross-fertilisation of approaches' adopted by awards:

> All of that said, the Tribunal considers that the debate as to the degree of overlap between an autonomous standard of FET and the minimum standard of treatment, or put another way, the differences between them, is in the present day context somewhat academic given the cross-fertilisation of approaches taken under differently worded treaties. Indeed, it is noteworthy that NAFTA awards rendered by tribunals that are instructed to apply the MST and rules of customary international law, such as Waste Management II, which summarised prior decisions of tribunals applying that standard with a view toward describing an emerging general standard under the NAFTA, have been cited with approval by many tribunals (including the present one) charged with applying an autonomous FET standard. What the Tribunal can say with confidence is that although there has been a substantial convergence between these two formulations, as a matter of pure treaty interpretation, 'fair and equitable treatment', unlinked to the minimum standard of treatment or customary international law, is a more capacious formulation.[67]

The argument is not convincing. The fact that tribunals examining stand-alone FET clauses referred to NAFTA awards does not support in any way the existence of a 'convergence'. As mentioned above, NAFTA awards were the first to address the nature, scope and content of FET clauses. It is only natural that tribunals have referred to them frequently. In any event, the argument would only work if there were opposing examples, i.e., examples of tribunals examining FET clauses linked to the MST looking at how other awards assessing stand-alone clause have interpreted the clause. I have found no such examples. NAFTA tribunals predominantly (63%) cite other NAFTA awards.[68] Alschner explains the reasoning behind this: 'NAFTA tribunals tend to accord considerable weight to the specific language of NAFTA in order to arrive at a correct interpretation,' adding that 'they are reluctant to admit precedent under third treaties with divergent wordings even where similar interpretive issues arise'.[69]

This is especially the case regarding the interpretation of the FET standard under Article 1105. In proceedings, NAFTA parties have repeatedly explained that awards examining stand-alone clauses were not relevant to interpreting Article 1105.[70] The *Glamis* Tribunal decided to 'look solely to arbitral awards – including BIT awards – that seek to be understood by reference to the customary international law minimum standard of treatment, as opposed to any autonomous standard'.[71] As recently explained

67. *Cairn Energy PLC and Cairn UK Holdings Limited (CUHL) v. India*, PCA Case No. 2016-07, Award, 21 Dec. 2020, para. 1704, fn 2146.
68. Alschner, *supra* n. 54, 248.
69. *Ibid.*, 249-250.
70. For a recent analysis, *see* Gaukrodger, *supra* n. 38, 32.
71. *Glamis*, *supra* n. 39, para. 611. *See also*, *Bilcon*, *supra* n. 48, para. 436 ('In light of the FTC Notes, it is important to emphasize that the trend in the wider world outside NAFTA is only relevant to the extent that such trend has affected the international minimum standard under customary international law').

in the *Lone Pine* award, the NAFTA Tribunal was 'not persuaded that awards which examine an autonomous standard of FET are relevant for the purposes of examining the content of custom'.[72] The same point was made in the *Cargill* award.[73] The Tribunal further explained that the Claimant's effort to establish the 'current customary content' of the FET 'relies rather heavily on the award rendered in *Tecmed*, a reliance that Respondent contends is misplaced'.[74] The Tribunal 'agreed' with the Respondent for the following reasons:

> The award and statements of the Teemed tribunal thus do not bear on the customary international law minimum standard of treatment, but rather reflect an autonomous standard based on an interpretation of the text. Thus, the Tribunal determines that the holding in Teemed is not instructive in this arbitration as to the scope and bounds of the fair and equitable treatment required by Article 1105 of the NAFTA.[75]

The same is true regarding CAFTA awards; they reference NAFTA awards.[76] In fact, CAFTA tribunals, and other tribunals examining similar FET clauses in other treaties,[77] *do not* refer to other awards which have assessed stand-alone FET clauses *precisely* because they deal with different FET clauses. This is because the *method* used by a tribunal to assess the existence of a rule of custom is 'fundamentally different' from that of examining a stand-alone FET clause not linked to custom.[78] For that reason, as explained by the *Glamis* Tribunal, the 'arbitral decisions that apply an autonomous standard provide no guidance inasmuch as the entire method of reasoning does not bear on an inquiry into custom'.[79]

72. *Lone Pine, supra* n. 48, 601.
73. *Cargill, supra* n. 38: 'In the Tribunal's view, these decisions are relevant to the issue presented in Article 1105(1) only if the fair and equitable treatment clause of the BIT in question was viewed by the Tribunal as involving, like Article 1105, an incorporation of the customary international law standard rather than autonomous treaty language.'
74. *Ibid.*, para. 279.
75. *Ibid.*, para. 280.
76. P. Dumberry, '*Cross Treaty Interpretation' en Bloc or How CAFTA Tribunals Are Systematically Interpreting the FET Standard Based NAFTA Case Law*, 22(2) LPICT 384-418 (2023) DOI: 10.1163/15718034-bja10093.
77. *See*, awards examined in Part II, Chapter III.
78. *Glamis, supra* n. 39, para. 20: 'Approaching the task of ascertaining the customary international law standard of "fair and equitable treatment", the Tribunal employs a mode of reasoning that differs from some of the awards it has reviewed. The Tribunal emphasizes that the task of seeking the meaning of "fair and equitable treatment" by way of treaty interpretation is fundamentally different from the task of ascertaining the content of custom. A tribunal confronted with a question of treaty interpretation can, with little input from the parties, provide a legal answer. It has the two necessary elements to do so, namely the language at issue and rules of interpretation. A tribunal confronted with the task of ascertaining custom, on the other hand, has a quite different task because ascertainment of the content of custom involves not only questions of law but also questions of fact, where custom is found in the practice of States regarded as legally required by them.'
79. *Ibid.*, para. 608.

3.4 A Higher Threshold of Gravity Applies to Find a Breach of the MST

Recent awards examining NAFTA-style FET clauses have explained that one of the main differences with stand-alone autonomous FET clauses is the high threshold of seriousness and gravity which is required to show that a breach has been committed. It is remarkable that (almost) all awards assessing FET clauses linked to the MST[80] have referred to the existence of such a high threshold.[81] In his dissenting opinion in the *Eco Oro* case, Sands clearly explained the point:

> In the past, certain tribunals have – accidentally or deliberately – sought to equate or meld the MST and FET standards. The two standards may share a common aim of imposing restrictions on the manner and extent to which a state is required to treat a foreign investor in its territory, but they do so to in different ways. A breach of the customary MST standard would invariably give rise to a breach of the FET standards, but the reverse is generally not the case. This is because the MST standard sets a much higher bar.[82]

According to the *Lopez* Tribunal, 'even if some tribunals have held that there is a convergence between the treatment guaranteed under MST and the FET, the majority view amongst investment tribunals is that the threshold for a breach of the MST is high'.[83] Speaking of this high threshold of severity, the Tribunal further explained that 'this approach is consistent with the growing understanding of the need to reduce the perception of an almost unfettered discretion of tribunals that may derive from a self-standing reference to fair and equitable treatment not anchored to the parameters of customary international law on the treatment of aliens'.[84] In other words, while arbitrators may have an 'almost unfettered discretion' to determine what they believe is unfair and unequitable under stand-alone FET clauses, the same cannot be said about clauses linked to the MST. Under such clauses, arbitrators do not have the same wide margin of appreciation; they can only arrive at the conclusion that the standard has been breached if a high threshold of gravity or seriousness has been reached.

80. *See*, awards examined in Part II, Chapter III.
81. *See*, for instance, *Adel A Hamadi Al Tamimi v. Oman*, ICSID Case No. ARB/11/33, Award, 27 Oct. 2015, para. 383, '[a]lthough a number of subsequent arbitral decisions have acknowledged that with the passage of time the standard has likely advanced beyond these basic requirements [set out in the Neer decision], tribunals have continued to employ descriptions which emphasize the high threshold for breach'. *See also*, *Lone Pine*, *supra* n. 48, para. 611 ('the Tribunal concludes that, notwithstanding an evolution from the Neer standard, the customary international law minimum standard of treatment for FET continues to bear a high threshold. This position has been consistently recognized by international arbitral tribunals').
82. *Eco Oro*, *supra* n. 60, dissenting opinion Sands, para. 7. *See also*, para. 10 ('the threshold for finding a breach of the MST nevertheless remains very high, such that a finding that it has been breached must be based on facts which are truly exceptional. Although the ordinary decision-making processes of states may result in a breach of the FET standard, a breach of the MST is not an everyday occurrence and should be found only in truly egregious circumstances'), para. 36 ('a finding that a state has breached the MST will be rare and extraordinary').
83. *Lopez*, *supra* n. 9, para. 413, citing NAFTA cases.
84. *Ibid.*, paras 413, 415.

3.5 Applying the Theory Would Be Contrary to States' Intention When Adopting FET Clauses Referring to the MST

States are increasingly adopting investment treaties that contain FET clauses which are explicitly linked to the MST.[85] No new treaty signed in the last five years contains a 'stand-alone' FET clause.[86] Why are States doing this? There is no doubt that their aim is precisely to limit the 'almost unfettered discretion' of arbitrators. In this context, the very idea that both standards may have hypothetically 'converged' is not only a rather artificial and baseless construction but also contrary to the intention of States when they design new FET clauses.

Ultimately, the way the contracting parties decide to draft their FET clauses in investment treaties matters. The variation in language in these clauses and, most importantly, whether or not the standard is anchored to that of 'international law' or the MST is central for any tribunal assessing its meaning. The standard of treatment under an autonomous stand-alone FET clause does not offer the same level of protection as under the MST. The two standards have not 'converged'. That does not mean of course that rules of custom do not evolve over time.[87] As explained by numerous tribunals, 'the customary international law minimum standard of treatment is not a static standard but is an evolutionary one'.[88] No one is suggesting that the level of treatment existing today is the same as the one 100 years ago. Yet, claims of any such evolution must be backed by some evidence of State practice and *opinio juris*.[89] There is no doubt, as acknowledged by many tribunals, that the parties may face difficulties when asserting evidence of the existence of a rule of custom.[90] Yet, there is no logical or realistic substitute to concretely show the evolution of international law. As the *Glamis* Tribunal noted, 'as an evidentiary matter, the evolution of a custom is a

85. OECD, *'Fair' and 'Equitable' Treatment Provisions in Investment Treaties; A Large-Sample Survey of Treaty Provisions* (2023), indicating that about half of all treaties concluded in the past decade and which include an FET clause have adopted this approach.
86. *Ibid.*, 15.
87. *ADF Group Inc. v. United States*, ICSID Case No. ARB(AF)/00/1, Award, 9 Jan. 2003, at para. 178: 'both customary international law and the minimum standard of treatment of aliens it incorporates, are constantly in a process of development'.
88. One recent example is *Lone Pine, supra* n. 48, para. 602.
89. *Resolute Forest Products Inc. v. Canada*, PCA Case No. 2016-1, Award, 25 Jul. 2022, para. 738, noting that the 'evolution of that standard has to be confirmed by customary international law developments'.
90. *Cargill, supra* n. 38, para. 273: 'The burden of establishing any new elements of this custom is on Claimant. The Tribunal acknowledges that the proof of change in a custom is not an easy matter to establish. However, the burden of doing so falls clearly on Claimant. If Claimant does not provide the Tribunal with the proof of such evolution, it is not the place of the Tribunal to assume this task. Rather the Tribunal, in such an instance, should hold that Claimant fails to establish the particular standard asserted.' *See also*, para. 274: 'The Tribunal acknowledges, however, that surveys of State practice are difficult to undertake and particularly difficult in the case of norms such as "fair and equitable treatment" where developed examples of State practice may not be many or readily accessible. Claimant has not provided the Tribunal with such a survey of recent State practice nor is the Tribunal aware of such a survey.' *See also, Glamis, supra* n. 39, para. 602 ('The Tribunal acknowledges that it is difficult to establish a change in customary international law'); *Lone Pine, supra* n. 48, para. 597.

proposition to be established'.[91] If the MST is to be taken seriously, any claim that the standard now 'provides for the fair and equitable treatment of alien investors within the confines of *reasonableness*'[92] should be challenged. As recently noted by the *Lone Pine* Tribunal, claimants have so far generally failed to 'cite' 'any persuasive evidence to demonstrate that the customary international law standard for FET is akin to the autonomous treaty standard of FET'.[93] Contrary to what the *Merrill & Ring* Tribunal said, the present survey of case law has shown that 'the name assigned to the standard' *does* matter.[94]

91. *Glamis*, *supra* n. 39, para. 20.
92. *Merrill & Ring*, *supra* n. 9, para. 213, emphasis added.
93. *Lone Pine*, *supra* n. 48, para. 613.
94. *Merrill & Ring*, *supra* n. 9, para. 210.

PART IV

'Conclusion'

In a 2012 Report, the United Nations Conference on Trade and Development (UNCTAD) noted a significant statistical difference between the lower success rate of Fair and Equitable Treatment (FET) claims under the North American Free Trade Agreement (NAFTA) when compared to the much higher one under Bilateral investment treaties (BITs). Only 22% of the NAFTA claims were successful (4 out of 18), and 62% of other BIT cases were accepted by tribunals (41 out of 66).[1] The goal of my research project was to assess whether this statement is still accurate 10 years later.

My survey of 279 relevant awards confirms the same patterns as those outlined in the UNCTAD Report some 10 years ago. I have also found some other trends which UNCTAD did not envisage in its Report.

The most significant findings of this book can be briefly summarised as follows:

(1) One of the surprising findings of this survey is that less than 25% of awards (29 out of 120) examining stand-alone FET clauses have addressed the question of its status and its relationship with the Minimum standard of treatment (MST). In fact, a larger number of awards (74 out of 120) did not mention the issue at all.

(2) The vast majority of awards where tribunals took a position on the issue have concluded that the clause should be interpreted to have an autonomous character (23 out of 29 awards, i.e., some 80% of awards). The same is true for awards examining the Energy Charter Treaty: almost all tribunals that took a position on the issue have adopted the same approach. Only a few awards considered that a stand-alone FET clause was a reference to the MST under custom.

1. UNCTAD, *Fair and Equitable Treatment*, UNCTAD Series on Issues in International Investment Agreements II (2012) 60-61, concluding that the NAFTA claimants' success rate is 'much lower than in cases under traditional BITs, where the FET provision is most often analysed as setting an autonomous standard not linked to the MST'.

(3) In any event, all awards assessing stand-alone FET clauses have adopted broad interpretations when defining their content. They have all concluded that the standard encompasses elements such as the protection of legitimate expectations (often defined narrowly) and many of them have referred to an obligation of transparency.
(4) The broad interpretation adopted by these tribunals has had, in turn, an impact on how they have decided matters of liability and compensation. The overall success rate for all 120 awards where tribunals have examined stand-alone FET clauses is high (63 awards out of 120). Claimants have a 50% chance of being successful. The success rate is even higher if one takes into account the 54 other awards rendered under the Energy Charter Treaty where claimants were successful in 60% of cases. In any case, the most important finding is that this success rate is much higher compared to that of awards examining FET clauses where the standard is expressly linked to the MST. These findings are in line with what the UNCTAD Report highlighted 10 years ago.
(5) My survey also shows some interesting patterns which, to the best of my knowledge, had not been empirically identified before. These developments concern FET clauses which refer to 'international law'. As further explained in the following paragraphs, the question of how a tribunal analyses the status of an FET clause containing a reference to 'international law' has a direct impact on the interpretation (broad or narrow) it gives to the content of the standard and, in turn, on how it addresses matters of liability and compensation.
(6) The vast majority of awards where tribunals have taken a position on the status of an 'in accordance with international law' FET clause concluded that this is *not* a reference to the MST under custom. They considered that under this clause the FET standard offers better protection than under the MST and have, in practice, interpreted the clause in very much the same way that other tribunals have regarding stand-alone FET clauses having an autonomous character. These broad interpretations led the majority of tribunals (two-thirds of awards) to find a breach of FET and to award compensation.
(7) Tribunals assessing 'no less' than international law FET clauses have been evenly divided on the interpretation to be given to this clause and its relation to the MST. Yet, there is also a clear link between the approach adopted by a tribunal regarding the status of a 'no less' FET clause (and its relationship with the MST) and how it assesses matters of liability and compensation. Those tribunals which have considered 'no less' clauses in the same way as autonomous stand-alone FET clauses have all given broad interpretations which led *all of them* to conclude that a breach had been committed. On the contrary, tribunals which have interpreted 'no less' clauses as meaning that the level of treatment is the same as the one existing under MST, have adopted narrower approaches which led the vast majority of them to not find a breach.

(8) Ultimately, what is clear is that a BIT that contains an FET clause with a reference to 'international law' (whether 'in accordance' or 'no less') does *not* provide any guarantee that a tribunal will interpret this wording as being synonymous with the MST under custom. Only a minority of tribunals have adopted this approach (15 out of 63 awards, i.e., 25%). In fact, it is much more likely that a tribunal will interpret such language similarly to a stand-alone FET clause containing no reference to 'international law' whatsoever. In practical terms, the vast majority of tribunals that have adopted this approach came to the conclusion that the FET clause had been breached and awarded compensation.

(9) All tribunals examining FET clauses expressly linked to the MST (or custom) followed the contracting parties' intention and applied a strict standard. I found no award interpreting this type of clause as a stand-alone 'autonomous' FET clause.

(10) Interpreting the clause in accordance with the MST leads tribunals to define the content of the FET standard narrowly. For instance, the majority of them did not consider legitimate expectations to be a stand-alone element, but rather a factor to be taken into account when assessing other elements. They also systematically applied a high threshold of severity to find a breach.

(11) As a result of this narrow interpretation, NAFTA tribunals came to the conclusion that the host State had violated the FET clause in a limited number of cases. The success rate of NAFTA claims (25%) is significantly lower when compared with awards interpreting other types of FET clauses. These findings are in line with what the UNCTAD Report highlighted 10 years ago. It should be added that for non-NAFTA tribunals interpreting treaties containing similar wording, the success rate is similar to that of awards assessing stand-alone FET clauses.

(12) These findings are important given that new trends are emerging regarding how States are drafting FET clauses in their new investment treaties. As mentioned in the Introduction, States are increasingly expressing their willingness to adopt new FET clauses (or to modify existing ones) to better protect their needs and interests.[2] In this context, there are several important facts highlighted in this survey that they may want to keep in mind:

- A stand-alone FET clause provides very limited protection for States against the possibility that a tribunal will adopt a broad interpretation and conclude that a breach has been committed. The same is true for clauses containing a reference to 'international law'. In most cases, tribunals have interpreted them in pretty much the same way as stand-alone 'autonomous' FET clauses.

2. *See*, OECD 'Track 2' program: https://www.oecd.org/investment/investment-policy/investment-treaties.htm.

- An FET clause explicitly linked to the MST is the only type of provision which can significantly reduce the possibility of a tribunal giving a broad interpretation of the FET standard and finding liability.

(13) Finally, my empirical analysis of awards does not support the 'convergence' theory whereby the standard of protection under an FET treaty clause is said to be the same as under the MST. In fact, the way tribunals have generally assessed the content of the FET standard (broad or narrow) and matters of liability very much depends on the specific type of FET clause they had to interpret.

Bibliography

Books

Diehl, A., *The Core Standard of International Investment Protection: Fair and Equitable Treatment*, Wolters Kluwer, 2012.

Dumberry, P., *The Fair and Equitable Treatment Standard: A Guide to NAFTA Case Law on Article 1105*, Kluwer Law International, 2013.

Dumberry, P., *The Formation and Identification of Rules of Customary International Law in International Investment Law*, Cambridge UP, 2016.

Dumberry, P., *Fair and Equitable Treatment: Its Interaction with the Minimum Standard and Its Customary Status*, Brill Research Perspectives in International Investment Law and Arbitration, 2018.

Islam, R., *The Fair and Equitable Treatment (FET) Standard in International Investment Arbitration: Developing Countries in Context*, Springer, 2018.

Kelsen, H., *Pure Theory of Law*, University of California Press, 1970.

Kinnear, M., A. Bjorklund & J.F.G. Hannaford, *Investment Disputes under NAFTA: An Annotated Guide to NAFTA Chapter 11*, Kluwer Law, 2006.

Kläger, R., *Fair and Equitable Treatment in International Investment Law*, Cambridge UP, 2011.

Paparinskis, M., *The International Minimum Standard and Fair and Equitable Treatment*, Oxford UP, 2013.

Schreuer, C. & Dolzer R., *Principles of International Investment Law*, Oxford UP, 2008.

Chapters in Book

Bondy, C., *Fair and Equitable Treatment: Ten Years On*, in: Jean Engelmayer Kalicki & Mohamed Abdel Raouf (eds), *Evolution and Adaptation: The Future of International Arbitration*, ICCA Congress Series, 2019.

De Brabandere, E., *States' Reassertion of Control Over International Investment Law: (Re)defining 'Fair and Equitable Treatment' and 'Indirect Expropriation'*, in: Andreas Kulick (ed.), *States' Reassertion of Control Over International Investment Agreements and International Investment Treaty Dispute Settlement*, Cambridge UP, 2016.

Dumberry, P., *Fair and Equitable Treatment*, in: Stefanie Schacherer & Makane Moïse Mbengue (eds), *Foreign Investment under the Comprehensive Economic and Trade Agreement (CETA)*, Springer 2018.

Dumberry, P., *Article 8.10: Treatment of Investors and of Covered Investments*, in: Marc Bungenberg & August Reinisch (eds), *CETA Investment Law: Article-by-Article Commentary*, Nomos-Hart 2021, 249-269.

Dupuy, F. & P.-M. Dupuy, *What to Expect from Legitimate Expectations? A Critical Appraisal and Look into the Future of the 'Legitimate Expectations' Doctrine in International Investment Law*, in: Mohamed, Abdel Raouf, Philippe Leboulanger & Nassib G. Ziade (eds), *Festschrift Ahmed Sadek El-Kosheri: From the Arab World to the Globalization of International Law and Arbitration*, Kluwer Law International, 2015.

Grisel, F., *Fair and Equitable Treatment: Ordering Chaos Through Precedent?*, in: D. Behn, O.K. Fauchald & M. Langford (eds), *The Legitimacy of Investment Arbitration: Empirical Perspectives*, Cambridge UP, 2022, 256-280.

Yannaca-Small, K., *Fair and Equitable Treatment Standard: Recent Developments*, in: August Reinisch (ed.), *Standards of Investment Protection*, Oxford UP, 2008.

Articles

Boone Barrera, E., *The Case for Removing the Fair and Equitable Treatment Standard from NAFTA*, CIGI Paper 128 (2017).

Carfagnini, M., *Too Low a Threshold: Bilcon v Canada and the International Minimum Standard of Treatment*, Canadian YIL 53 (2016), 244-277.

Denza, E. & S. Brooks, *Investment Protection Treaties: United Kingdom Experience*, International & Comparative Law Quarterly 36(4) (1987), 908-923.

Dumberry, P., *The Prohibition Against Arbitrary Conduct and the Fair and Equitable Treatment Standard under NAFTA Article 1105*, J. World Invest. & Trade 15(1) (2014), 117-151.

Dumberry, P., *Moving the Goal Post! How Some NAFTA Tribunals have Challenged the FTC Note of Interpretation on the Fair and Equitable Treatment Standard under NAFTA Article 1105*, World Arbitration and Mediation Review 9(2) (2014).

Dumberry, P., *The Protection of Investors' Legitimate Expectations and the Fair and Equitable Treatment Standard under NAFTA Article 1105*, J. Int. Arb. 31(1) (2014), 47-74.

Dumberry, P., *Cross Treaty Interpretation en Bloc or How CAFTA Tribunals are Systematically Interpreting the FET Standard Based NAFTA Case Law*, LPICT 22(2) (2023), 384-418.

Emami, M. & R. Gul, *Diversity in the Formulation of Fair and Equitable Treatment in International Investment Agreements*, J E Asia & Int'l L. 14(1) (2021), 79-100.

Gantz, David A., *Settlement of Disputes under the Central America-Dominican Republic – United States Free Trade Agreement*, B C Int'l & Comp L Rev. 30(2) (2007), 331-410.

Gélinas, F. & F. Jadeau, *CETA's Definition of the Fair and Equitable Treatment Standard: Toward a Guided and Constrained Interpretation*, TDM 13(1) (2016), 10.

Mann, F.A., *British Treaties for the Promotion and Protection of Investment*, British YIL 52 (1981), 241-254.

Picherack, J.R., *The Expanding Scope of the Fair and Equitable Treatment Standard: Have Recent Tribunals Gone Too Far?*, J. World Invest. & Trade 9(4) (2008), 257-291.

Schreurer, C., *Fair and Equitable Treatment in Arbitral Practice*, J World Investment & Trade 6(3) (2005), 357-386.

Schacherer, S., *TPP, CETA and TTIP Between Innovation and Consolidation – Resolving Investor–State Disputes under Mega-regionals*, Journal of International Dispute Settlement 7(3) (2016), 628-653.

Van Harten, G., *ISDS in the Revised CETA: Positive Steps, But is it the 'Gold Standard'?*, Centre for International Governance Innovation (CIGI), Investor-State Arbitration Commentary Series 6 (2016).

Reports

Gaukrodger, D., *Addressing the Balance of Interests in Investment Treaties; The Limitation of Fair and Equitable Treatment Provisions to the Minimum Standard of Treatment under Customary International Law*, OECD Working Papers on International Investment (2017).

OECD, *Draft Convention on the Protection of Foreign Property*, 7 ILM 117 (1967).

OECD, *Fair and Equitable Treatment Standard in International Investment Law*, Working Papers on International Investment Law, No. 2004/3 (2004).

OECD, *International Investment Law: A Changing Landscape – A Companion Volume to International Investment Perspectives* (2005).

OECD, *'Fair' and 'Equitable' Treatment Provisions in Investment Treaties; A Large-Sample Survey of Treaty Provisions* (2023).

UNCTAD, *Fair and Equitable Treatment*, Series on Issues in International Investment Agreements (1999).

UNCTAD, *Fair and Equitable Treatment*, UNCTAD series on issues in international investment agreements II, United Nations, Geneva (2012).

Table of Cases

Case Law

Investor-State Arbitration Arbitral Awards

ICSID Cases

Alex Genin, Eastern Credit Limited, Inc. and A.S. Baltoil Genin v. Estonia, ICSID Case No. ARB/99/2, Award, 25 June 2001, 116, 118, 119, 139

Alpha Projektholding GmbH v. Ukraine, ICSID Case No. ARB/07/16, Award, 8 November 2010, 78, 82

American Manufacturing & Trading v. Republic of Zaire (AMT), ICSID Case No. ARB/93/1, Award, 21 February 1997, 117, 120

Anglo American PLC v. Bolivarian Republic of Venezuela, ICSID Case No. ARB(AF)/14/1, Award, 18 January 2019, 95, 98, 104-106

Antoine Abou Lahoud and Leila Bounafeh-Abou Lahoud v. Democratic Republic of the Congo, ICSID Case No. ARB/10/4, Award, 7 February 2014, 49

Apotex Holdings Inc & Apotex Inc. v. United States, ICSID Case No. ARB(AF)/12/1, Award, 25 August 2014, 11, 124, 130, 131, 136

Azurix Corp. v. The Argentine Republic, ICSID Case No. ARB/01/12, Award, 14 July 2006, 10, 86, 111-113, 115, 120, 157

B3 Croatian Courier Coöperatief U.A. v. Republic of Croatia, ICSID Case No. ARB/15/5, Award, 5 April 2019, 77, 82

Banco Bilbao Vizcaya Argentaria S.A. v. Plurinational State of Bolivia, ICSID Case No. ARB(AF)/18/5, Award, 12 July 2022, 109, 120

Bayindir Insaat Turizm Ticaret ve Sanayi AS v. Pakistan, ICSID Case No. ARB/03/29, Award, 27 August 2009, 10-11, 63, 66, 82

Bay View Group LLC and The Spalena Company LLC v. Republic of Rwanda, ICSID Case No. ARB/18/21, Award, 30 March 2022, 143

BayWa r.e. Renewable Energy GmbH and BayWa r.e. Asset Holding GmbH v. Kingdom of Spain, ICSID Case No. ARB/15/16, Decision on Jurisdiction, Liability and Directions on Quantum, 2 December 2019, 85, 88, 89

Bear Creek Mining Corporation v. Republic of Peru, ICSID Case No. ARB/14/21480, Award, 30 November 2017, 143

Belenergia S.A. v. Italian Republic, ICSID Case No. ARB/15/40, Award, 6 August 2019, 12, 86, 88, 89

Bernhard von Pezold and Others v. Zimbabwe, ICSID Case No. ARB/10/15, Award, 28 July 2015, 77, 82

Big Sky Energy Corporation v. Republic of Kazakhstan, ICSID Case No. ARB/17/22, Award, 1 November 2012, 107

Biwater Gauff (Tanzania) Limited v. United Republic of Tanzania, ICSID Case No. ARB/05/22, Award, 24 July 2008, 11, 59, 60, 64-66, 157

Blusun S.A., Jean-Pierre Lecorcier and Michael Stein v. Italian Republic, ICSID Case No. ARB/14/3, Award, 27 December 2016, 33, 87-89

Bosh International, Inc and B&P Ltd Foreign Investments Enterprise v. Ukraine, ICSID Case No. ARB/08/11, Award, 25 October 2012, 107

Bridgestone Licensing Services, Inc. and Bridgestone Americas, Inc. v. Republic of Panama, ICSID Case No. ARB/16/34, Award, 14 August 2020, 143

Burlington Resources Inc. v. Republic of Ecuador, ICSID Case No. ARB/08/5, Decision on Reconsideration and Award, 7 February 2017, 116, 120

Casinos Austria International GmbH and Casinos Austria Aktiengesellschaft v. Argentine Republic, ICSID Case No. ARB/14/32, Award, 5 November 2021, 50

Duke Energy International Peru Investments No. 1 Ltd. v. Republic of Peru, ICSID Case No. ARB/03/28, Award, 18 August 2008, 49, 157

Eco Oro Minerals Corp. v. Colombia, ICSID Case No. ARB/16/41, Decision on Jurisdiction, Liability and Directions on Quantum, 9 September 2021, 147-151, 154, 162, 166

EDF (Services) Limited v. Romania, ICSID Case No. ARB/05/13, Award, 8 October 2009, 79, 81

EDF International S.A., SAUR International S.A. and León Participaciones Argentinas S.A. v. Argentine Republic, ICSID Case No. ARB/03/23, Award, 11 June 2012, 11, 95

Eiser Infrastructure Limited and Energía Solar Luxembourg S.à r.l. v. Kingdom of Spain, ICSID Case No. ARB/13/36, Award, 4 May 2017, 83, 85, 89

Electrabel v. Hungary, ICSID Case No. ARB/07/19, Decision on Jurisdiction, Applicable Law and Liability, 30 November 2012, 11, 12, 87, 89

El Paso Energy International Co. v. Argentina, ICSID Case No. ARB/03/15, Award, 31 October 2011, 11, 12, 71, 73, 108, 117, 118, 120

Emilio Agustín Maffezini v. The Kingdom of Spain, ICSID Case No. ARB/97/7, Award, 13 November 2000, 77, 78, 82

Enron Creditors Recovery Corporation (formerly Enron Corporation) and Ponderosa Assets, L.P. v. Argentine Republic, ICSID Case No. ARB/01/3, Award, 22 May 2007, 11, 110, 120

Eskosol S.p.A. in liquidazione v. Italian Republic, ICSID Case No. ARB/15/50, Award, 4 September 2020, 88, 89

ESPF Beteiligungs GmbH, ESPF Nr. 2 Austria Beteiligungs GmbH, and InfraClass Energie 5 GmbH & Co. KG v. Italian Republic, ICSID Case No. ARB/16/5, Award, 14 September 2020, 84

Eurus Energy Holdings Corporation v. Kingdom of Spain, ICSID Case No. ARB/16/4, Decision on Jurisdiction and Liability, 17 March 2021, 84, 85, 89

Eutelsat S.A. v. United Mexican States, ICSID Case No. ARB(AF)/17/2, Award, 15 September 2021, 93, 105

Fouad Alghanim & Sons Co. for General Trading & Contracting, W.L.L. and Mr. Fouad Mohammed Thunyan Alghanim v. Hashemite Kingdom of Jordan, ICSID Case No. ARB/13/38, Award, 14 December 2017, 77, 82

Franck Charles Arif v. Republic of Moldova, ICSID Case No. ARB/11/23, Award, 8 April 2013, 12, 94, 95, 97, 104, 106

Flughafen Zürich A.G. and Gestión e Ingenería IDC S.A. v. Bolivarian Republic of Venezuela, ICSID Case No. ARB/10/19, Award, 12 November 2014, 12, 100, 106

Gardabani And Silk Road v. Georgia, ICSID Case No. ARB/17/29, Final Award, 27 October 2022, 59, 60, 64-66

Garanti Koza LLP v. Turkmenistan, ICSID Case No. ARB/11/20, Award, 19 December 2016, 77, 82

GEA Group Aktiengesellschaft v. Ukraine, ICSID Case No. ARB/08/16, Award, 31 March, 2011, 77, 81

Gemplus S.A., SLP S.A., Gemplus Industrial S.A. de C.V. v. The United Mexican States, ICSID Case No. ARB(AF)/04/3, Award, 16 June 2010, 77, 82

Georg Gavrilovic and Gavrilovic d.o.o. v. Republic of Croatia, ICSID Case No. ARB/12/39, Award, 26 July 2018, 81

Glencore International A.G. y C.I. Prodeco S.A. c. La República de Colombia, ICSID Case No. ARB/16/6, Award, 27 August 2019, 80, 82

Global Telecom Holding S.A.E. v. Canada, ICSID Case No. ARB/16/16, Award, 27 March 2020, 95, 96, 104-106

Gold Reserve Inc. v. Venezuela, ICSID Case No. ARB(AF)/09/1, Award, 22 September 2014, 18, 93, 102, 104, 106

Gramercy Funds Management LLC and Gramercy Peru Holdings LLC v. Republic of Peru, ICSID Case No. UNCT/18/2, 6 December 2022, 145

Helnan International Hotels v. Arab Republic of Egypt, ICSID Case No. ARB/05/19, Award, 3 July 2008, 49

HOCHTIEF Aktiengesellschaft v. Argentine Republic, ICSID Case No. ARB/07/31, Decision on Liability, 29 December 2014, 77-78, 82

Hydro Energy 1 S.à.r.l and Hydroxana Sweden AB v. Kingdom of Spain, ICSID Case No. ARB/15/42, Decision on Jurisdiction, Liability and Directions on Quantum, 9 March 2020, 84, 85, 88, 89

Iberdrola Energia, S.A. v. Republic of Guatemala, ICSID Case No. ARB/09/5, Award, 17 August 2012, 12, 117

İçkale İnşaat Limited Şirketi v. Turkmenistan, ICSID Case No. ARB/10/24, Award, 8 March 2016, 25, 50

Impregilo S.p.A. v. Argentine Republic I, ICSID Case No. ARB/07/17, Award, 21 June 2011, 11, 79-80, 82

Infinito Gold Ltd. v. Republic of Costa Rica, ICSID Case No. ARB/14/5, Award, 3 June 2021, 94, 95, 98-100, 103, 104, 106

Infracapital F1 S.à r.l. and Infracapital Solar B.V. v. Kingdom of Spain, ICSID Case No. ARB/16/18, Decision on Jurisdiction, Liability, and Directions on Quantum, 13 September 2021, 85, 88, 89

InfraRed Environmental Infrastructure GP Limited and others v. Kingdom of Spain, ICSID Case No. ARB/14/12, Award, 2 August 2019, 87-89

Inmaris Perestroika Sailing Maritime Services GmbH and others v. Ukraine, ICSID Case No. ARB/08/8, Award, 1 March 2012, 59, 64-66

Interocean Oil Development Company and Interocean Oil Exploration Company v. Federal Republic of Nigeria, ICSID Case No. ARB/13/20, Award, 6 October 2020, 49

Infrastructure Services Luxembourg S.à.r.l. and Energia Termosolar B.V. (formerly Antin Infrastructure Services Luxembourg S.à.r.l. and Antin Energia Termosolar B.V.) v. Kingdom of Spain, ICSID Case No. ARB/13/31, Award, 15 June 2018, 85

Ioan Micula, Viorel Micula, S.C. European Food S.A, S.C. Starmill S.R.L. and S.C. Multipack S.R.L. v. Romania, ICSID Case No. ARB/05/20, Final Award, 11 December 2013, 62, 65, 66

Ioan Micula, Viorel Micula and others v. Romania [II], ICSID Case No. ARB/14/29, Award, 5 March, 2020, 80

Ioannis Kardassopoulos v. The Republic of Georgia, ICSID Case No. ARB/05/18, Award, 3 March 2010, 11, 78, 82

UNCITRAL Cases

PCA Cases

Other Arbitral Awards or Cases

Domestic Court Decisions

Case Reports

Index

www.ingramcontent.com/pod-product-compliance
Lightning Source LLC
LaVergne TN
LVHW020638300926
849161LV00004B/746
* 9 7 8 9 4 0 3 5 2 5 0 8 2 *